Archie® and Katy Keene™

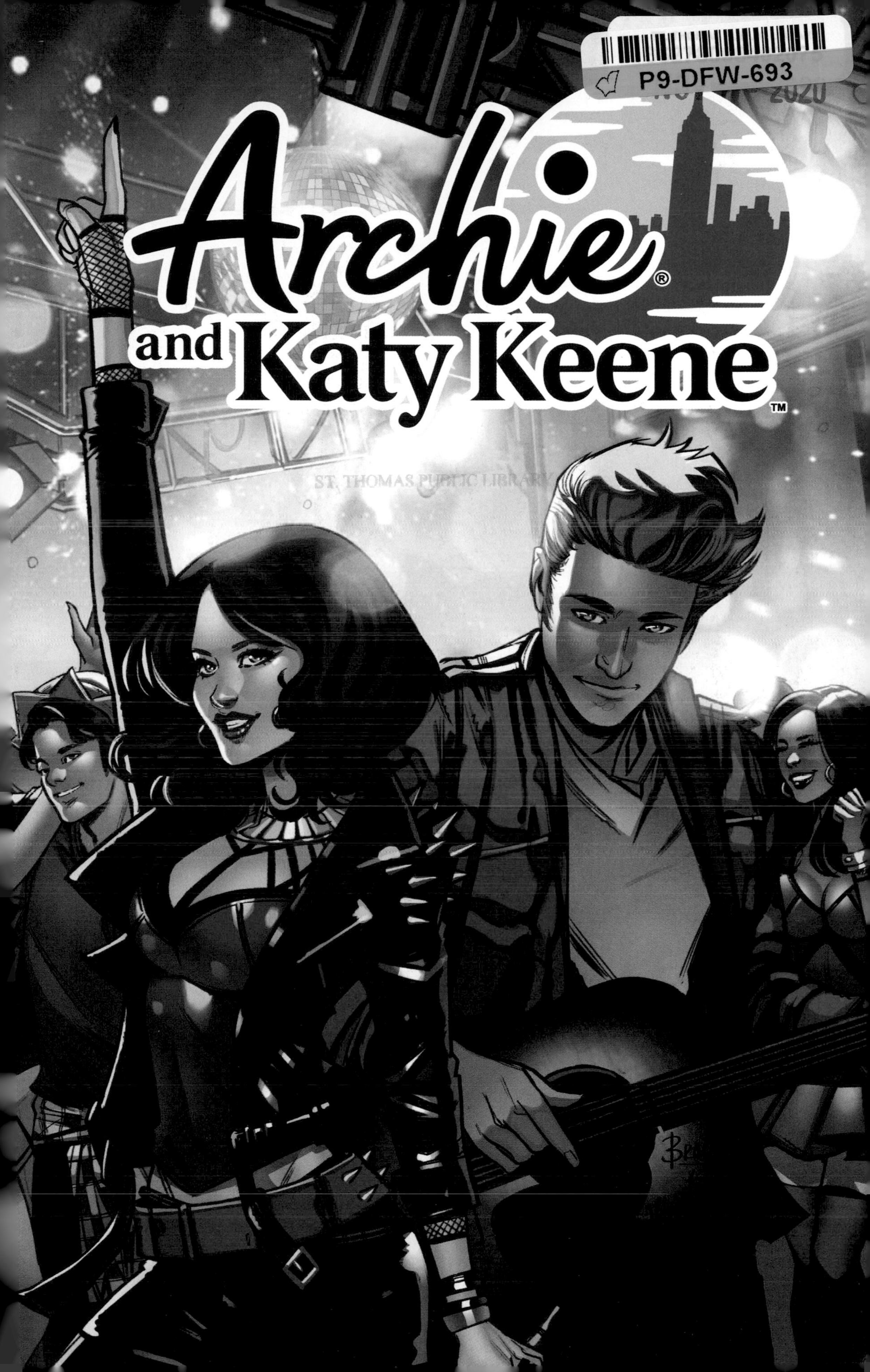

STORY BY
**MARIKO TAMAKI
& KEVIN PANETTA**

ART BY
LAURA BRAGA

LETTERING BY
JACK MORELLI

COLORS BY
MATT HERMS

GRAPHIC DESIGN BY
KARI McLACHLAN

EDITORS
**ALEX SEGURA
& JAMIE LEE ROTANTE**

ASSOCIATE EDITOR
STEPHEN OSWALD

CO-PRESIDENT
MIKE PELLERITO

ASSISTANT EDITOR
VINCENT LOVALLO

EDITOR-IN-CHIEF
VICTOR GORELICK

PUBLISHER
JON GOLDWATER

PREVIOUSLY IN RIVERDALE...

After **Archie Andrews**' lonely summer, love struck our redheaded teen like a bolt of magic... little did he know, it was more magical than he ever could have imagined! A chance encounter with (unbeknownst to him) teen witch **Sabrina Spellman** led the two into a whirlwind, magical and—most importantly—secret romance. Keeping their secret was a challenge—especially with former girlfriends **Betty Cooper** and **Veronica Lodge** on the case. But it was just one of the many mysteries plaguing the quiet town of **Riverdale** at the time—along with **Reggie Mantle**'s missing father, **Ricky**, and the strange secrets being harbored in **Fox Forest**. Unfortunately Sabrina's aunts, **Hilda** and **Zelda**, were not keen on their witch niece dating a mortal teenager. While Archie took some time to understand what it means to date a witch, the police set their sights on Sabrina as a possible suspect in the case of Ricky Mantle—but without much to go on, their investigation went quiet.

Now that some time has passed and the dust has settled, Archie and Sabrina are finally able to pursue their relationship *without* having to keep it a secret, allowing them to focus on their romantic life and Archie's hope to have a blooming musical career. But things are never really quiet in Riverdale, and the appearance of a new mystery fashionista named **Katy Keene** has got everyone talking. Who is she, where did she come from and, more importantly, *why* is she in Riverdale?

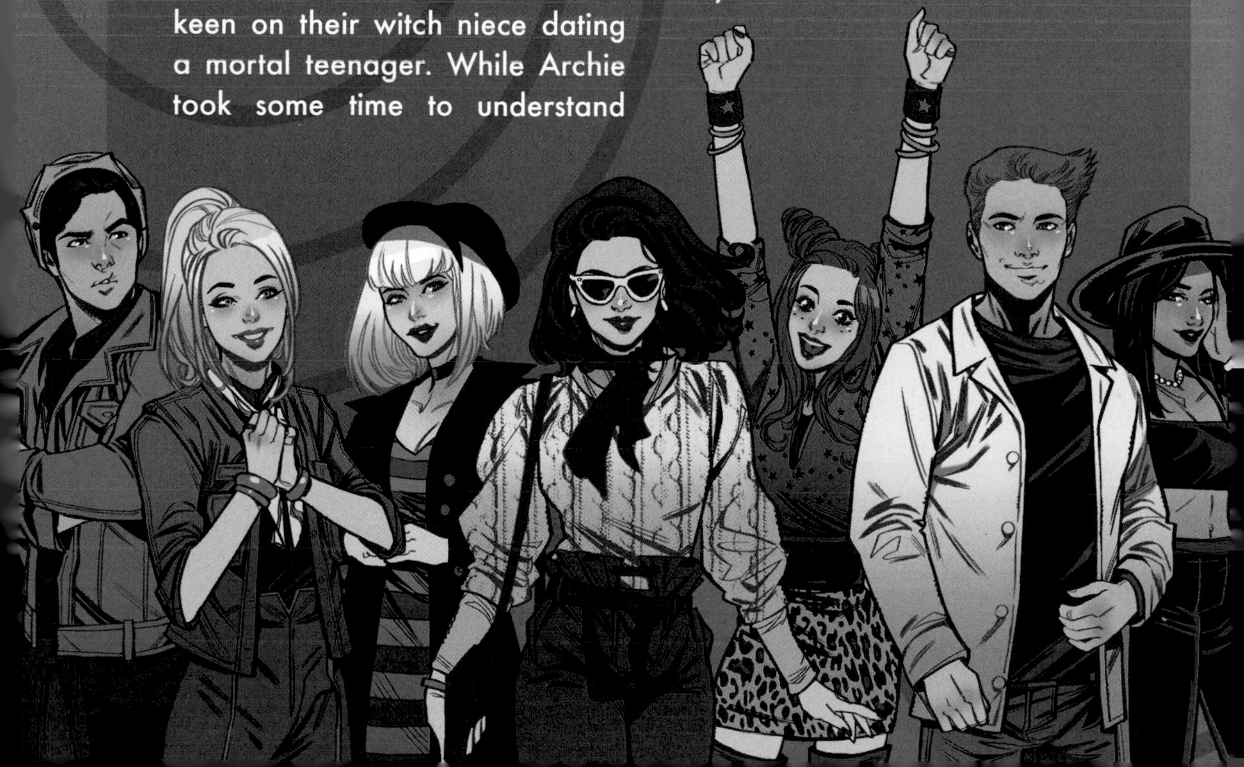

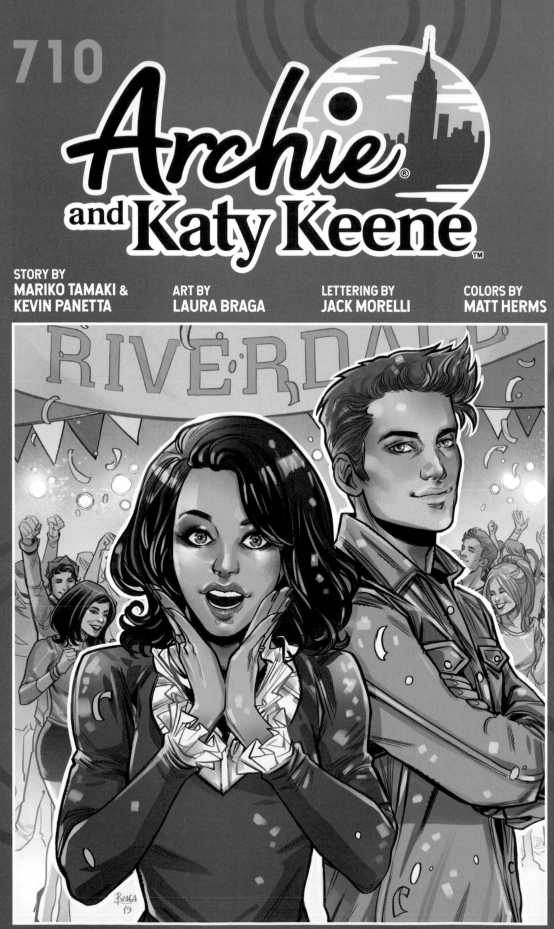

710

Archie® and Katy Keene™

STORY BY
**MARIKO TAMAKI &
KEVIN PANETTA**

ART BY
LAURA BRAGA

LETTERING BY
JACK MORELLI

COLORS BY
MATT HERMS

COVER ART: **LAURA BRAGA**

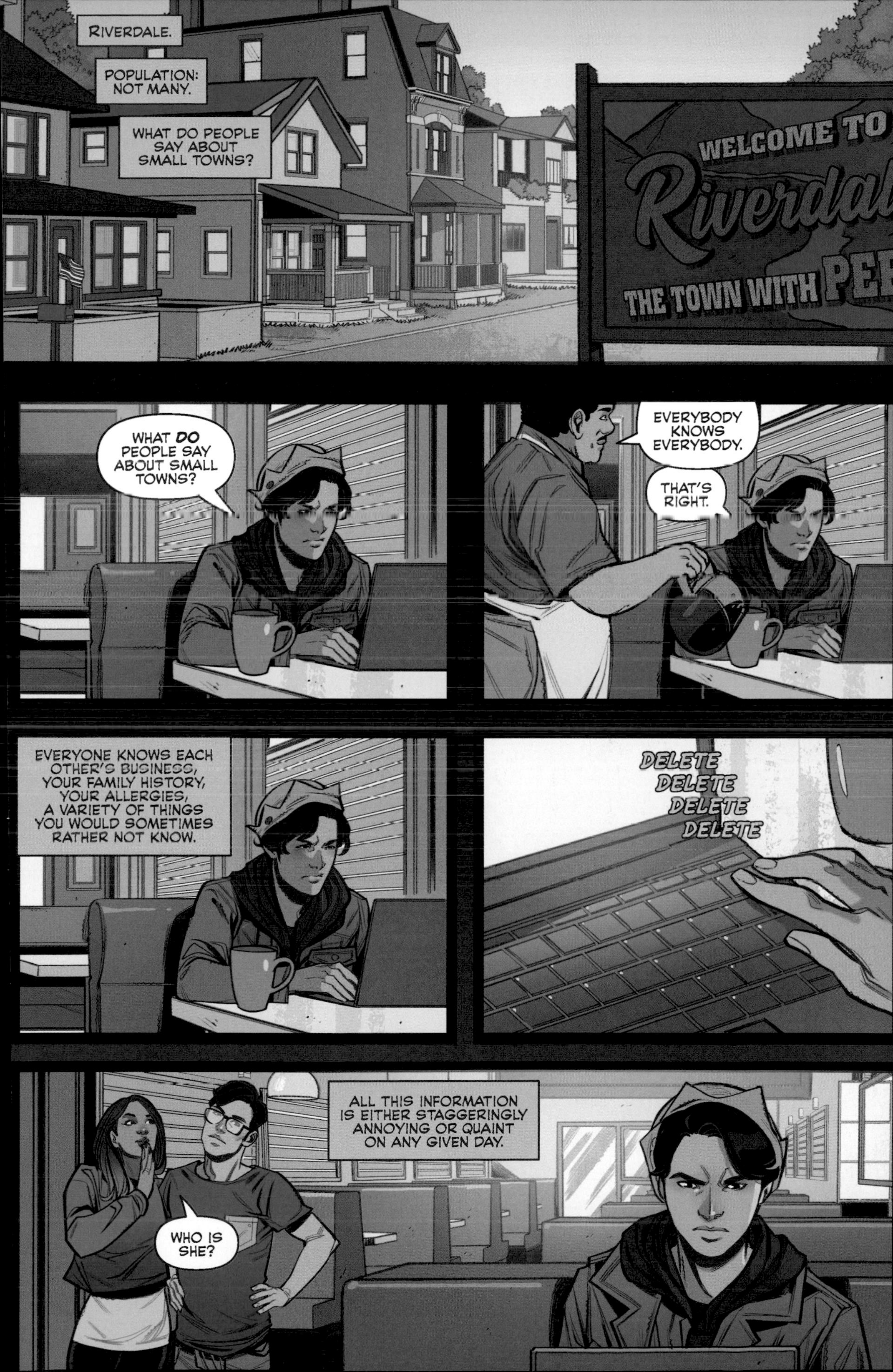
RIVERDALE.
POPULATION: NOT MANY.
WHAT DO PEOPLE SAY ABOUT SMALL TOWNS?
WELCOME TO
Riverdal
THE TOWN WITH PE
WHAT **DO** PEOPLE SAY ABOUT SMALL TOWNS?
EVERYBODY KNOWS EVERYBODY.
THAT'S RIGHT.
EVERYONE KNOWS EACH OTHER'S BUSINESS, YOUR FAMILY HISTORY, YOUR ALLERGIES, A VARIETY OF THINGS YOU WOULD SOMETIMES RATHER NOT KNOW.
DELETE
DELETE
DELETE
DELETE
ALL THIS INFORMATION IS EITHER STAGGERINGLY ANNOYING OR QUAINT ON ANY GIVEN DAY.
WHO IS SHE?

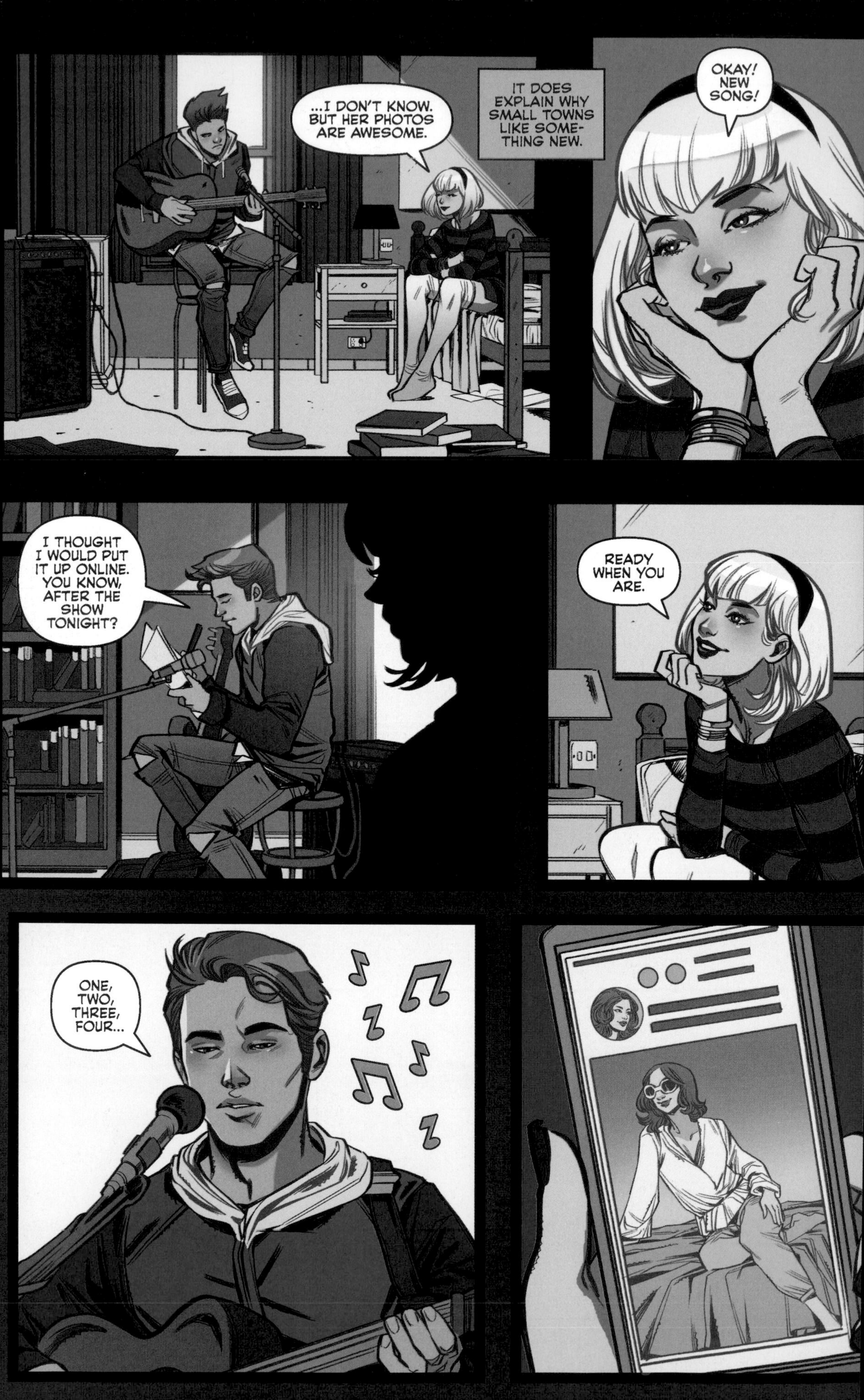
...I DON'T KNOW. BUT HER PHOTOS ARE AWESOME.
IT DOES EXPLAIN WHY SMALL TOWNS LIKE SOME-THING NEW.
OKAY! NEW SONG!
I THOUGHT I WOULD PUT IT UP ONLINE. YOU KNOW, AFTER THE SHOW TONIGHT?
READY WHEN YOU ARE.
ONE, TWO, THREE, FOUR...

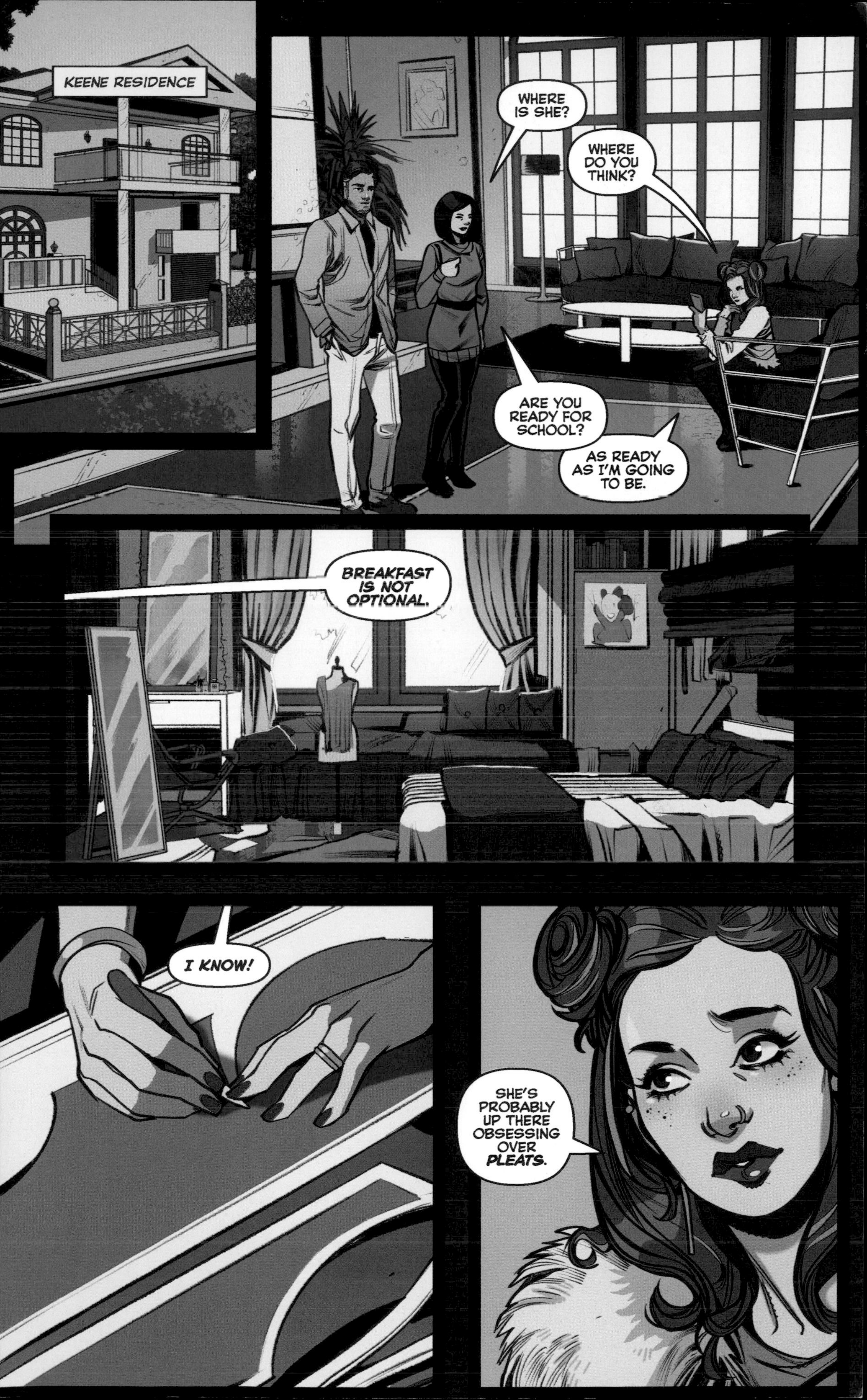
KEENE RESIDENCE
WHERE IS SHE?
WHERE DO YOU THINK?
ARE YOU READY FOR SCHOOL?
AS READY AS I'M GOING TO BE.
BREAKFAST IS NOT OPTIONAL.
I KNOW!
SHE'S PROBABLY UP THERE OBSESSING OVER PLEATS.

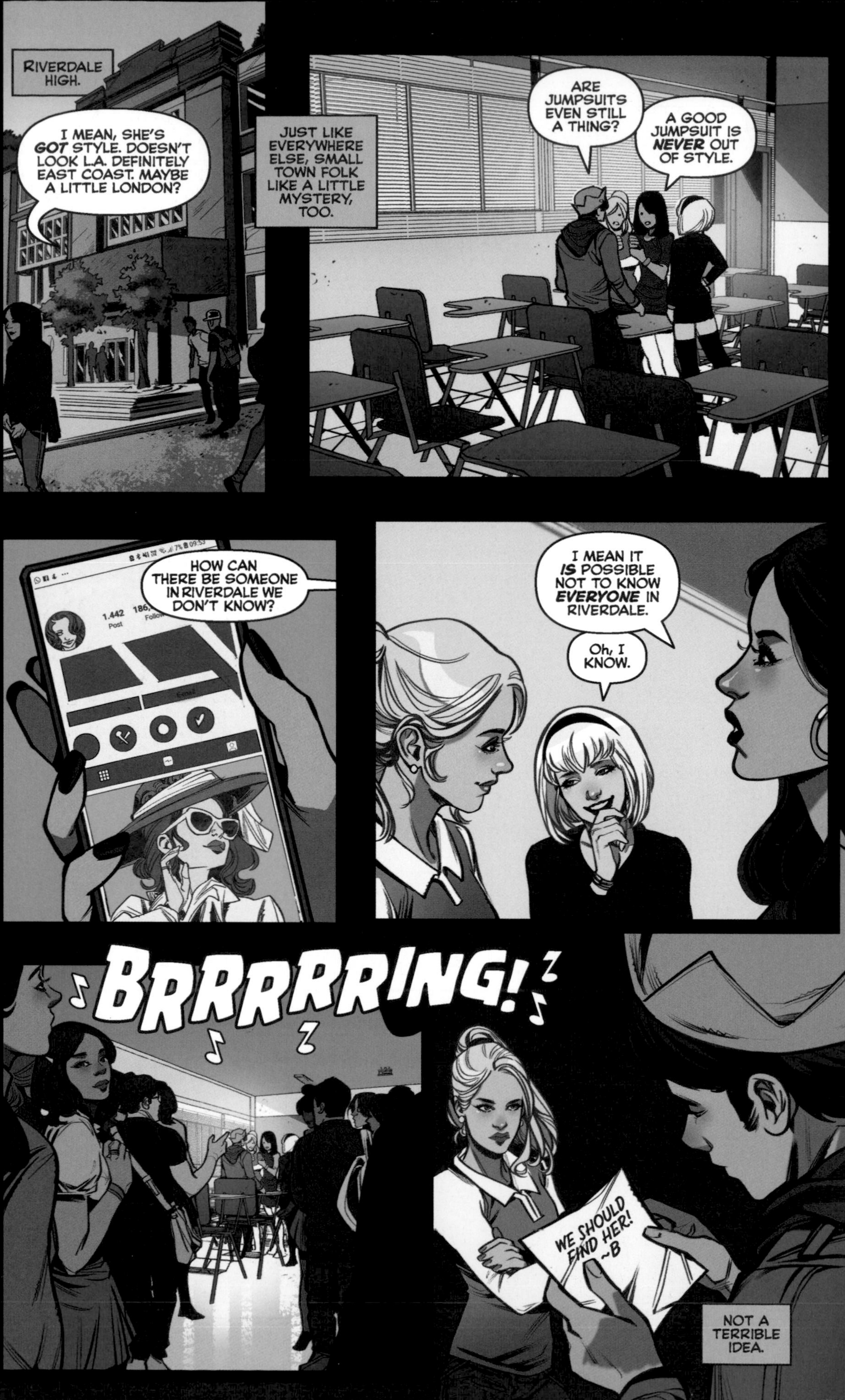
RIVERDALE HIGH.
I MEAN, SHE'S GOT STYLE. DOESN'T LOOK L.A. DEFINITELY EAST COAST. MAYBE A LITTLE LONDON?
JUST LIKE EVERYWHERE ELSE, SMALL TOWN FOLK LIKE A LITTLE MYSTERY, TOO.
ARE JUMPSUITS EVEN STILL A THING?
A GOOD JUMPSUIT IS NEVER OUT OF STYLE.
HOW CAN THERE BE SOMEONE IN RIVERDALE WE DON'T KNOW?
I MEAN IT IS POSSIBLE NOT TO KNOW EVERYONE IN RIVERDALE.
Oh, I KNOW.
BRRRRRING!
WE SHOULD FIND HER! ~B
NOT A TERRIBLE IDEA.

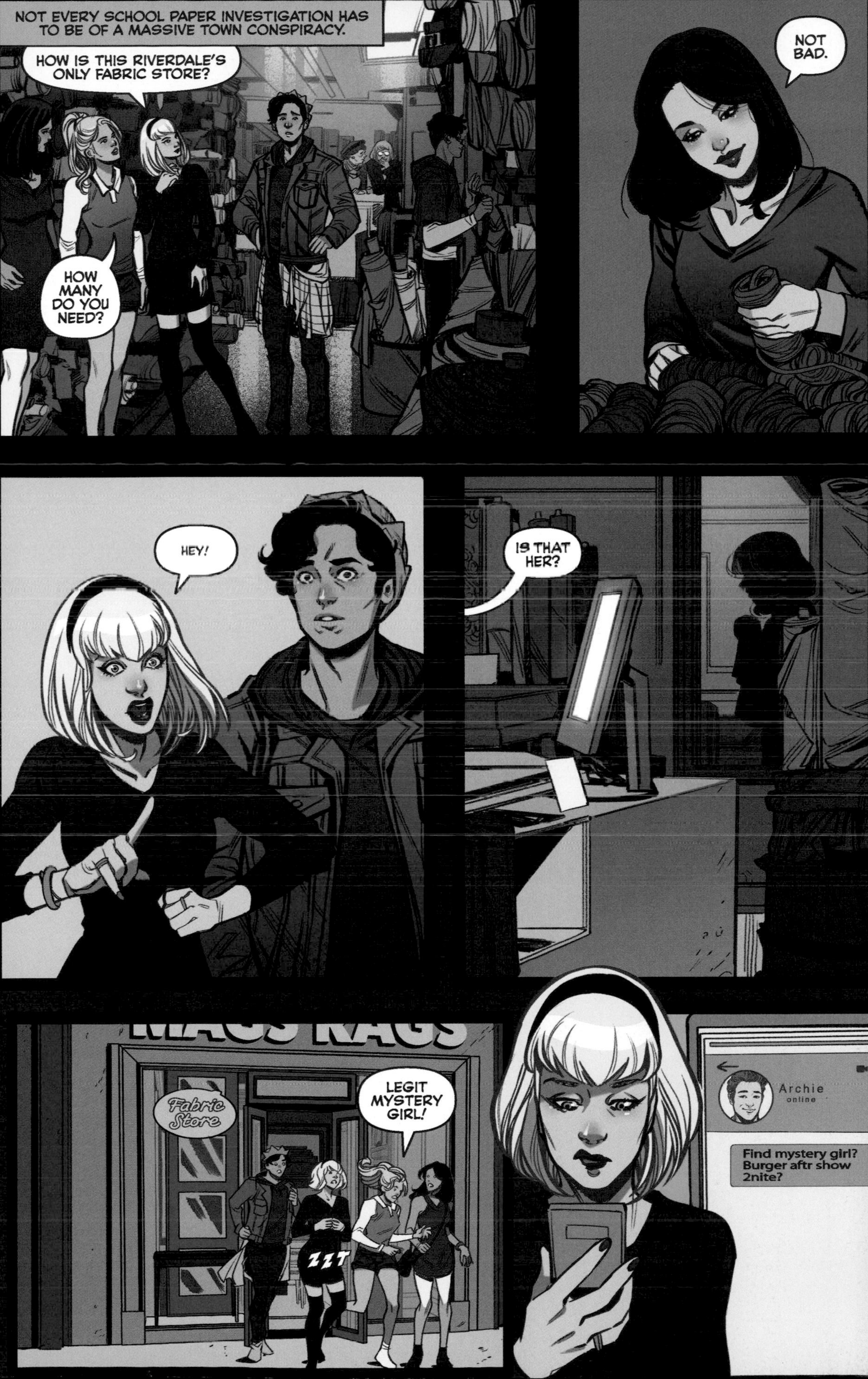
NOT EVERY SCHOOL PAPER INVESTIGATION HAS TO BE OF A MASSIVE TOWN CONSPIRACY.
HOW IS THIS RIVERDALE'S ONLY FABRIC STORE?
HOW MANY DO YOU NEED?
NOT BAD.
HEY!
IS THAT HER?
MAGS RAGS
Fabric Store
LEGIT MYSTERY GIRL!
ZZT
Archie
online
Find mystery girl? Burger aftr show 2nite?

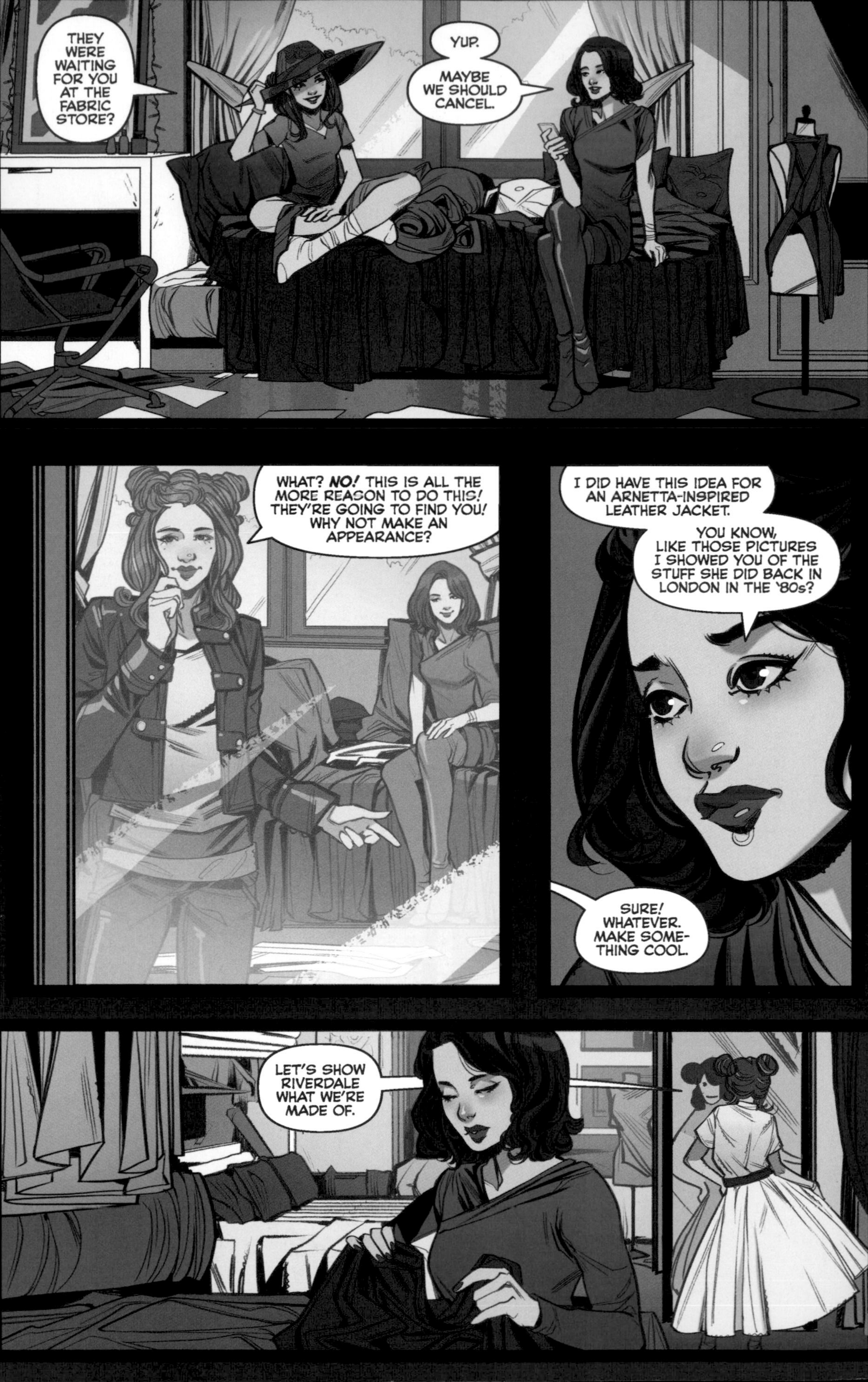
THEY WERE WAITING FOR YOU AT THE FABRIC STORE?
YUP.
MAYBE WE SHOULD CANCEL.
WHAT? NO! THIS IS ALL THE MORE REASON TO DO THIS! THEY'RE GOING TO FIND YOU! WHY NOT MAKE AN APPEARANCE?
I DID HAVE THIS IDEA FOR AN ARNETTA-INSPIRED LEATHER JACKET.
YOU KNOW, LIKE THOSE PICTURES I SHOWED YOU OF THE STUFF SHE DID BACK IN LONDON IN THE '80s?
SURE! WHATEVER. MAKE SOME-THING COOL.
LET'S SHOW RIVERDALE WHAT WE'RE MADE OF.

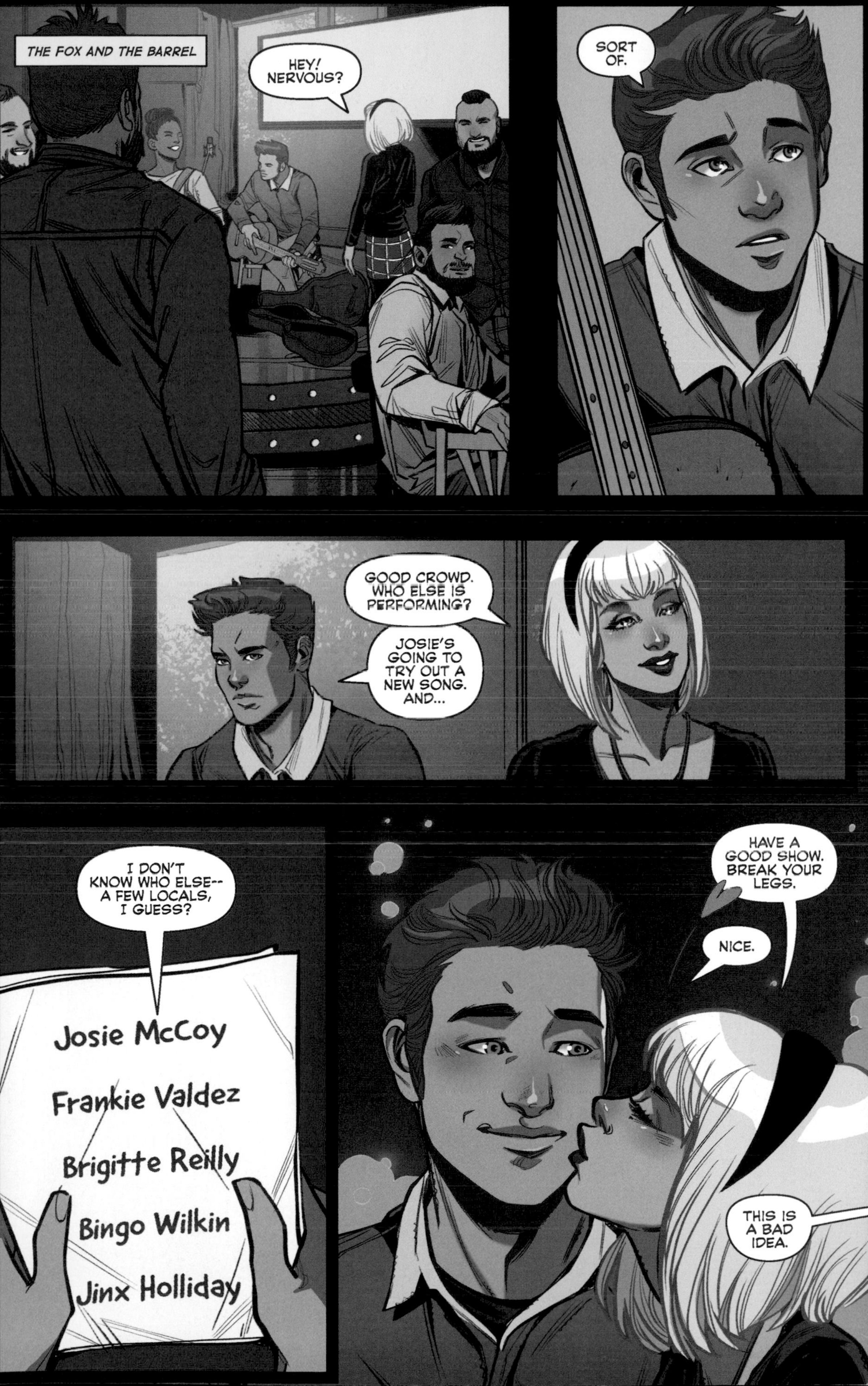
THE FOX AND THE BARREL
HEY! NERVOUS?
SORT OF.
GOOD CROWD. WHO ELSE IS PERFORMING?
JOSIE'S GOING TO TRY OUT A NEW SONG. AND...
I DON'T KNOW WHO ELSE-- A FEW LOCALS, I GUESS?
Josie McCoy
Frankie Valdez
Brigitte Reilly
Bingo Wilkin
Jinx Holliday
HAVE A GOOD SHOW. BREAK YOUR LEGS.
NICE.
THIS IS A BAD IDEA.

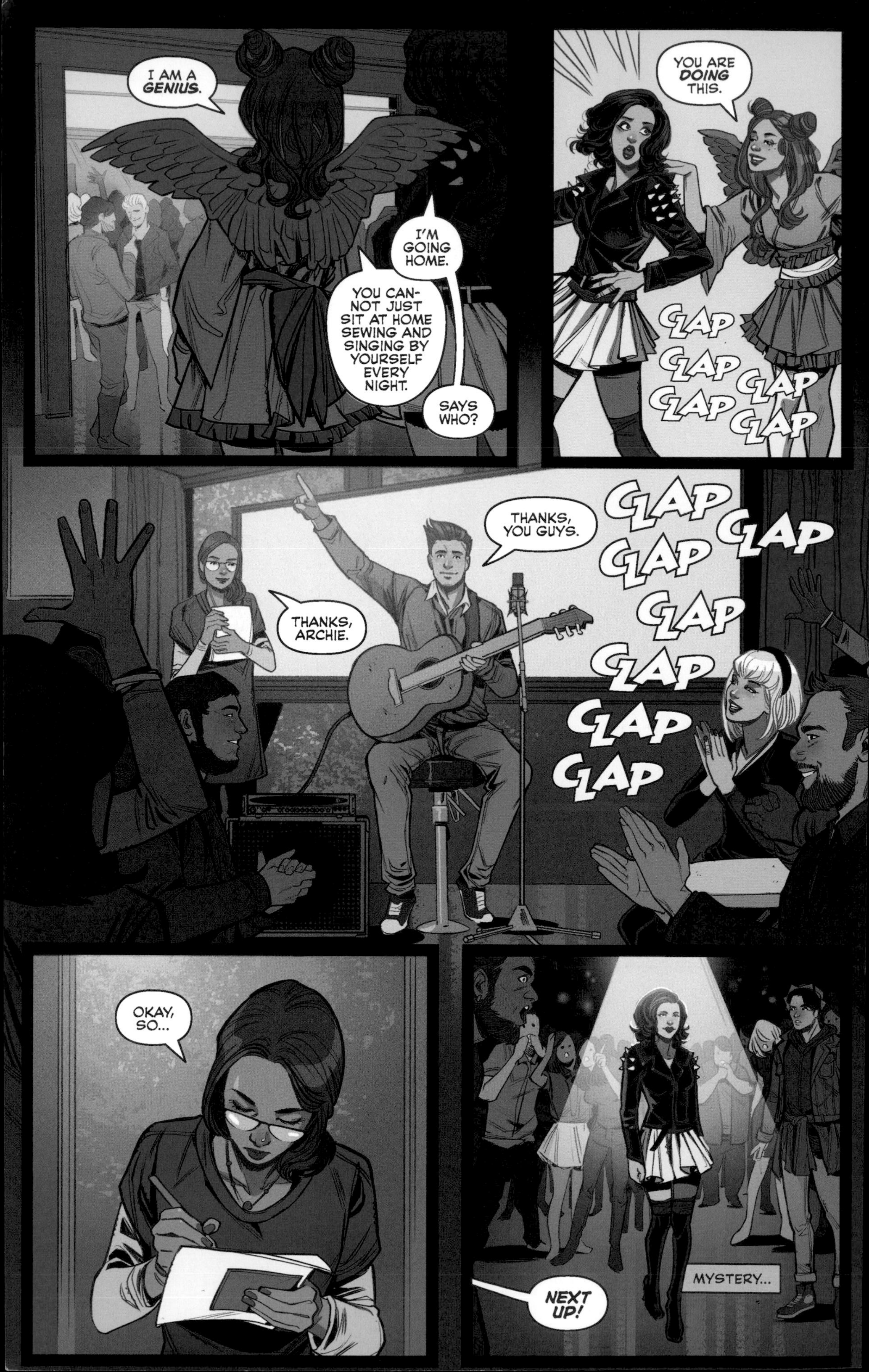
I AM A *GENIUS*.
I'M GOING HOME.
YOU CAN-NOT JUST SIT AT HOME SEWING AND SINGING BY YOURSELF EVERY NIGHT.
SAYS WHO?
YOU ARE *DOING* THIS.
CLAP CLAP CLAP CLAP CLAP
THANKS, YOU GUYS.
THANKS, ARCHIE.
CLAP CLAP CLAP CLAP CLAP CLAP CLAP
OKAY, SO...
MYSTERY...
NEXT UP!

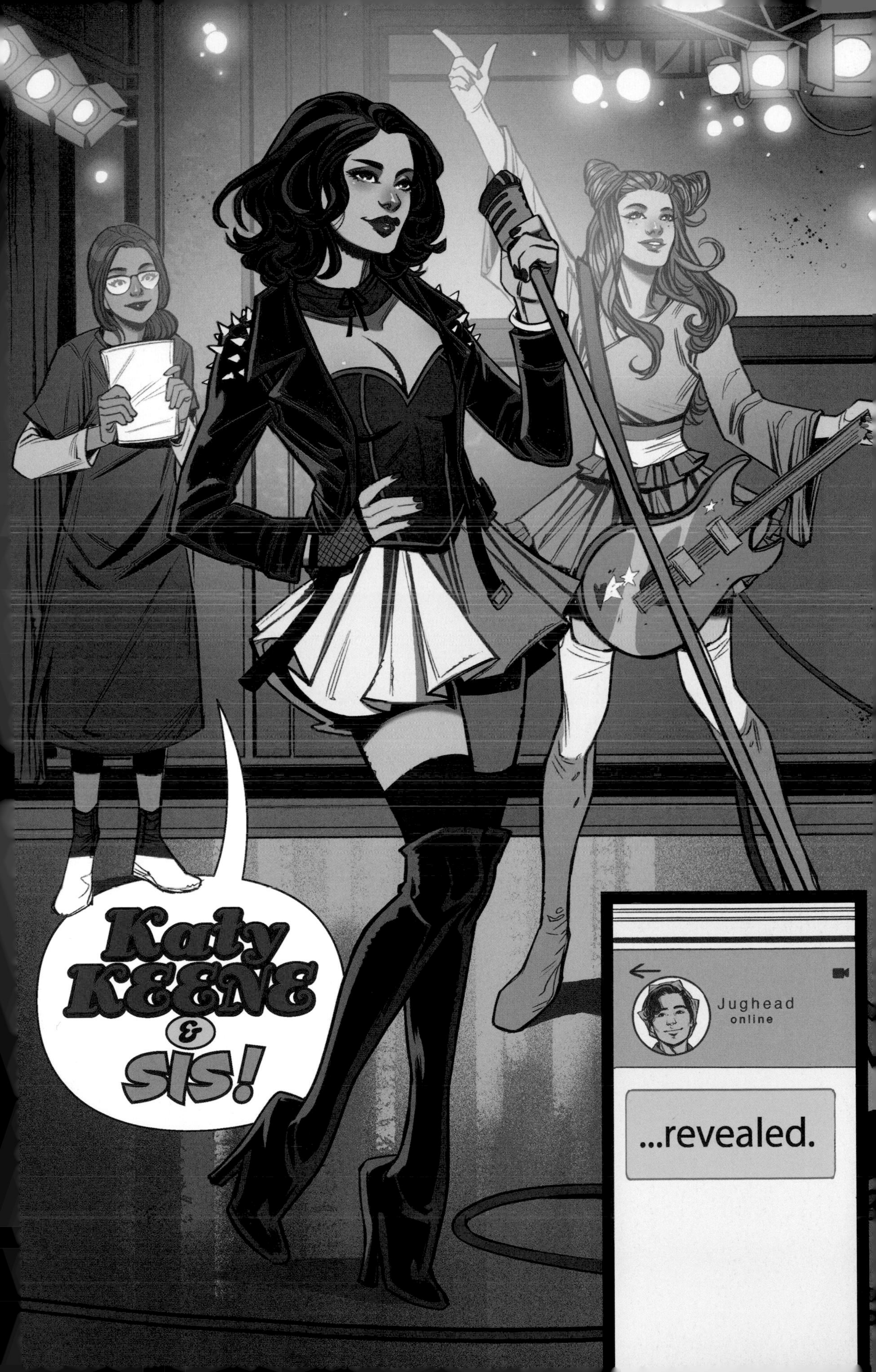
Katy KEENE & SIS!
Jughead
online
...revealed.

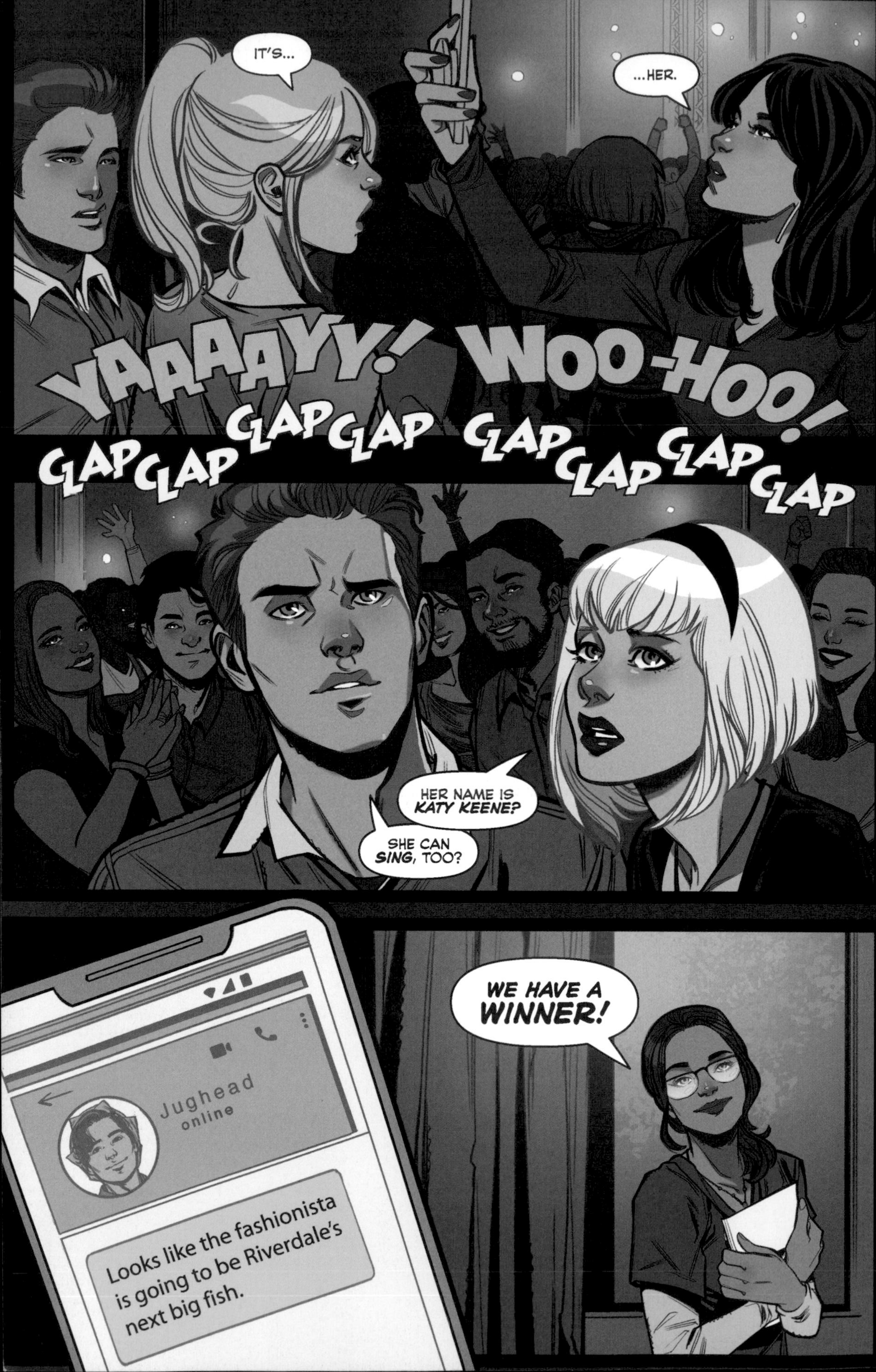
IT'S...
...HER.
YAAAAYY!
WOO-HOO!
CLAP CLAP CLAP CLAP
CLAP CLAP CLAP CLAP
HER NAME IS *KATY KEENE?*
SHE CAN **SING**, TOO?
Jughead
online
Looks like the fashionista is going to be Riverdale's next big fish.
WE HAVE A WINNER!

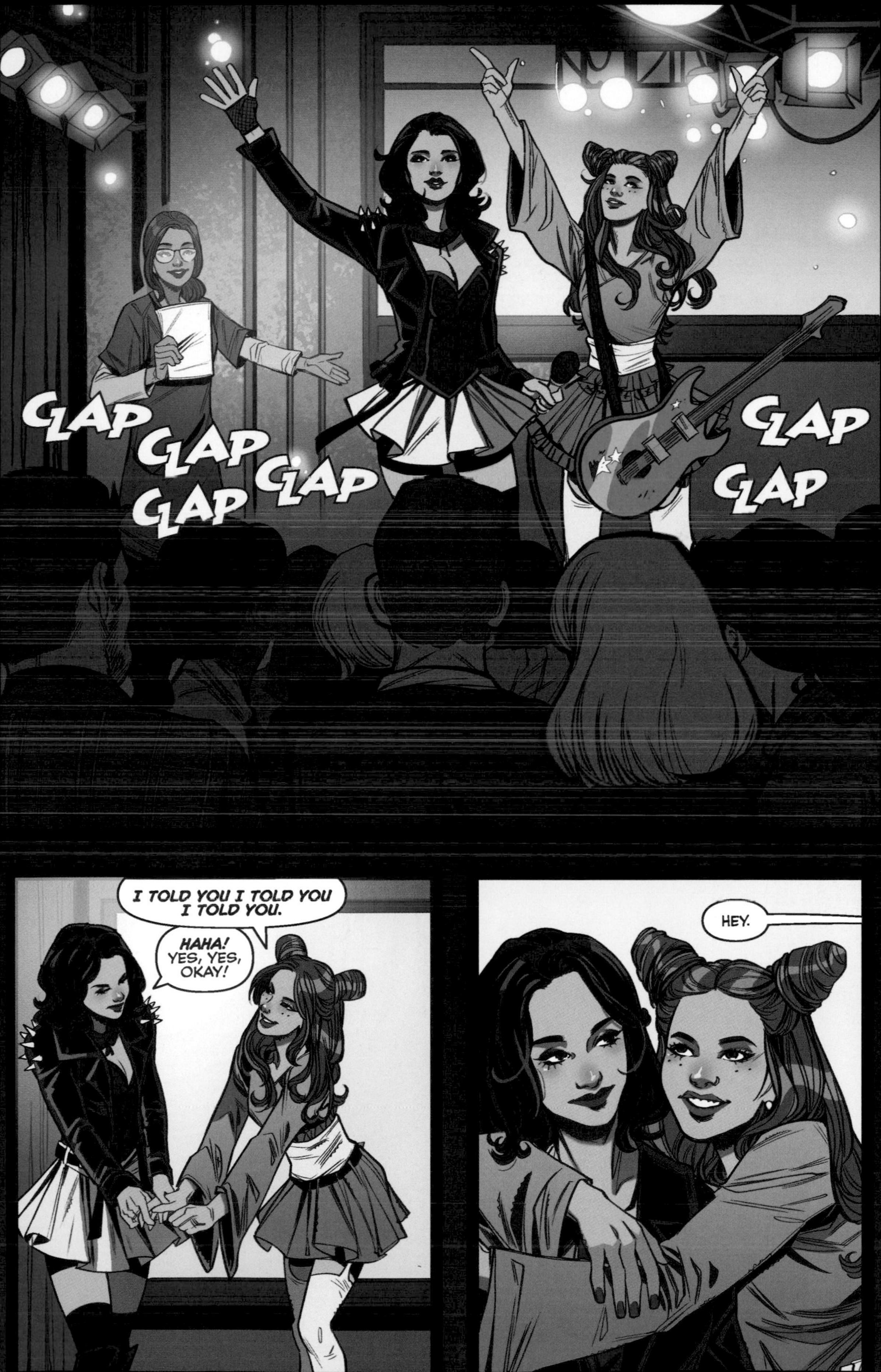
CLAP
CLAP
CLAP
CLAP
CLAP
CLAP
I TOLD YOU I TOLD YOU I TOLD YOU.
HAHA! YES, YES, OKAY!
HEY.

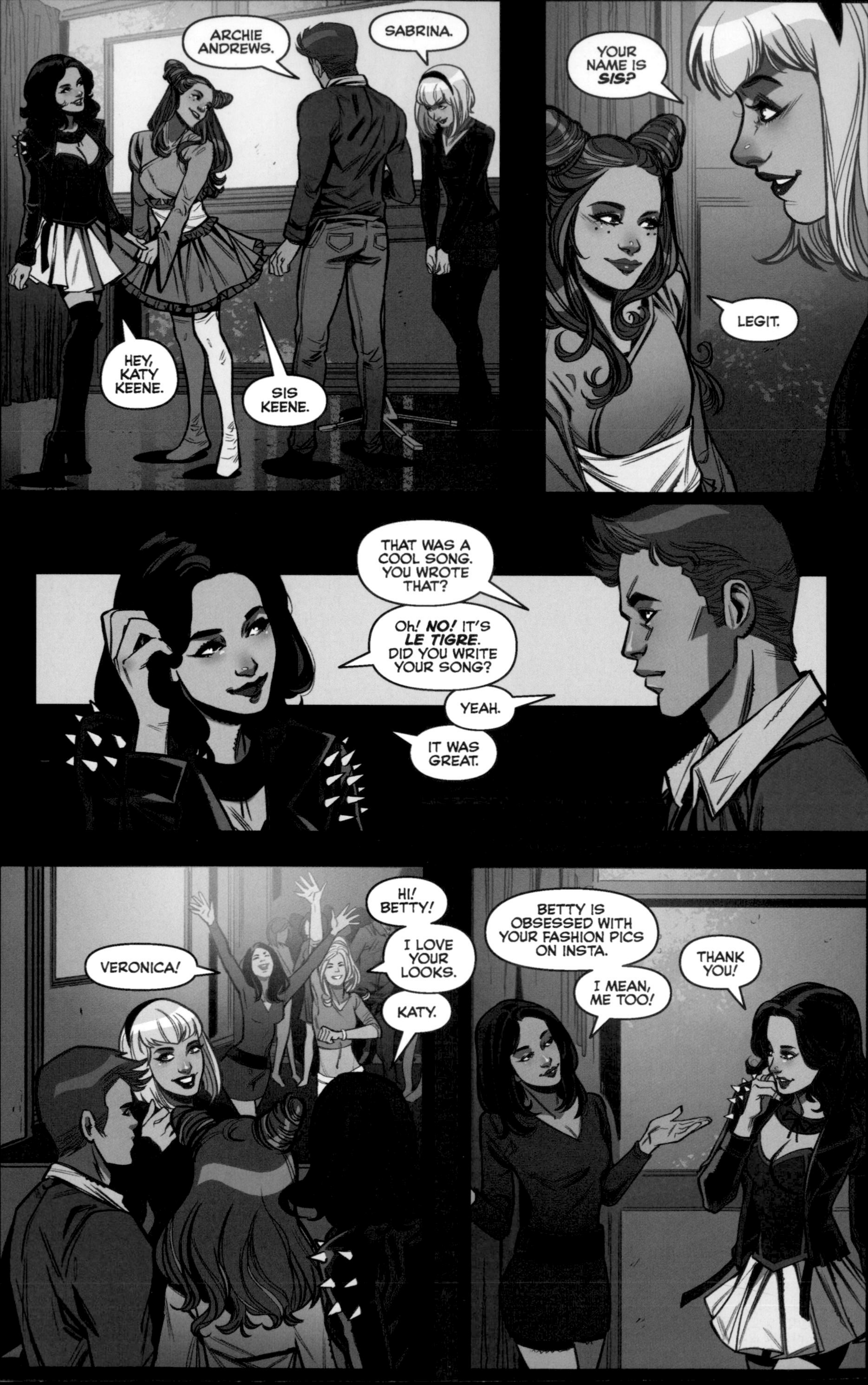
ARCHIE ANDREWS.
SABRINA.
HEY, KATY KEENE.
SIS KEENE.
YOUR NAME IS *SIS?*
LEGIT.
THAT WAS A COOL SONG. YOU WROTE THAT?
Oh! ***NO!*** IT'S ***LE TIGRE***. DID YOU WRITE YOUR SONG?
YEAH.
IT WAS GREAT.
VERONICA!
HI! BETTY!
I LOVE YOUR LOOKS.
KATY.
BETTY IS OBSESSED WITH YOUR FASHION PICS ON INSTA.
I MEAN, ME TOO!
THANK YOU!

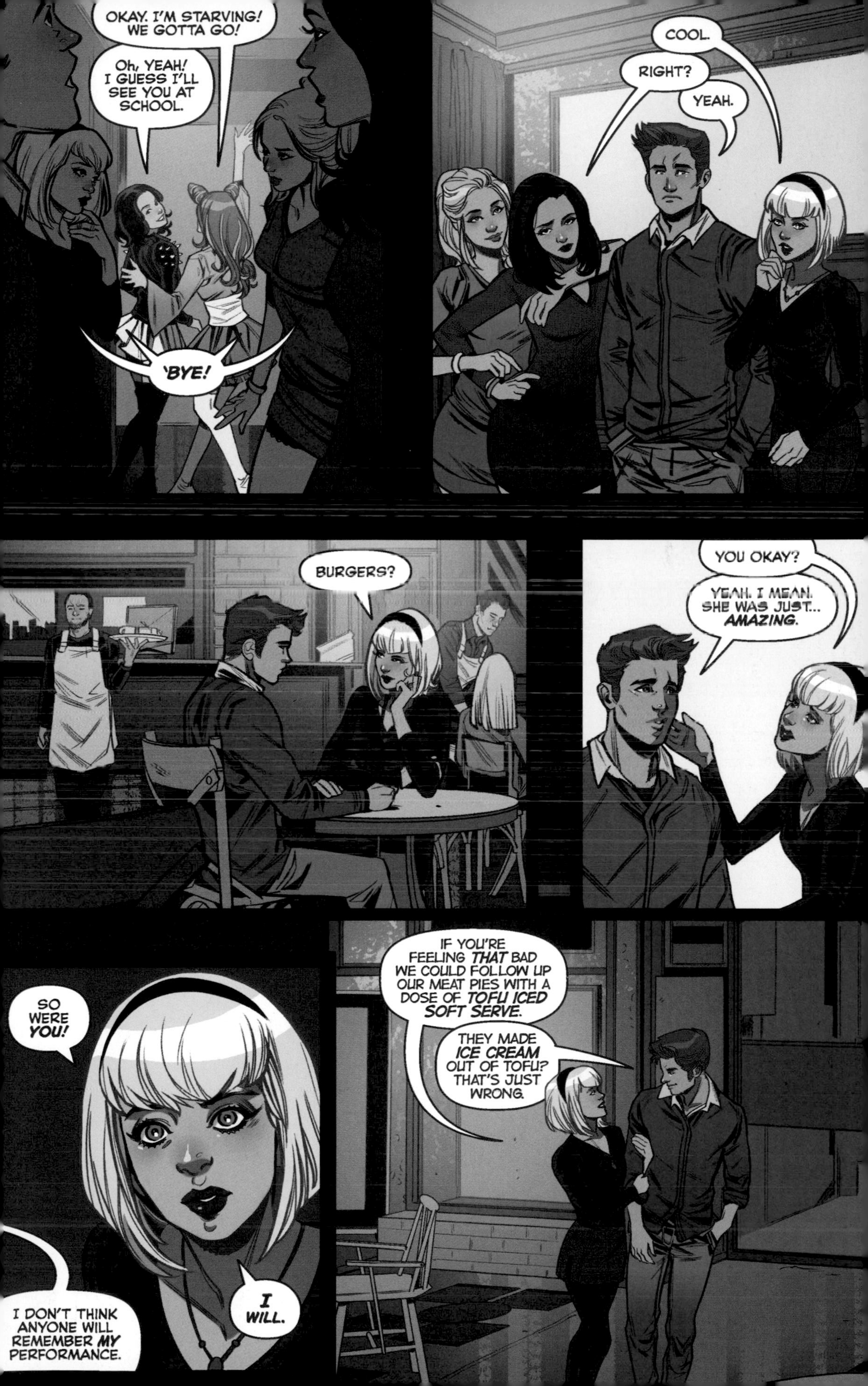
OKAY. I'M STARVING! WE GOTTA GO!
Oh, YEAH! I GUESS I'LL SEE YOU AT SCHOOL.
'BYE!
COOL.
RIGHT?
YEAH.
BURGERS?
YOU OKAY?
YEAH. I MEAN. SHE WAS JUST... AMAZING.
SO WERE YOU!
I DON'T THINK ANYONE WILL REMEMBER MY PERFORMANCE.
I WILL.
IF YOU'RE FEELING THAT BAD WE COULD FOLLOW UP OUR MEAT PIES WITH A DOSE OF TOFU ICED SOFT SERVE.
THEY MADE ICE CREAM OUT OF TOFU? THAT'S JUST WRONG.

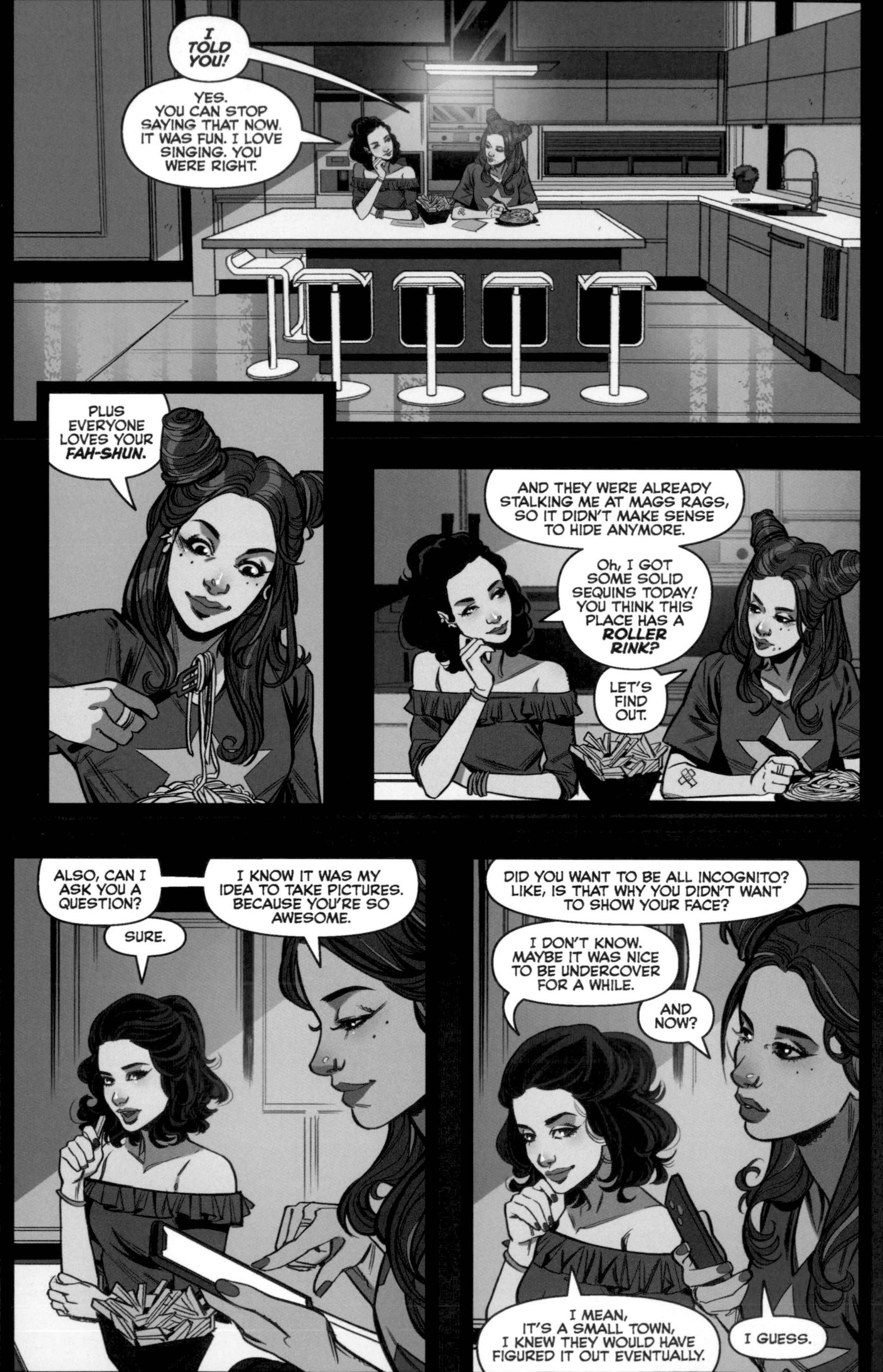
I TOLD YOU!
YES. YOU CAN STOP SAYING THAT NOW. IT WAS FUN. I LOVE SINGING. YOU WERE RIGHT.
PLUS EVERYONE LOVES YOUR FAH-SHUN.
AND THEY WERE ALREADY STALKING ME AT MAGS RAGS, SO IT DIDN'T MAKE SENSE TO HIDE ANYMORE.
Oh, I GOT SOME SOLID SEQUINS TODAY! YOU THINK THIS PLACE HAS A ROLLER RINK?
LET'S FIND OUT.
ALSO, CAN I ASK YOU A QUESTION?
SURE.
I KNOW IT WAS MY IDEA TO TAKE PICTURES. BECAUSE YOU'RE SO AWESOME.
DID YOU WANT TO BE ALL INCOGNITO? LIKE, IS THAT WHY YOU DIDN'T WANT TO SHOW YOUR FACE?
I DON'T KNOW. MAYBE IT WAS NICE TO BE UNDERCOVER FOR A WHILE.
AND NOW?
I MEAN, IT'S A SMALL TOWN, I KNEW THEY WOULD HAVE FIGURED IT OUT EVENTUALLY.
I GUESS.

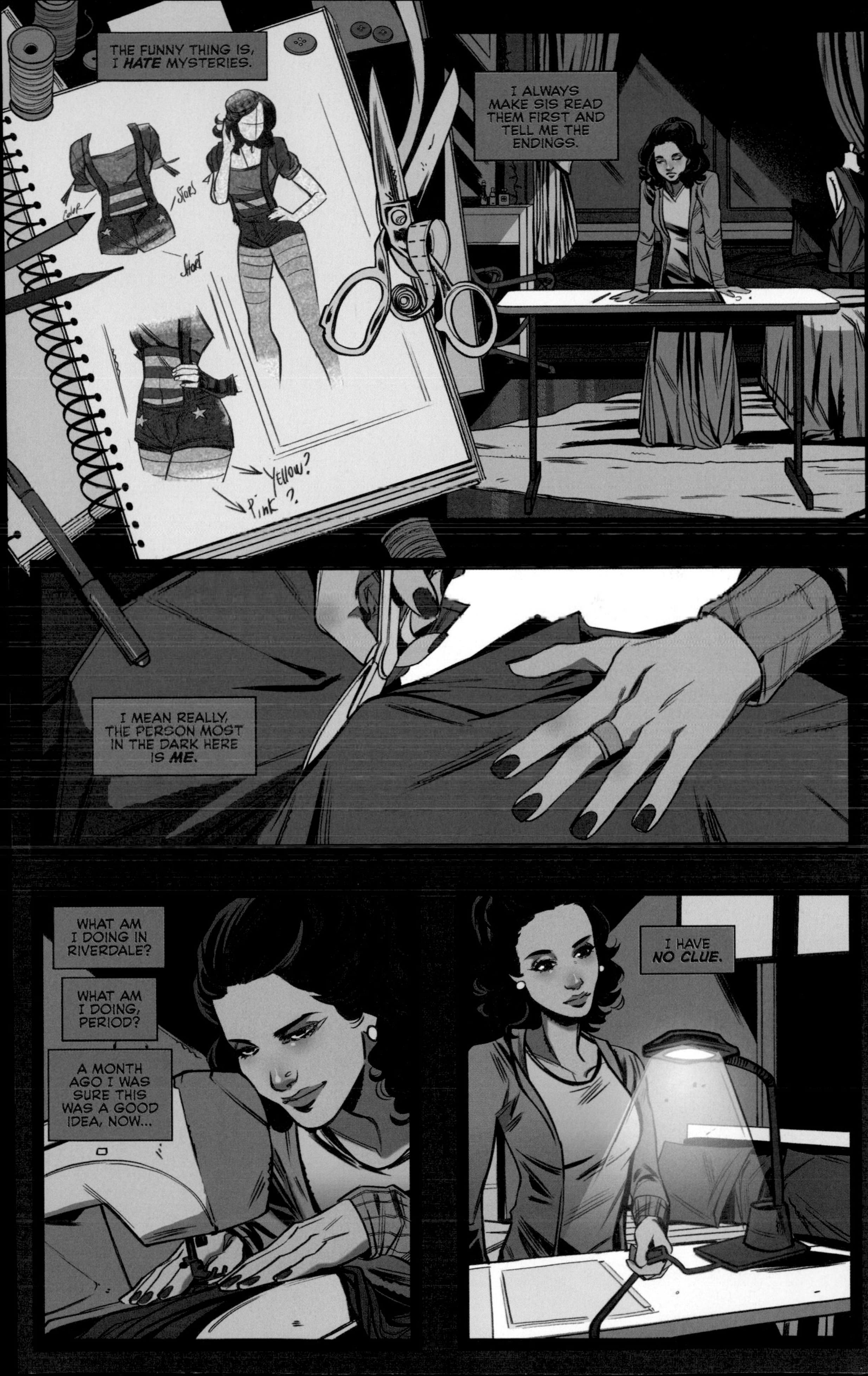
THE FUNNY THING IS, I HATE MYSTERIES.
Color
Stars
Short
Yellow?
Pink?
I ALWAYS MAKE SIS READ THEM FIRST AND TELL ME THE ENDINGS.
I MEAN REALLY, THE PERSON MOST IN THE DARK HERE IS ME.
WHAT AM I DOING IN RIVERDALE?
WHAT AM I DOING, PERIOD?
A MONTH AGO I WAS SURE THIS WAS A GOOD IDEA, NOW...
I HAVE NO CLUE.

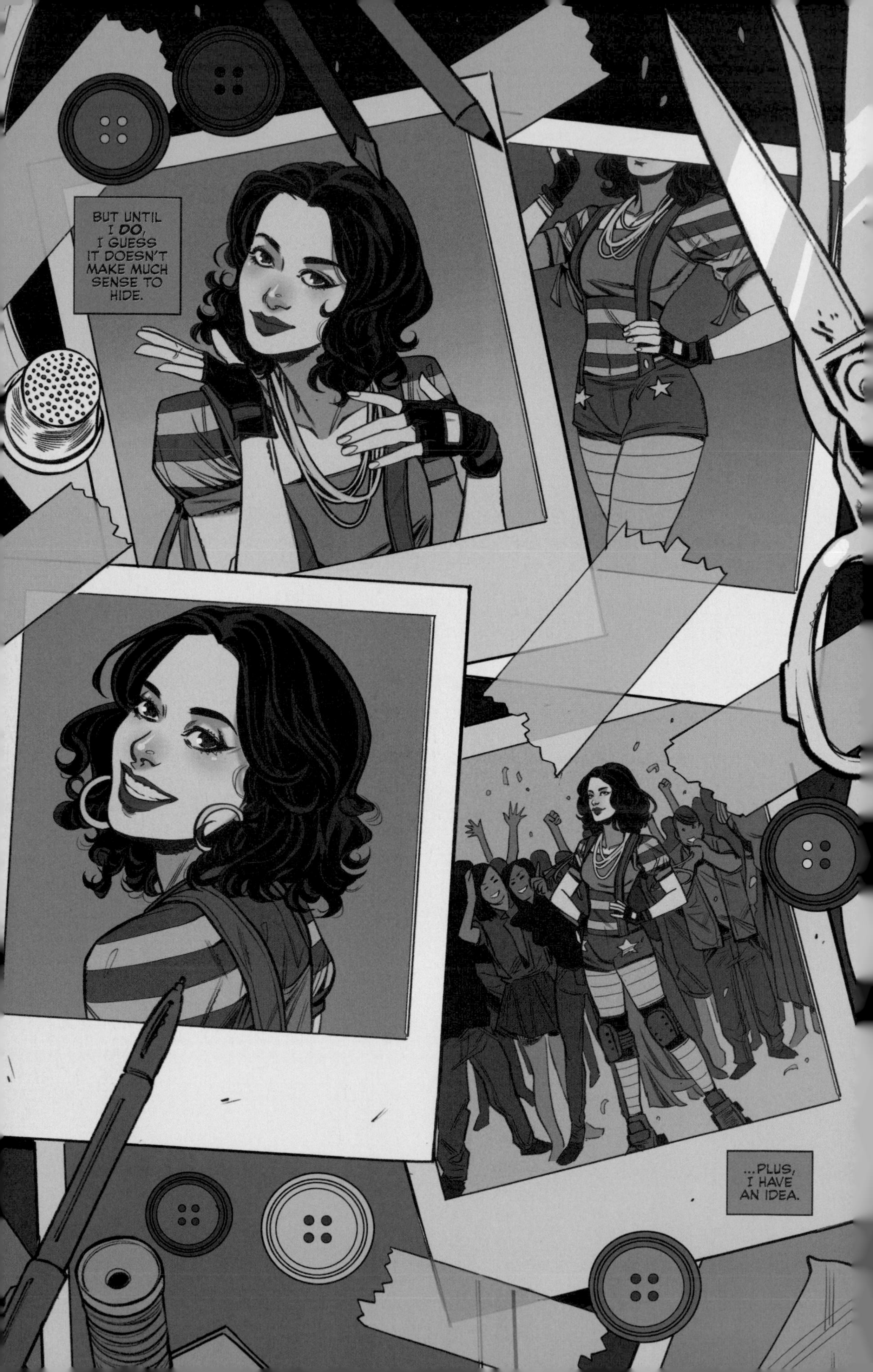
BUT UNTIL I *DO*, I GUESS IT DOESN'T MAKE MUCH SENSE TO HIDE.
...PLUS, I HAVE AN IDEA.

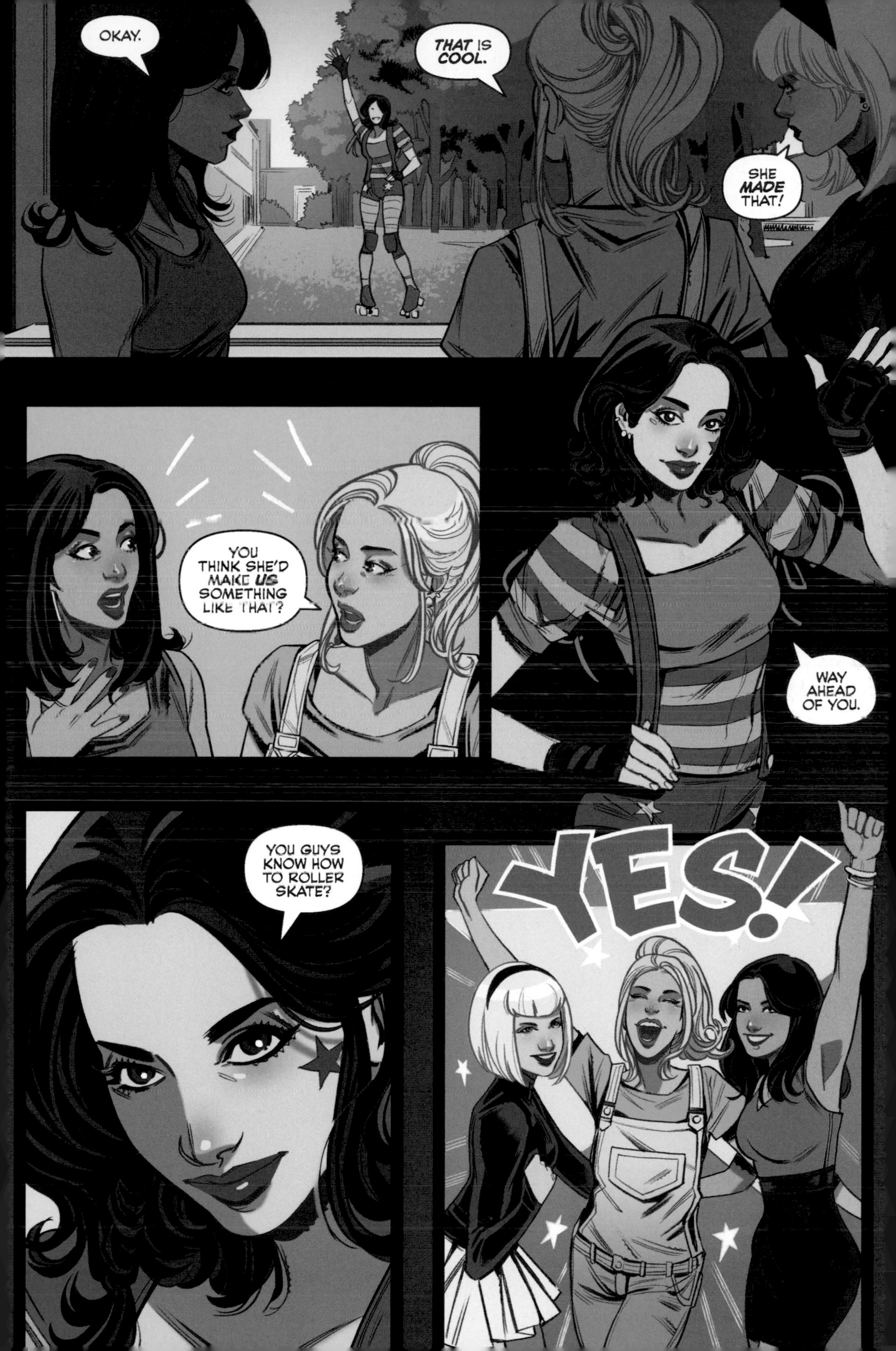
OKAY.
THAT IS COOL.
SHE MADE THAT!
YOU THINK SHE'D MAKE US SOMETHING LIKE THAT?
WAY AHEAD OF YOU.
YOU GUYS KNOW HOW TO ROLLER SKATE?
YES!

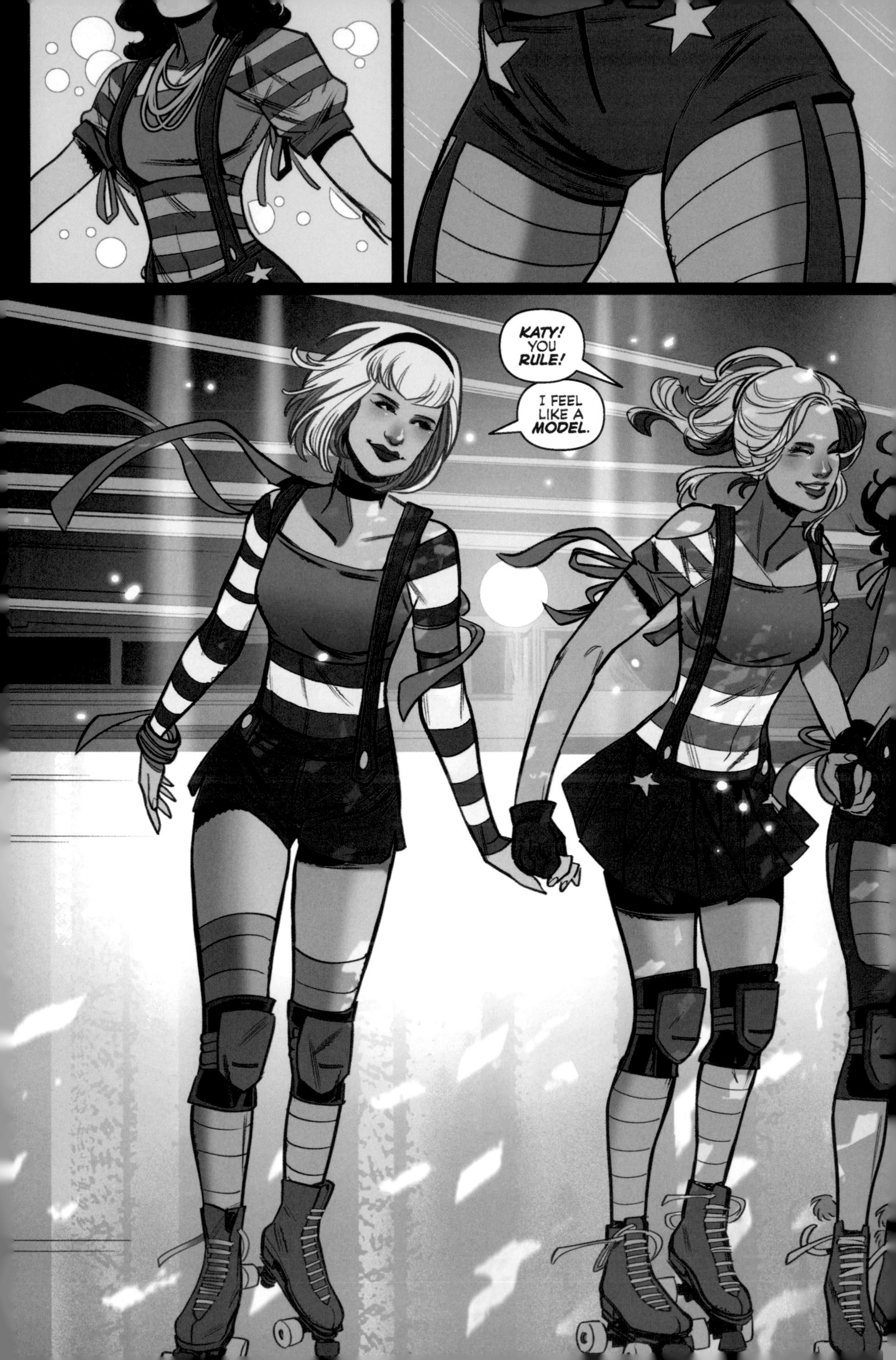
KATY! YOU RULE!
I FEEL LIKE A MODEL.

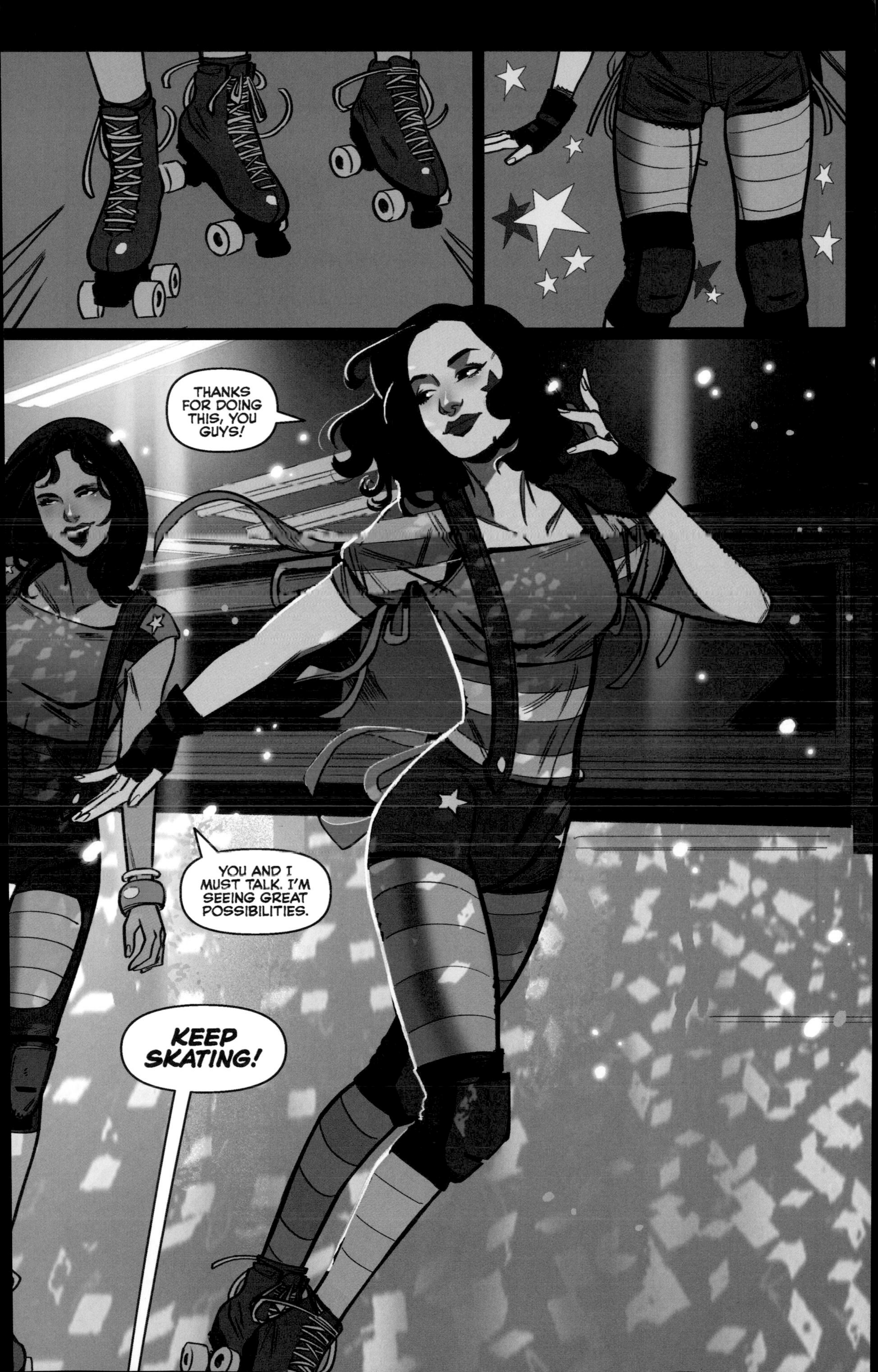

THANKS FOR DOING THIS, YOU GUYS!
YOU AND I MUST TALK. I'M SEEING GREAT POSSIBILITIES.
KEEP SKATING!

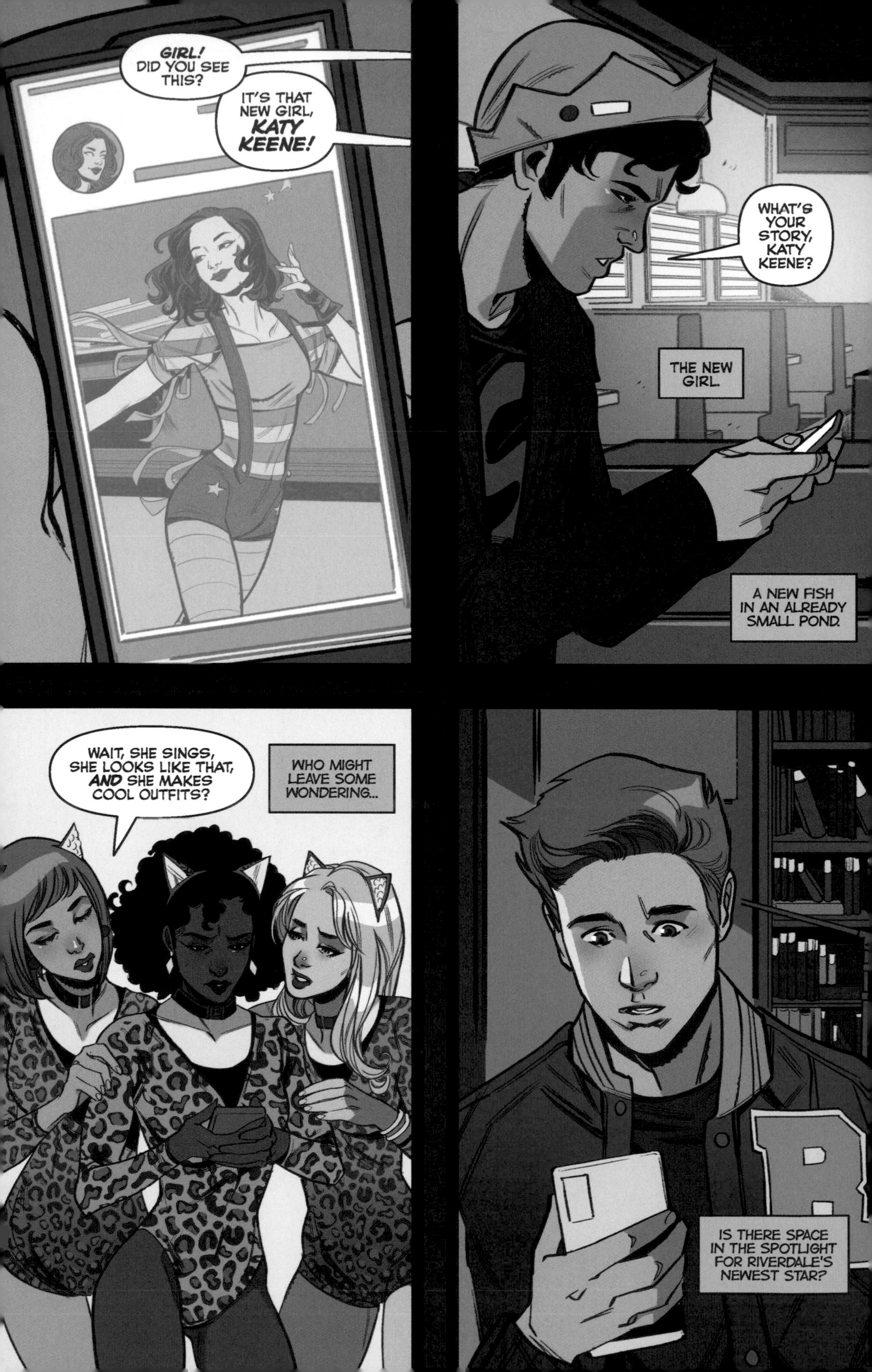
GIRL! DID YOU SEE THIS?
IT'S THAT NEW GIRL, KATY KEENE!
WHAT'S YOUR STORY, KATY KEENE?
THE NEW GIRL.
A NEW FISH IN AN ALREADY SMALL POND.
WAIT, SHE SINGS, SHE LOOKS LIKE THAT, AND SHE MAKES COOL OUTFITS?
WHO MIGHT LEAVE SOME WONDERING...
IS THERE SPACE IN THE SPOTLIGHT FOR RIVERDALE'S NEWEST STAR?

TO BE CONTINUED...

711

Archie® and Katy Keene™

STORY BY
MARIKO TAMAKI &
KEVIN PANETTA

ART BY
LAURA BRAGA

LETTERING BY
JACK MORELLI

COLORS BY
MATT HERMS

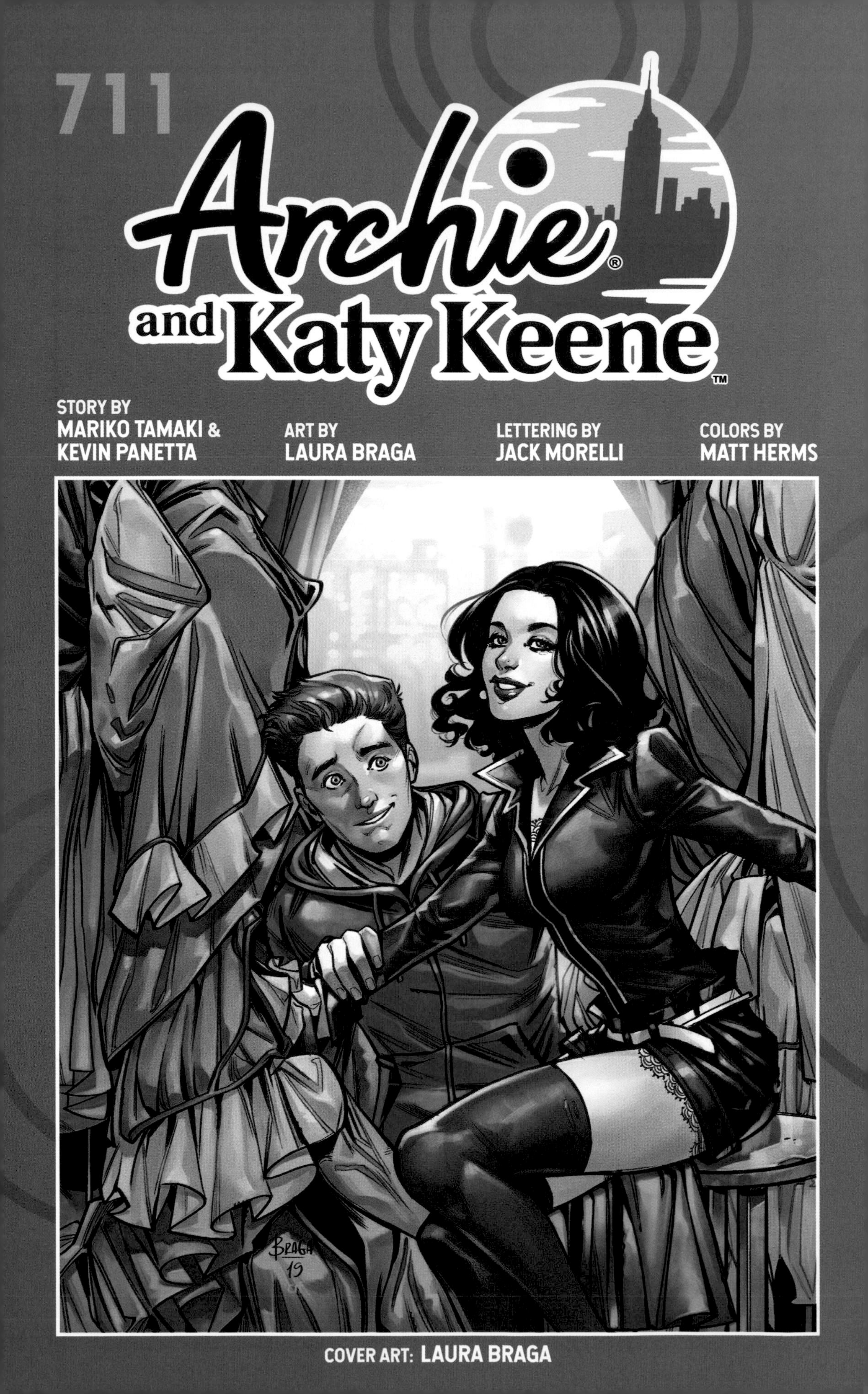
BRAGA
19

COVER ART: LAURA BRAGA

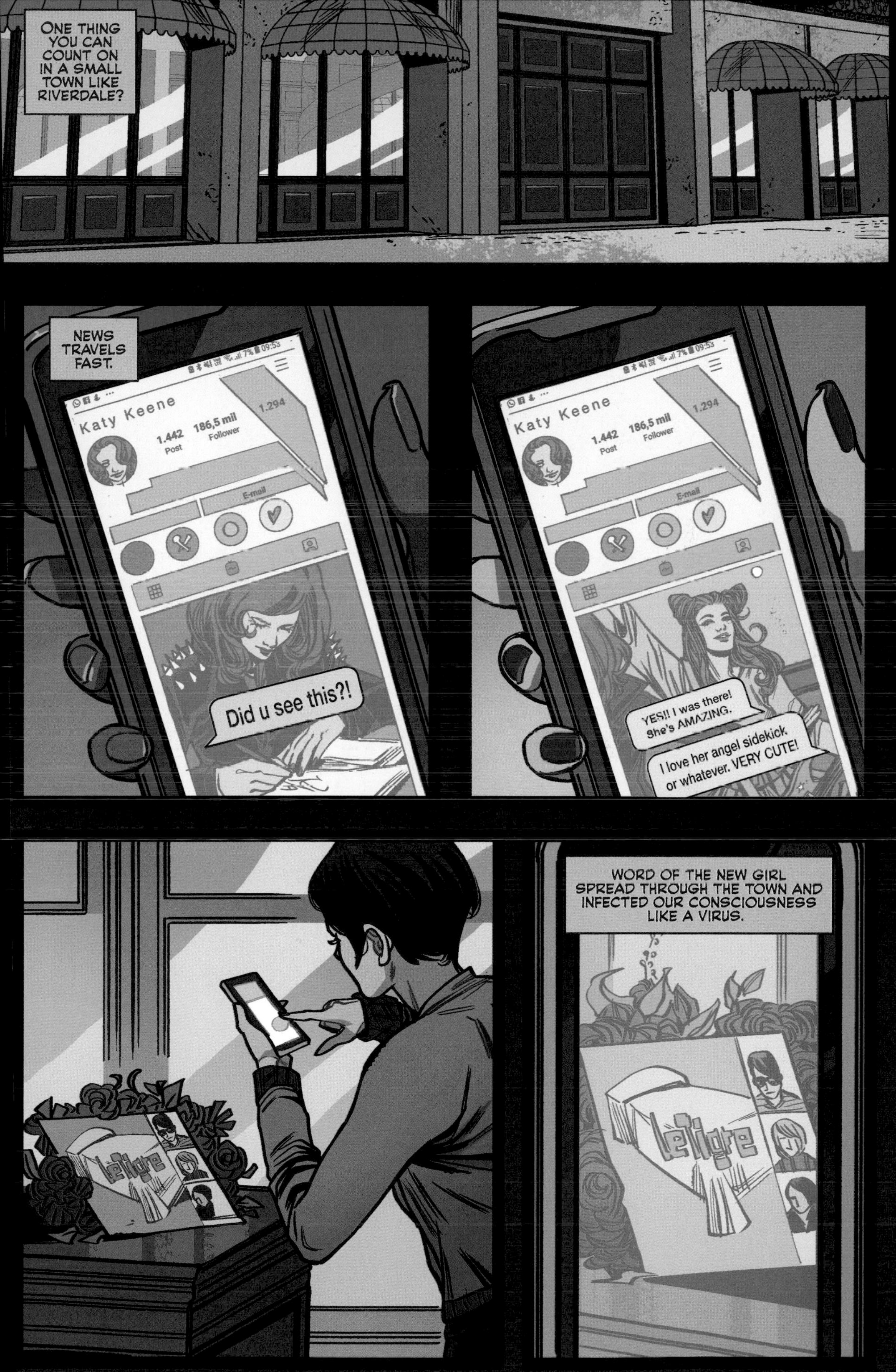

ONE THING YOU CAN COUNT ON IN A SMALL TOWN LIKE RIVERDALE?
NEWS TRAVELS FAST.
Katy Keene
1.442 Post
186,5 mil Follower
1.294
E-mail
Did u see this?!
Katy Keene
1.442 Post
186,5 mil Follower
1.294
E-mail
YES!! I was there! She's AMAZING.
I love her angel sidekick or whatever. VERY CUTE!
WORD OF THE NEW GIRL SPREAD THROUGH THE TOWN AND INFECTED OUR CONSCIOUSNESS LIKE A VIRUS.
le Tigre
le Tigre

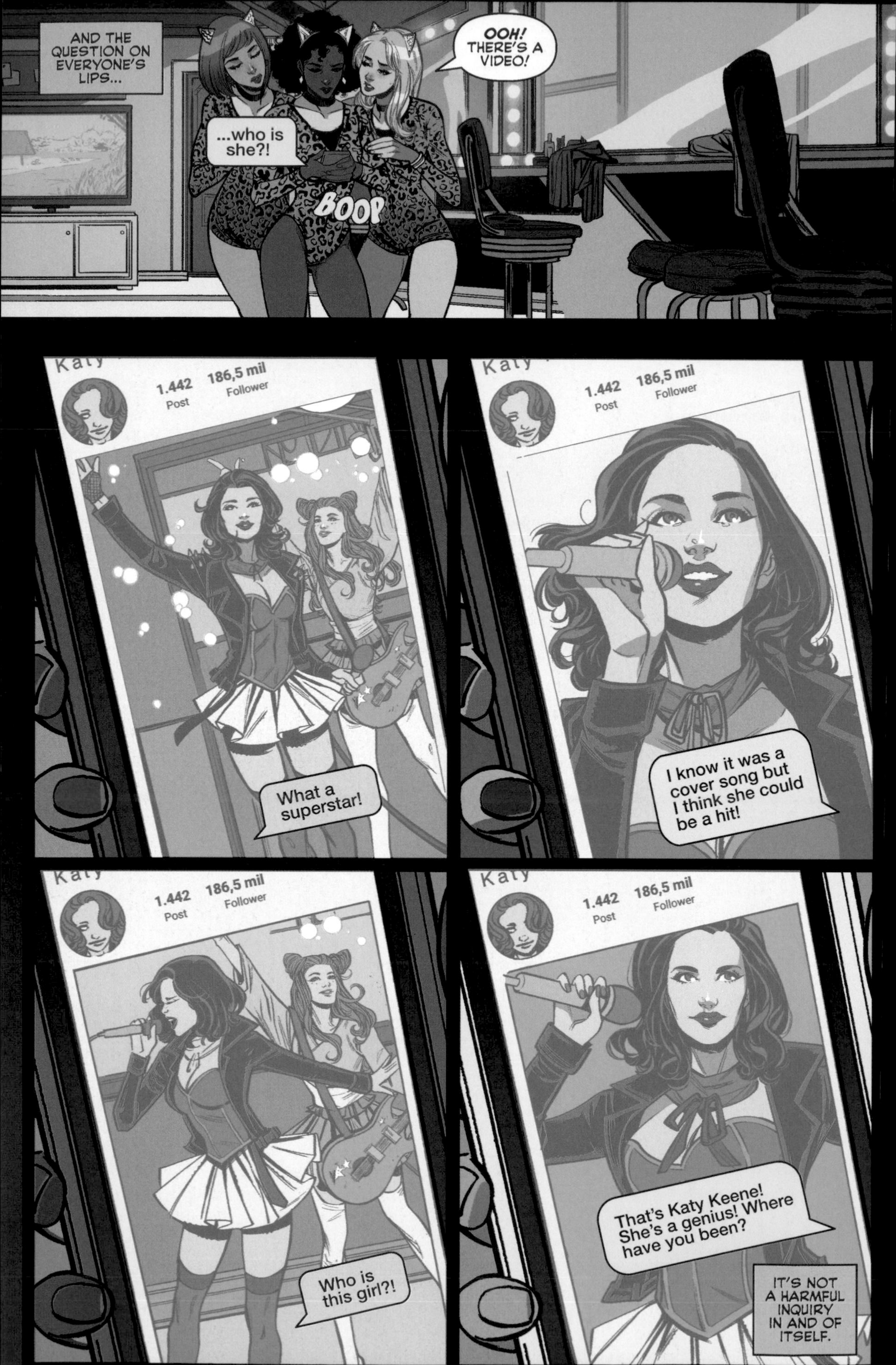

AND THE QUESTION ON EVERYONE'S LIPS...
...who is she?!
OOH! THERE'S A VIDEO!
BOOP
Katy
1.442 Post
186,5 mil Follower
What a superstar!
Katy
1.442 Post
186,5 mil Follower
I know it was a cover song but I think she could be a hit!
Katy
1.442 Post
186,5 mil Follower
Who is this girl?!
Katy
1.442 Post
186,5 mil Follower
That's Katy Keene! She's a genius! Where have you been?
IT'S NOT A HARMFUL INQUIRY IN AND OF ITSELF.

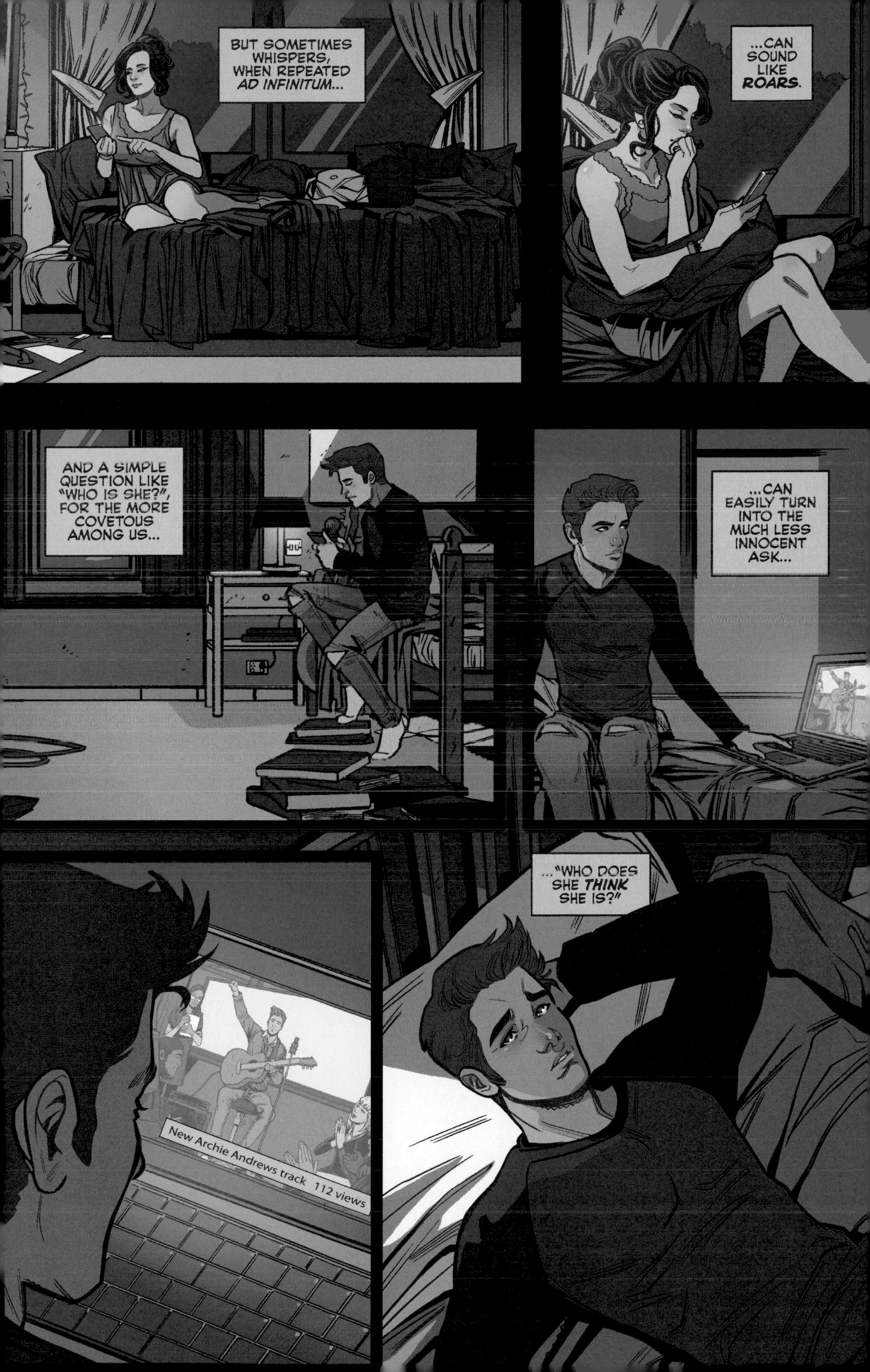
BUT SOMETIMES WHISPERS, WHEN REPEATED *AD INFINITUM*...
...CAN SOUND LIKE **ROARS**.
AND A SIMPLE QUESTION LIKE "WHO IS SHE?", FOR THE MORE COVETOUS AMONG US...
...CAN EASILY TURN INTO THE MUCH LESS INNOCENT ASK...
New Archie Andrews track 112 views
..."WHO DOES SHE *THINK* SHE IS?"

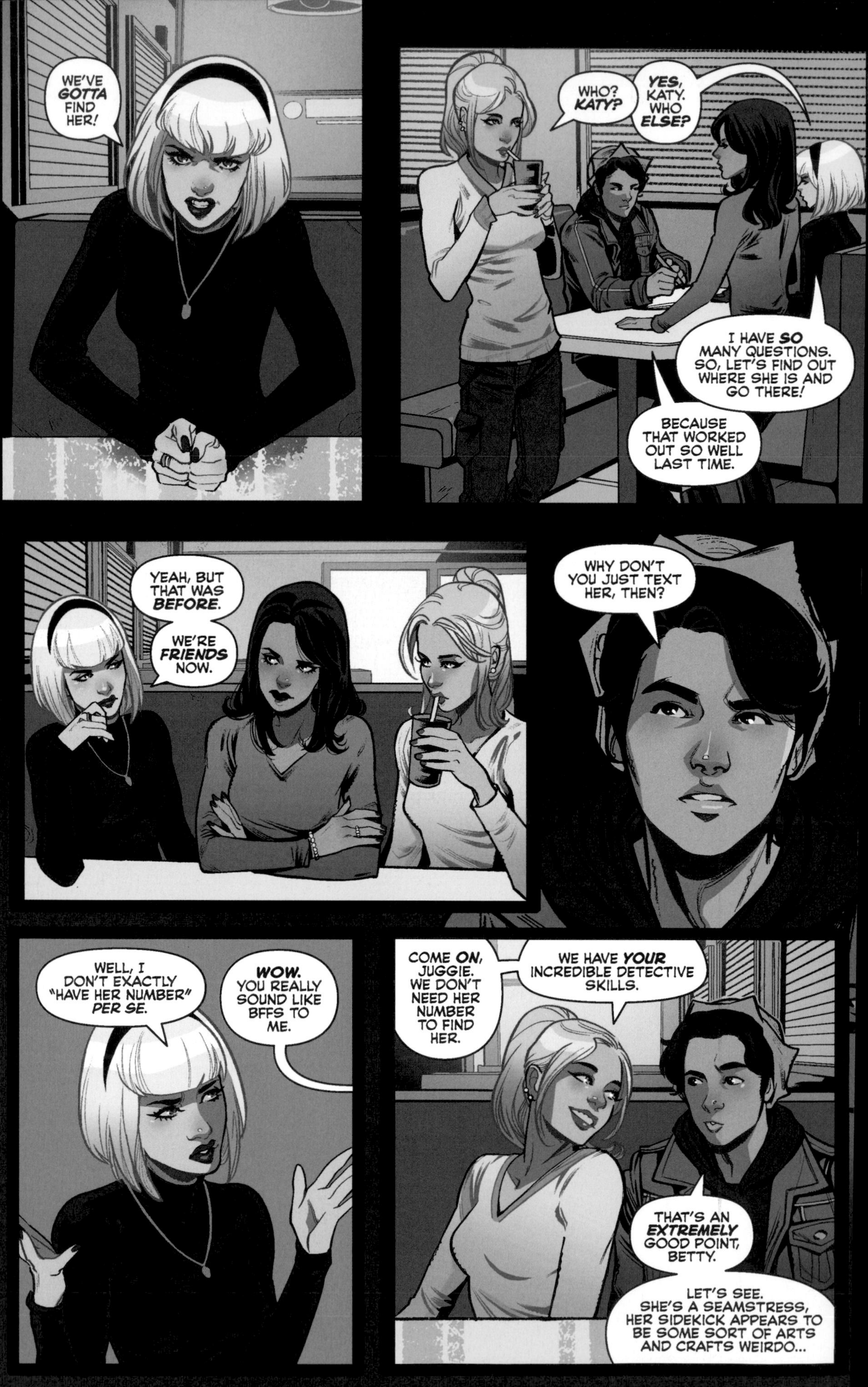
WE'VE GOTTA FIND HER!
WHO? KATY?
YES, KATY. WHO ELSE?
I HAVE SO MANY QUESTIONS. SO, LET'S FIND OUT WHERE SHE IS AND GO THERE!
BECAUSE THAT WORKED OUT SO WELL LAST TIME.
YEAH, BUT THAT WAS BEFORE.
WE'RE FRIENDS NOW.
WHY DON'T YOU JUST TEXT HER, THEN?
WELL, I DON'T EXACTLY "HAVE HER NUMBER" PER SE.
WOW. YOU REALLY SOUND LIKE BFFS TO ME.
COME ON, JUGGIE. WE DON'T NEED HER NUMBER TO FIND HER.
WE HAVE YOUR INCREDIBLE DETECTIVE SKILLS.
THAT'S AN EXTREMELY GOOD POINT, BETTY.
LET'S SEE. SHE'S A SEAMSTRESS, HER SIDEKICK APPEARS TO BE SOME SORT OF ARTS AND CRAFTS WEIRDO...

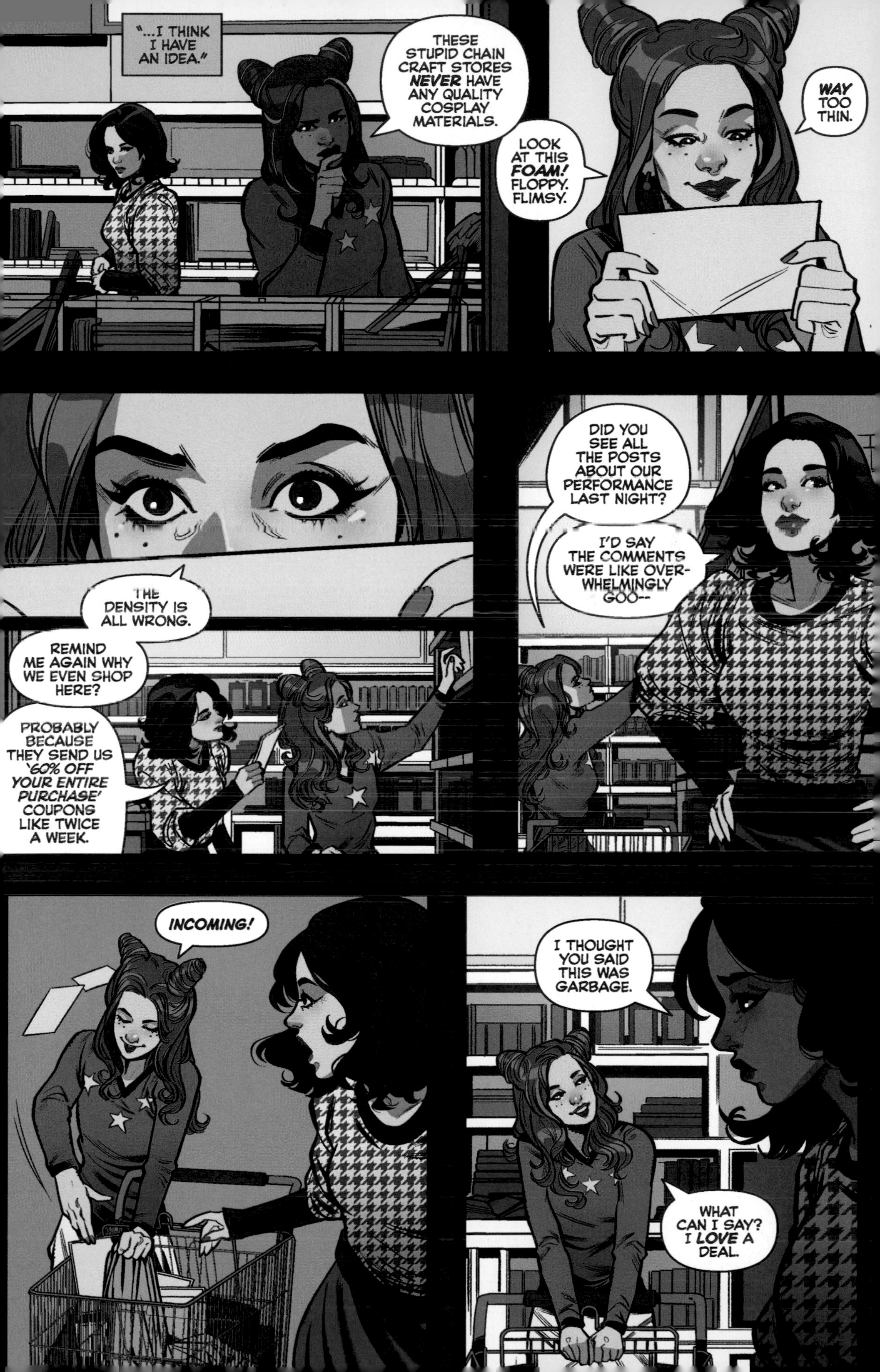
"...I THINK I HAVE AN IDEA."
THESE STUPID CHAIN CRAFT STORES **NEVER** HAVE ANY QUALITY COSPLAY MATERIALS.
LOOK AT THIS **FOAM!** FLOPPY. FLIMSY.
WAY TOO THIN.
THE DENSITY IS ALL WRONG.
REMIND ME AGAIN WHY WE EVEN SHOP HERE?
PROBABLY BECAUSE THEY SEND US *'60% OFF YOUR ENTIRE PURCHASE'* COUPONS LIKE TWICE A WEEK.
DID YOU SEE ALL THE POSTS ABOUT OUR PERFORMANCE LAST NIGHT?
I'D SAY THE COMMENTS WERE LIKE OVER-WHELMINGLY GOO--
INCOMING!
I THOUGHT YOU SAID THIS WAS GARBAGE.
WHAT CAN I SAY? I **LOVE** A DEAL.

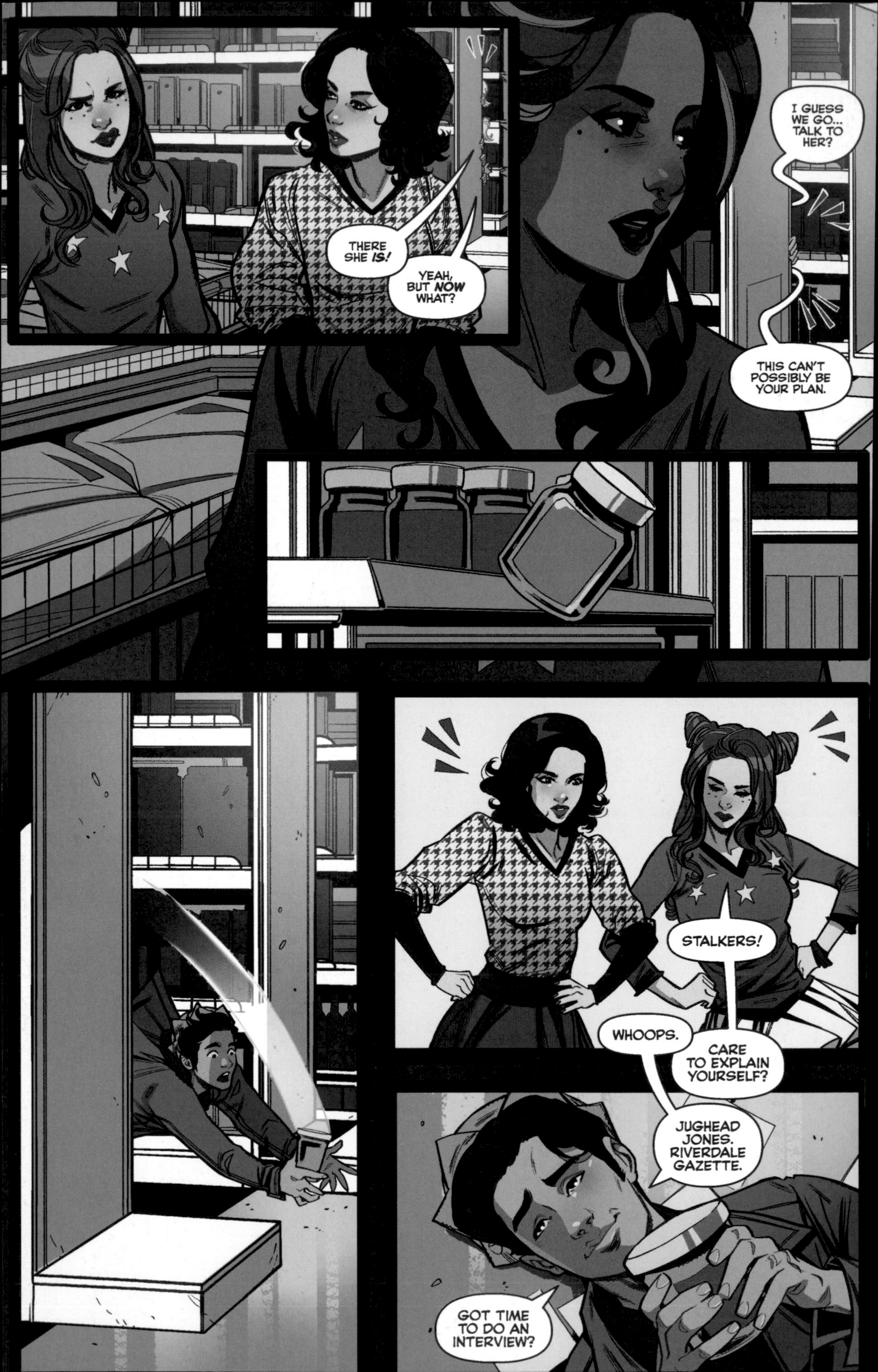
THERE SHE IS!
YEAH, BUT NOW WHAT?
I GUESS WE GO... TALK TO HER?
THIS CAN'T POSSIBLY BE YOUR PLAN.
STALKERS!
WHOOPS.
CARE TO EXPLAIN YOURSELF?
JUGHEAD JONES. RIVERDALE GAZETTE.
GOT TIME TO DO AN INTERVIEW?

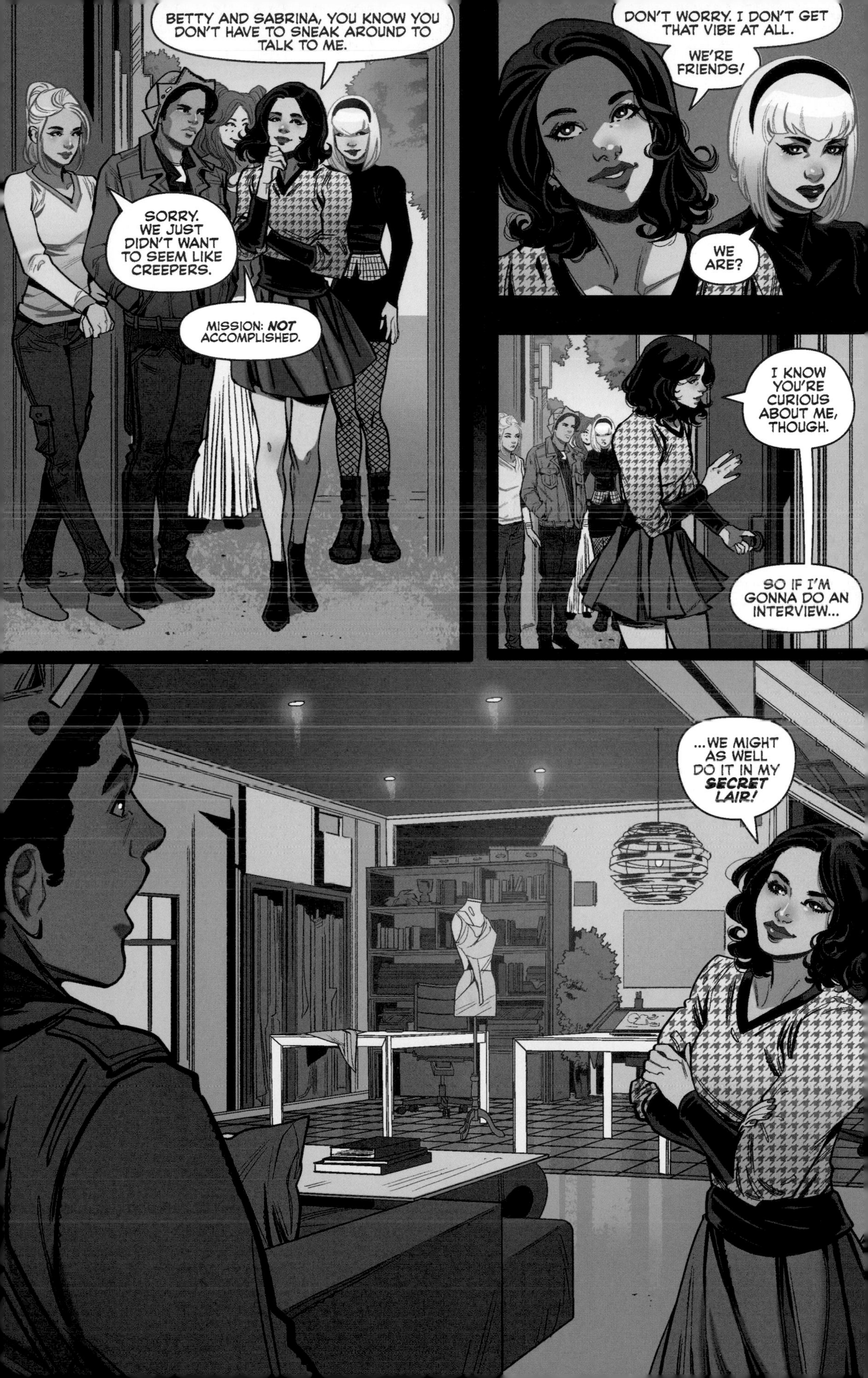
BETTY AND SABRINA, YOU KNOW YOU DON'T HAVE TO SNEAK AROUND TO TALK TO ME.
SORRY. WE JUST DIDN'T WANT TO SEEM LIKE CREEPERS.
MISSION: ***NOT*** ACCOMPLISHED.
DON'T WORRY. I DON'T GET THAT VIBE AT ALL.
WE'RE FRIENDS!
WE ARE?
I KNOW YOU'RE CURIOUS ABOUT ME, THOUGH.
SO IF I'M GONNA DO AN INTERVIEW...
...WE MIGHT AS WELL DO IT IN MY ***SECRET LAIR!***

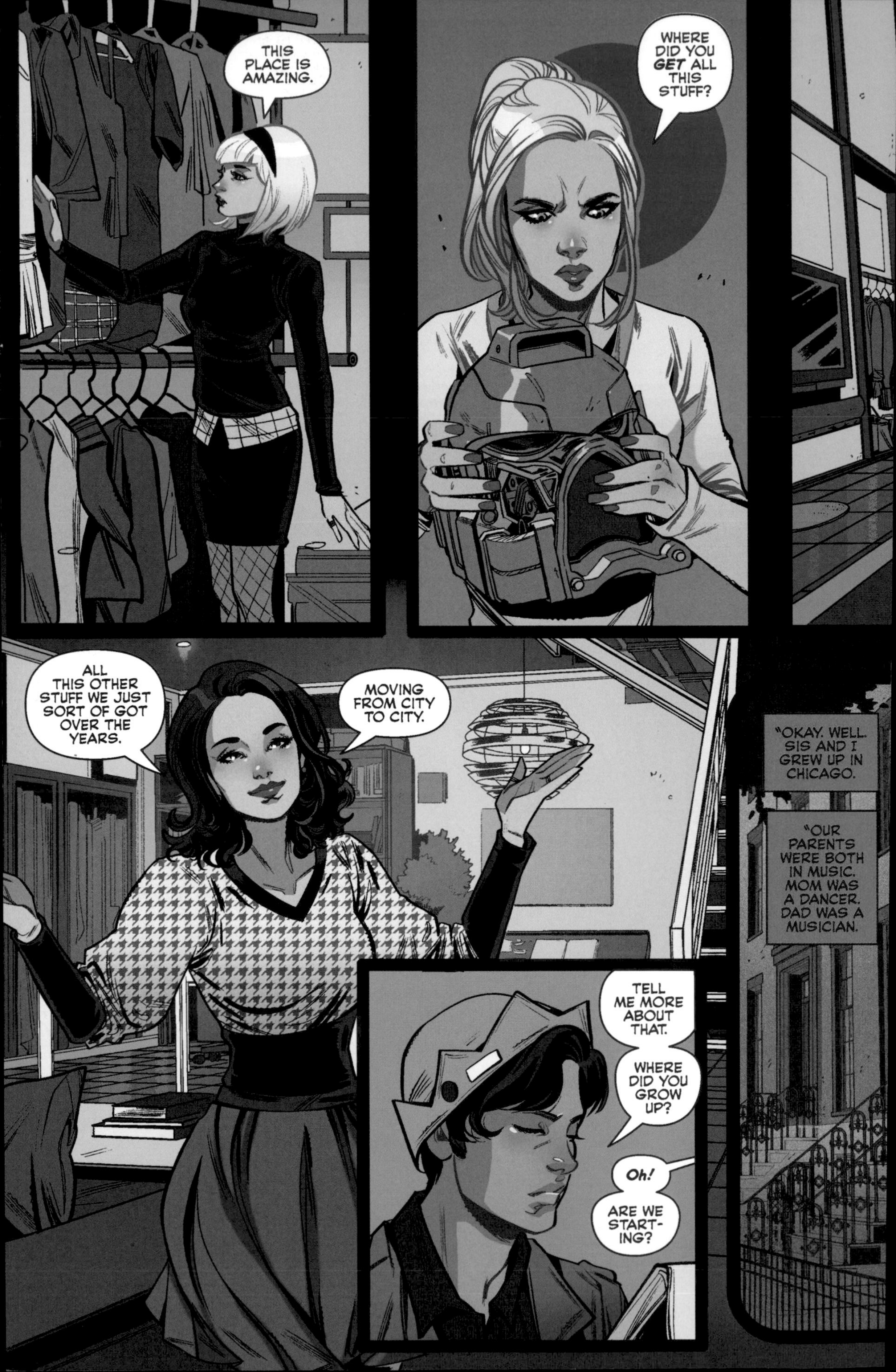
THIS PLACE IS AMAZING.
WHERE DID YOU **GET** ALL THIS STUFF?
ALL THIS OTHER STUFF WE JUST SORT OF GOT OVER THE YEARS.
MOVING FROM CITY TO CITY.
"OKAY. WELL. SIS AND I GREW UP IN CHICAGO.
"OUR PARENTS WERE BOTH IN MUSIC. MOM WAS A DANCER. DAD WAS A MUSICIAN.
TELL ME MORE ABOUT THAT.
WHERE DID YOU GROW UP?
Oh!
ARE WE STARTING?

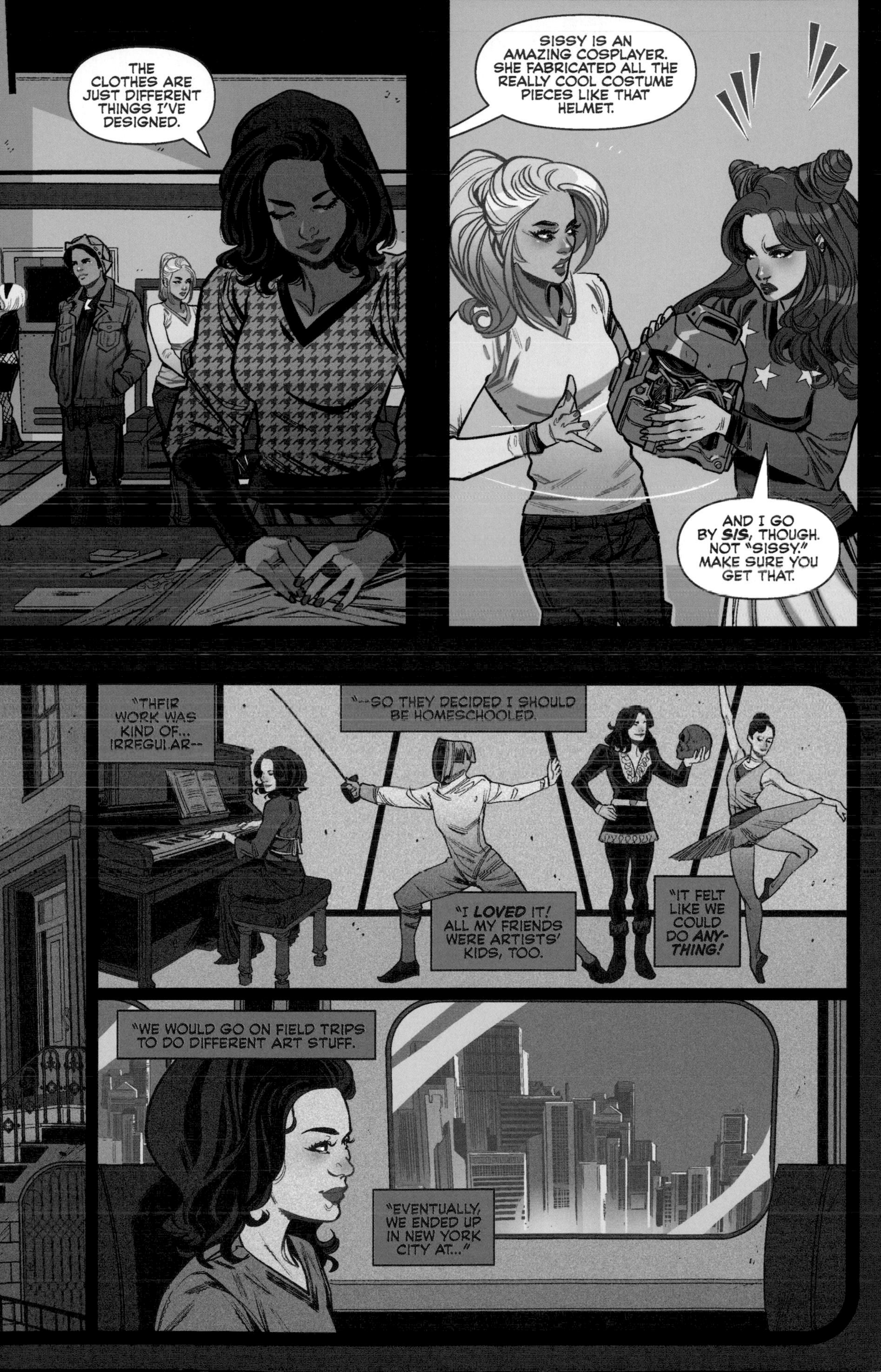
THE CLOTHES ARE JUST DIFFERENT THINGS I'VE DESIGNED.
SISSY IS AN AMAZING COSPLAYER. SHE FABRICATED ALL THE REALLY COOL COSTUME PIECES LIKE THAT HELMET.
AND I GO BY SIS, THOUGH. NOT "SISSY." MAKE SURE YOU GET THAT.
"THEIR WORK WAS KIND OF... IRREGULAR--
"--SO THEY DECIDED I SHOULD BE HOMESCHOOLED.
"I LOVED IT! ALL MY FRIENDS WERE ARTISTS' KIDS, TOO.
"IT FELT LIKE WE COULD DO ANYTHING!
"WE WOULD GO ON FIELD TRIPS TO DO DIFFERENT ART STUFF.
"EVENTUALLY, WE ENDED UP IN NEW YORK CITY AT..."

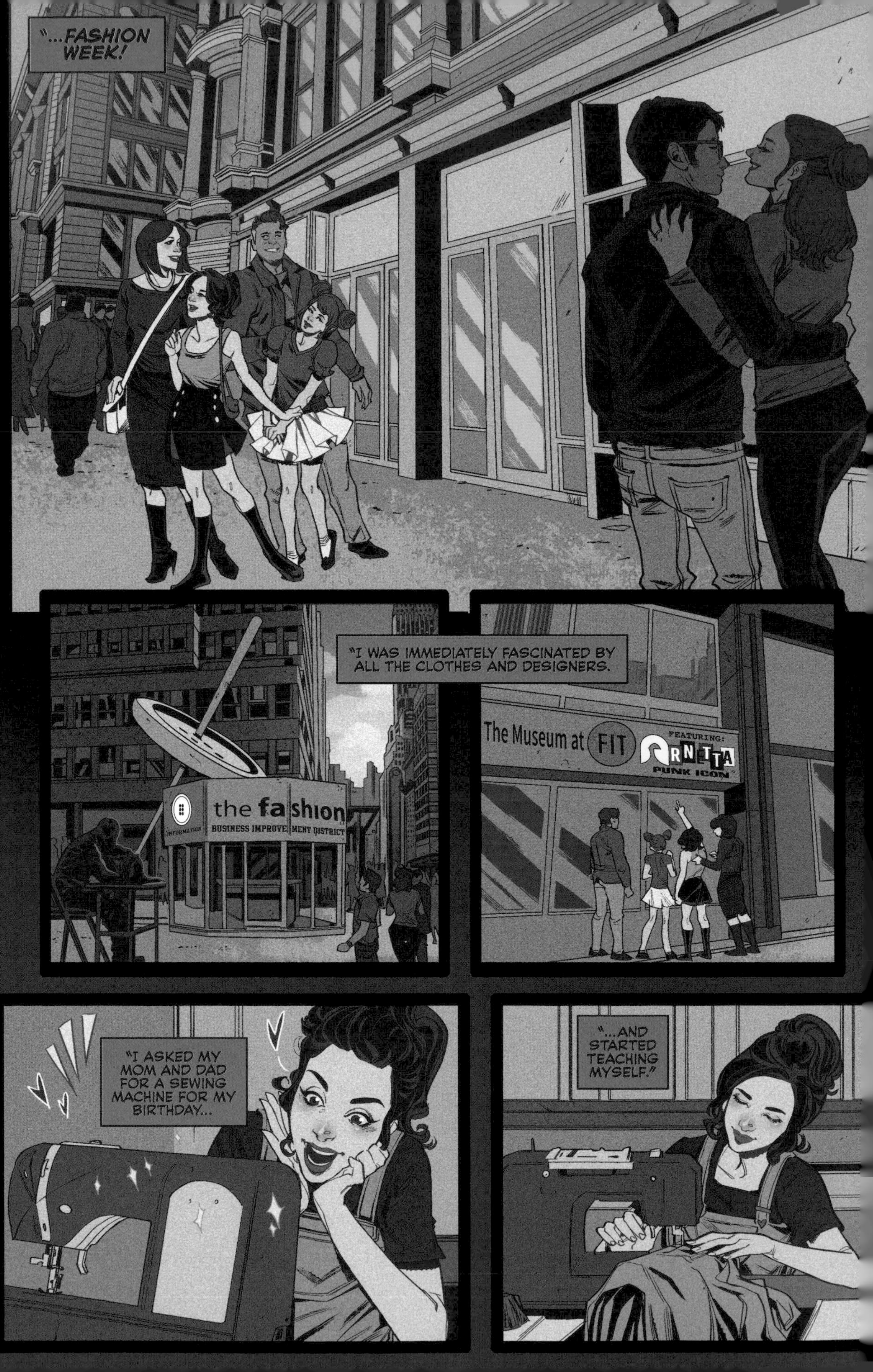
"...FASHION WEEK!
"I WAS IMMEDIATELY FASCINATED BY ALL THE CLOTHES AND DESIGNERS.
INFORMATION
the fashion
BUSINESS IMPROVEMENT DISTRICT
The Museum at FIT
FEATURING:
ARNETTA
PUNK ICON
"I ASKED MY MOM AND DAD FOR A SEWING MACHINE FOR MY BIRTHDAY...
"...AND STARTED TEACHING MYSELF."

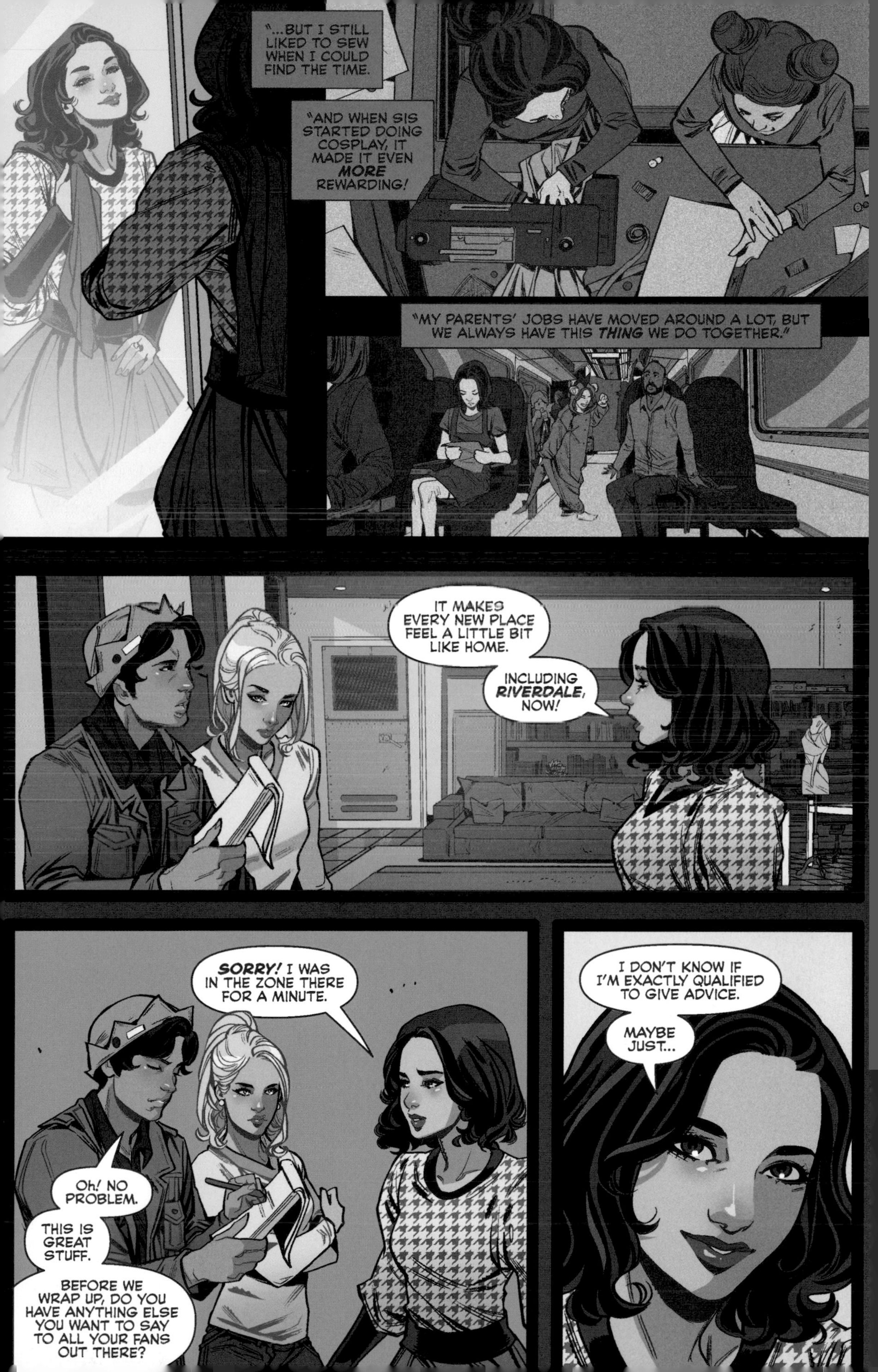

"...BUT I STILL LIKED TO SEW WHEN I COULD FIND THE TIME.
"AND WHEN SIS STARTED DOING COSPLAY, IT MADE IT EVEN MORE REWARDING!
"MY PARENTS' JOBS HAVE MOVED AROUND A LOT, BUT WE ALWAYS HAVE THIS THING WE DO TOGETHER."
IT MAKES EVERY NEW PLACE FEEL A LITTLE BIT LIKE HOME.
INCLUDING RIVERDALE, NOW!
SORRY! I WAS IN THE ZONE THERE FOR A MINUTE.
...
Oh! NO PROBLEM.
THIS IS GREAT STUFF.
BEFORE WE WRAP UP, DO YOU HAVE ANYTHING ELSE YOU WANT TO SAY TO ALL YOUR FANS OUT THERE?
I DON'T KNOW IF I'M EXACTLY QUALIFIED TO GIVE ADVICE.
MAYBE JUST...

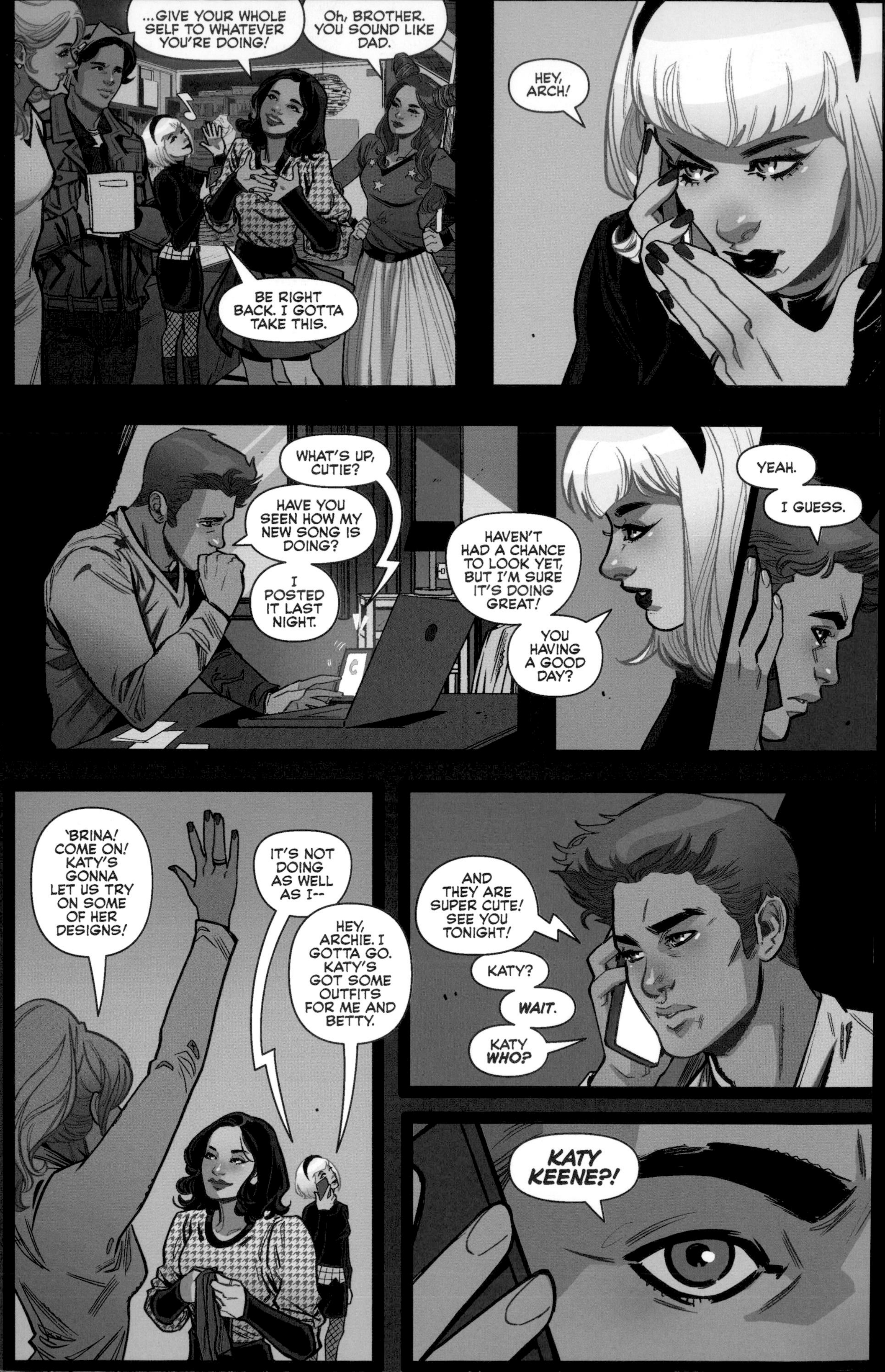
...GIVE YOUR WHOLE SELF TO WHATEVER YOU'RE DOING!
Oh, BROTHER. YOU SOUND LIKE DAD.
BE RIGHT BACK. I GOTTA TAKE THIS.
HEY, ARCH!
WHAT'S UP, CUTIE?
HAVE YOU SEEN HOW MY NEW SONG IS DOING?
I POSTED IT LAST NIGHT.
HAVEN'T HAD A CHANCE TO LOOK YET, BUT I'M SURE IT'S DOING GREAT!
YOU HAVING A GOOD DAY?
YEAH.
I GUESS.
'BRINA! COME ON! KATY'S GONNA LET US TRY ON SOME OF HER DESIGNS!
IT'S NOT DOING AS WELL AS I--
HEY, ARCHIE. I GOTTA GO. KATY'S GOT SOME OUTFITS FOR ME AND BETTY.
AND THEY ARE SUPER CUTE! SEE YOU TONIGHT!
KATY?
WAIT.
KATY WHO?
KATY KEENE?!

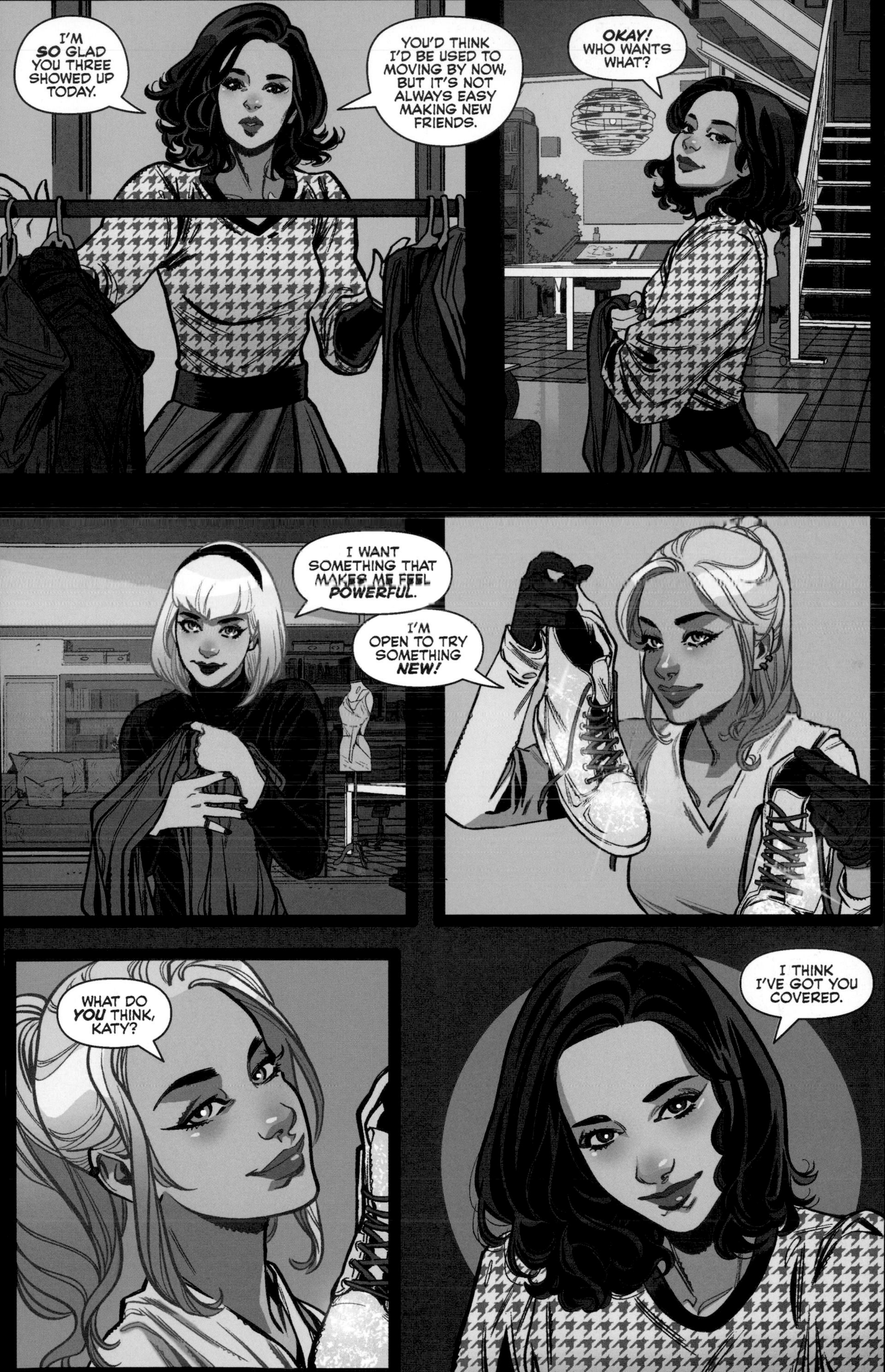
I'M *SO* GLAD YOU THREE SHOWED UP TODAY.
YOU'D THINK I'D BE USED TO MOVING BY NOW, BUT IT'S NOT ALWAYS EASY MAKING NEW FRIENDS.
OKAY! WHO WANTS WHAT?
I WANT SOMETHING THAT MAKES ME FEEL *POWERFUL*.
I'M OPEN TO TRY SOMETHING *NEW!*
WHAT DO *YOU* THINK, KATY?
I THINK I'VE GOT YOU COVERED.

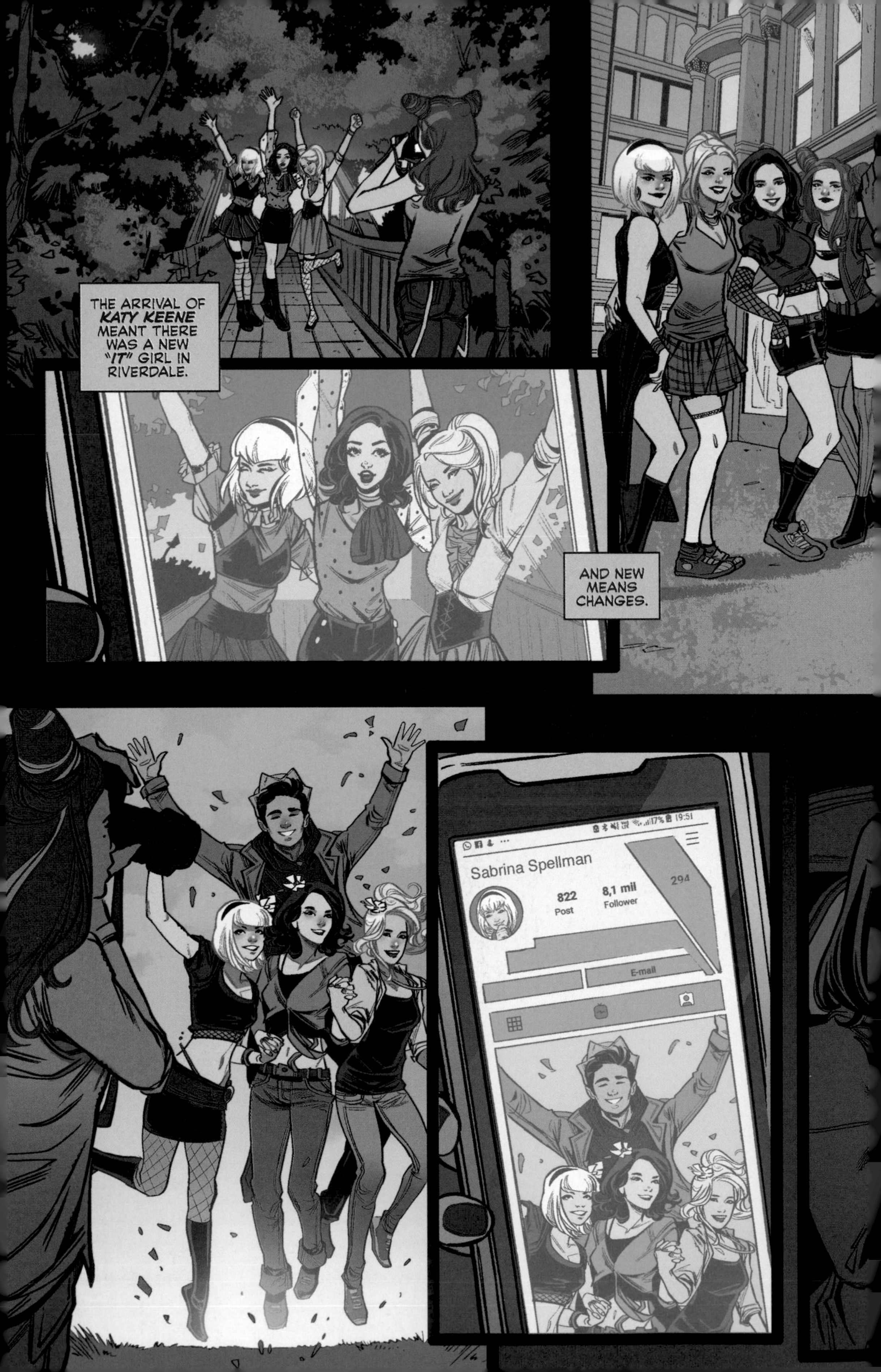

THE ARRIVAL OF KATY KEENE MEANT THERE WAS A NEW "IT" GIRL IN RIVERDALE.
AND NEW MEANS CHANGES.
Sabrina Spellman
822
Post
8,1 mil
Follower
294
E-mail

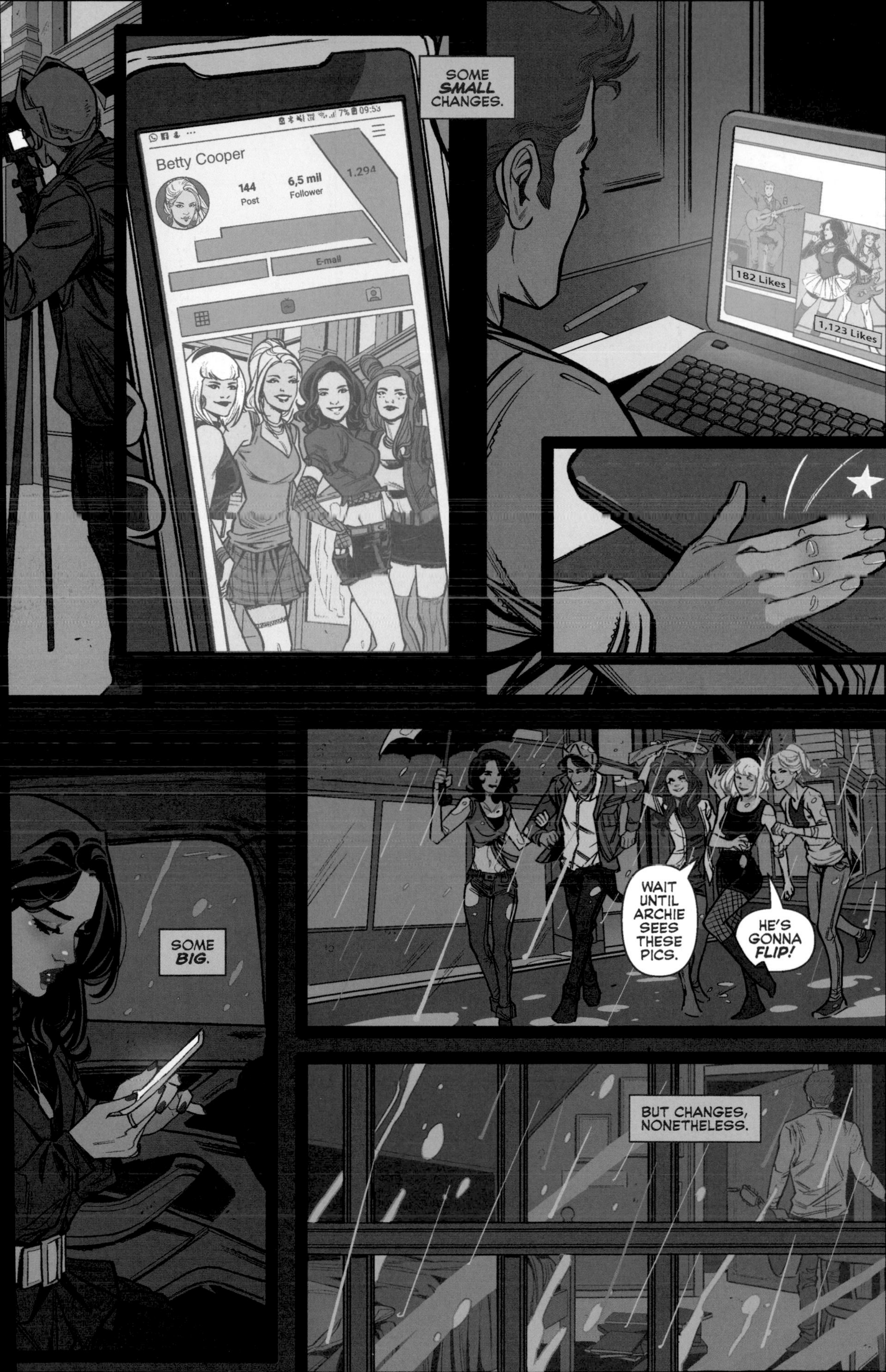

SOME SMALL CHANGES.
Betty Cooper
144 Post
6,5 mil Follower
1,294
E-mail
182 Likes
1,123 Likes
SOME BIG.
WAIT UNTIL ARCHIE SEES THESE PICS.
HE'S GONNA FLIP!
BUT CHANGES, NONETHELESS.

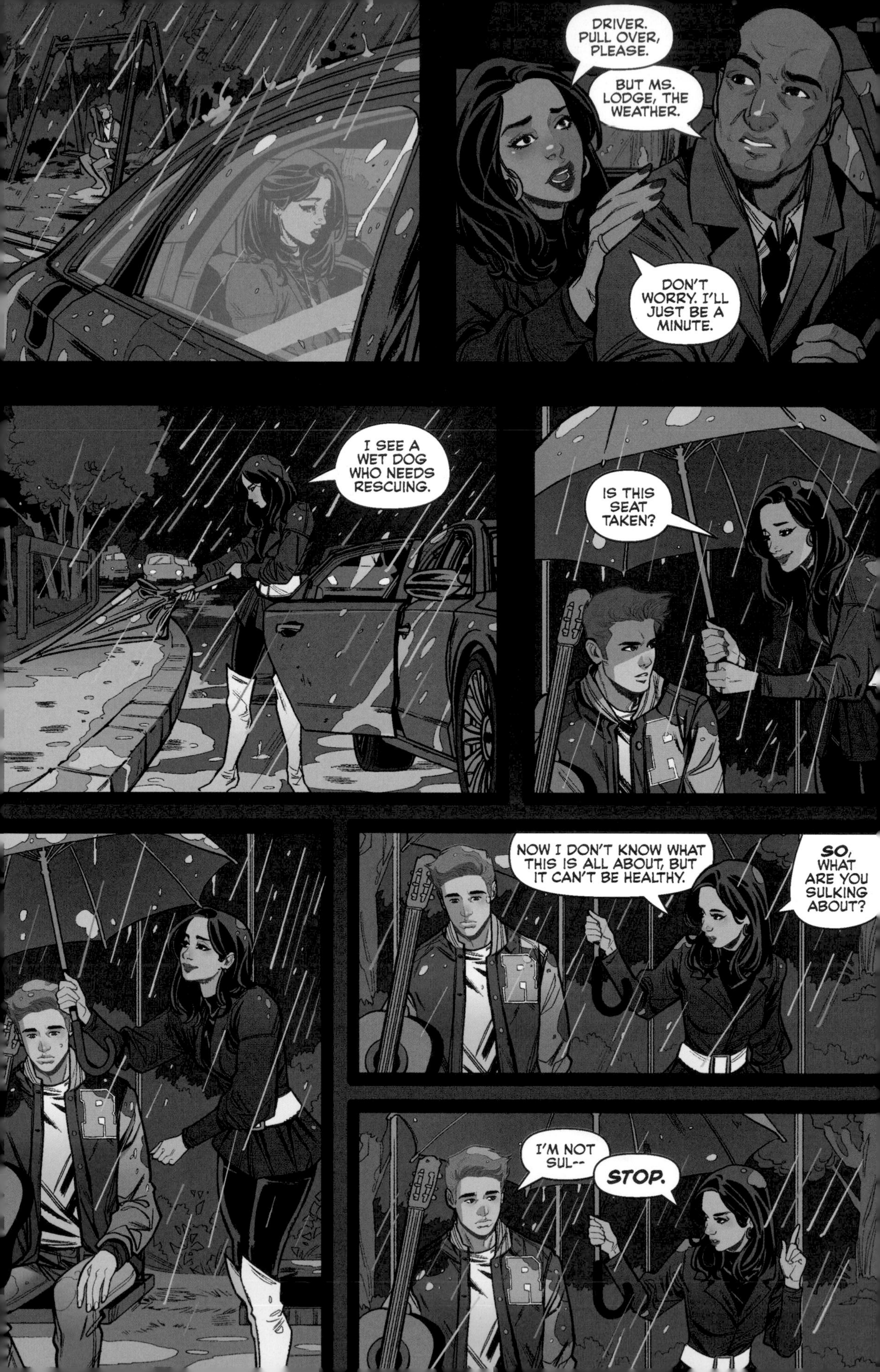
DRIVER. PULL OVER, PLEASE.
BUT MS. LODGE, THE WEATHER.
DON'T WORRY. I'LL JUST BE A MINUTE.
I SEE A WET DOG WHO NEEDS RESCUING.
IS THIS SEAT TAKEN?
NOW I DON'T KNOW WHAT THIS IS ALL ABOUT, BUT IT CAN'T BE HEALTHY.
SO, WHAT ARE YOU SULKING ABOUT?
I'M NOT SUL--
STOP.

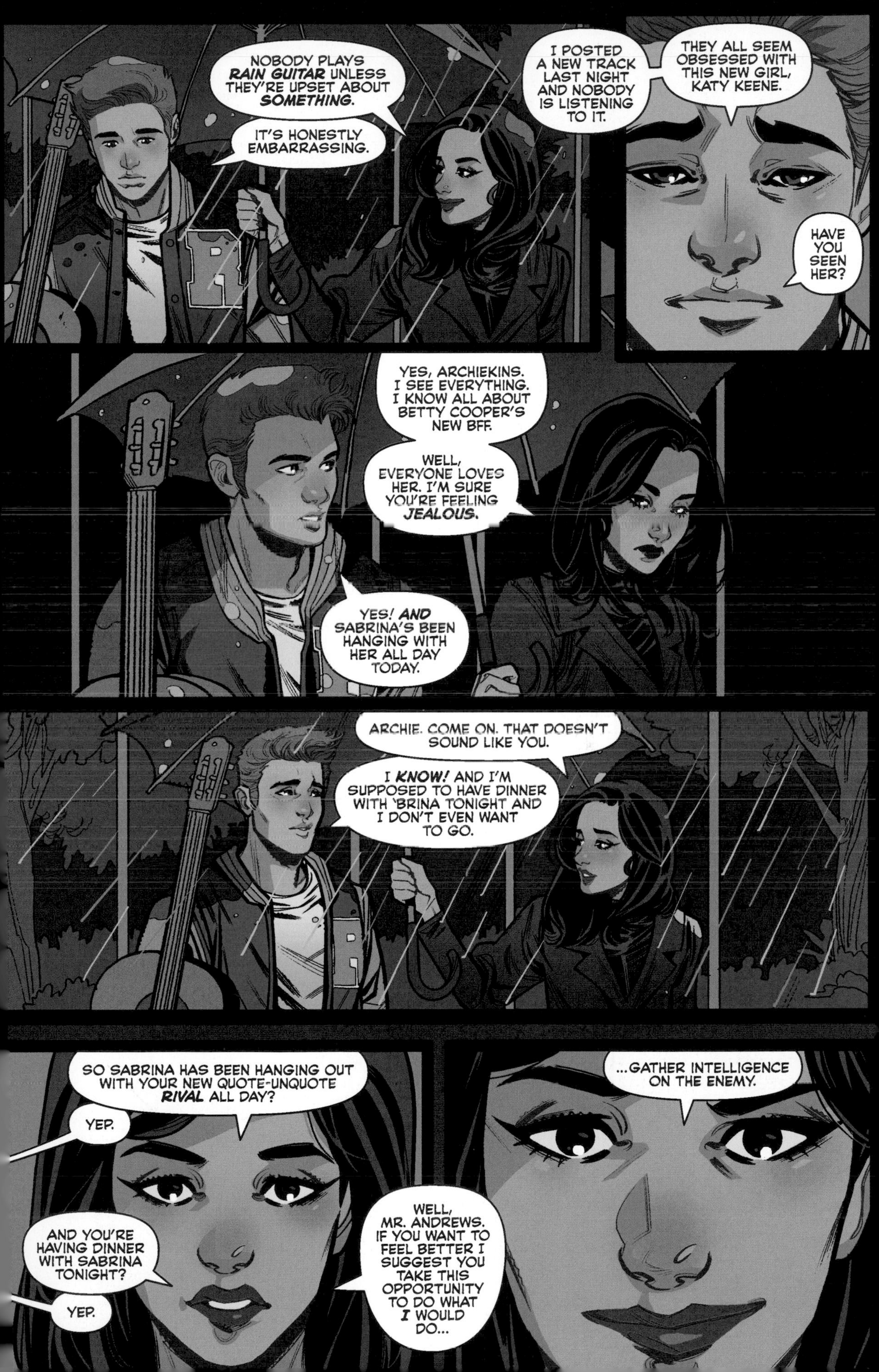
NOBODY PLAYS **RAIN GUITAR** UNLESS THEY'RE UPSET ABOUT **SOMETHING**.
IT'S HONESTLY EMBARRASSING.
I POSTED A NEW TRACK LAST NIGHT AND NOBODY IS LISTENING TO IT.
THEY ALL SEEM OBSESSED WITH THIS NEW GIRL, KATY KEENE.
HAVE YOU SEEN HER?
YES, ARCHIEKINS. I SEE EVERYTHING. I KNOW ALL ABOUT BETTY COOPER'S NEW BFF.
WELL, EVERYONE LOVES HER. I'M SURE YOU'RE FEELING **JEALOUS**.
YES! **AND** SABRINA'S BEEN HANGING WITH HER ALL DAY TODAY.
ARCHIE. COME ON. THAT DOESN'T SOUND LIKE YOU.
I **KNOW!** AND I'M SUPPOSED TO HAVE DINNER WITH 'BRINA TONIGHT AND I DON'T EVEN WANT TO GO.
SO SABRINA HAS BEEN HANGING OUT WITH YOUR NEW QUOTE-UNQUOTE **RIVAL** ALL DAY?
YEP.
AND YOU'RE HAVING DINNER WITH SABRINA TONIGHT?
YEP.
WELL, MR. ANDREWS. IF YOU WANT TO FEEL BETTER I SUGGEST YOU TAKE THIS OPPORTUNITY TO DO WHAT **I** WOULD DO...
...GATHER INTELLIGENCE ON THE ENEMY.

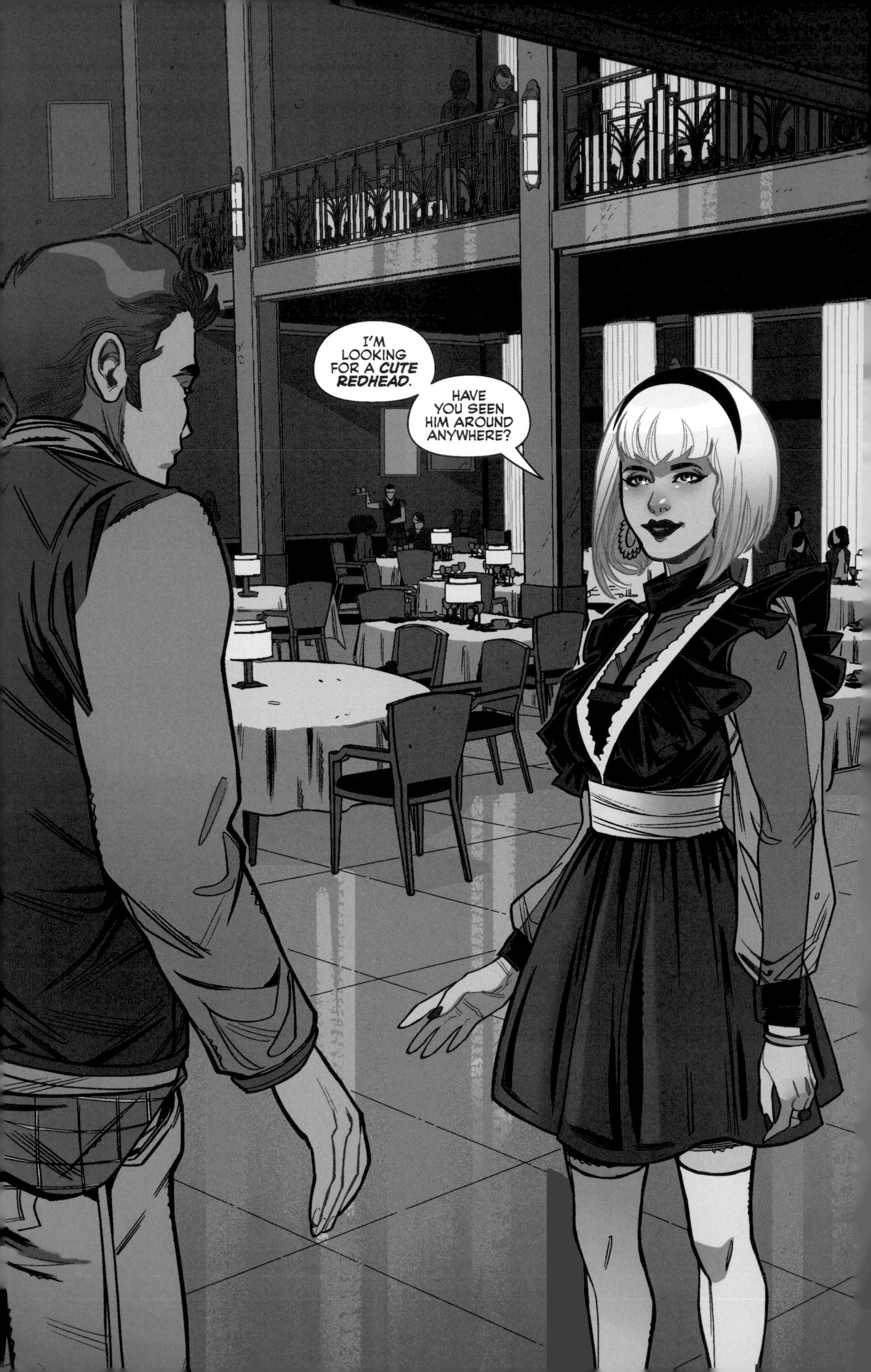
I'M LOOKING FOR A *CUTE REDHEAD*.
HAVE YOU SEEN HIM AROUND ANYWHERE?

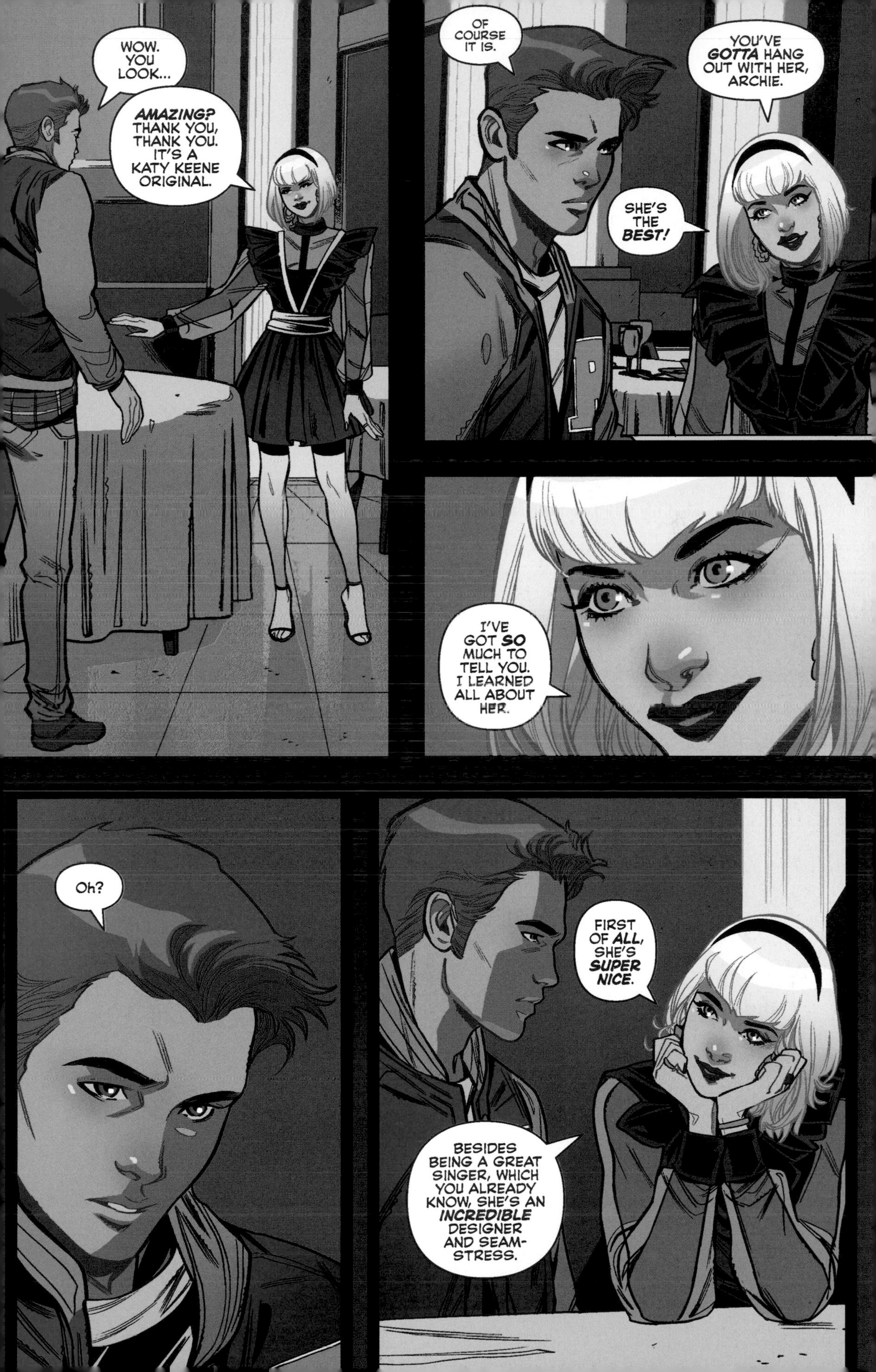
WOW. YOU LOOK...
AMAZING? THANK YOU, THANK YOU. IT'S A KATY KEENE ORIGINAL.
OF COURSE IT IS.
YOU'VE GOTTA HANG OUT WITH HER, ARCHIE.
SHE'S THE BEST!
I'VE GOT SO MUCH TO TELL YOU. I LEARNED ALL ABOUT HER.
Oh?
FIRST OF ALL, SHE'S SUPER NICE.
BESIDES BEING A GREAT SINGER, WHICH YOU ALREADY KNOW, SHE'S AN INCREDIBLE DESIGNER AND SEAM-STRESS.

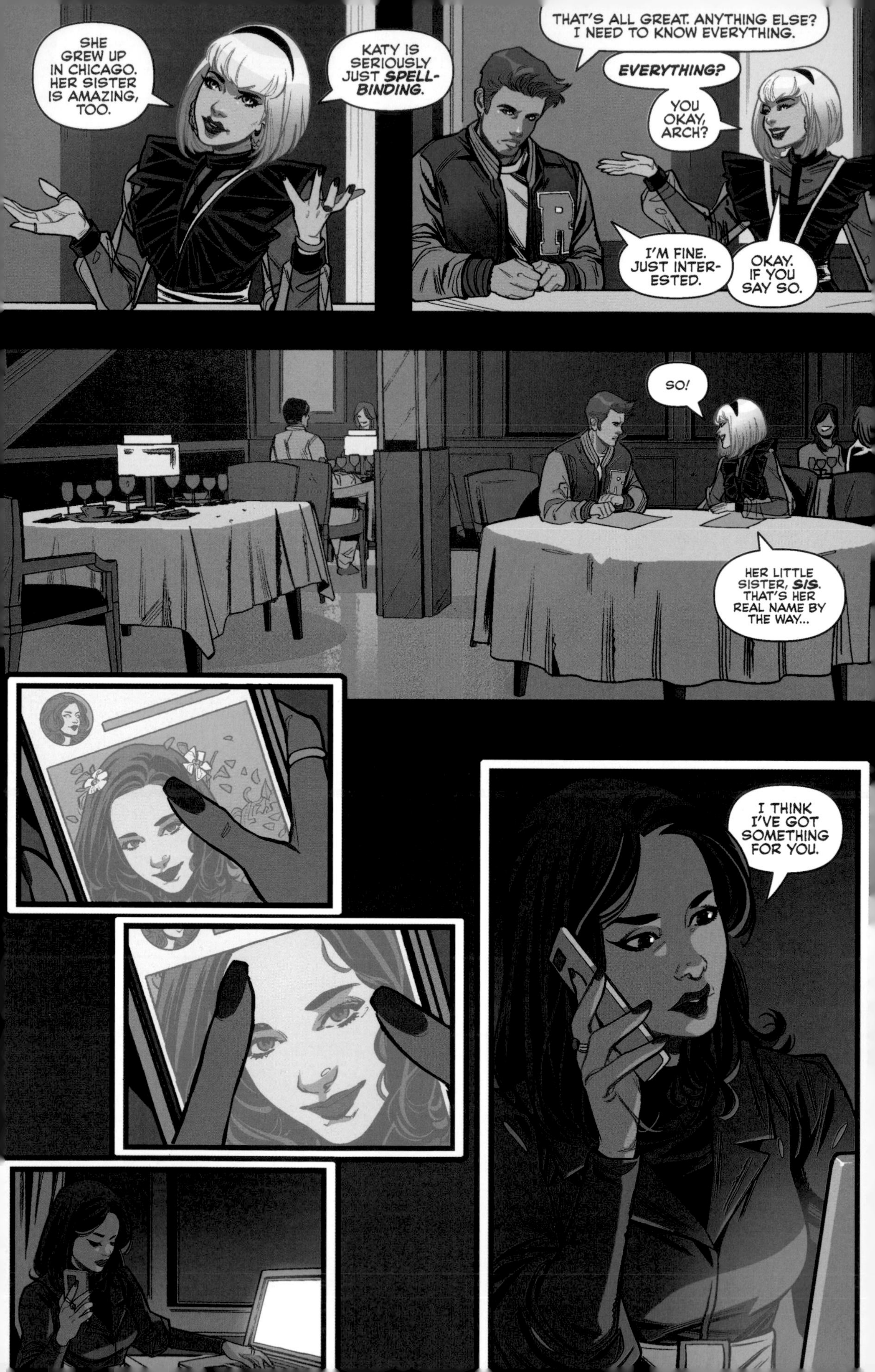
SHE GREW UP IN CHICAGO. HER SISTER IS AMAZING, TOO.
KATY IS SERIOUSLY JUST ***SPELL-BINDING***.
THAT'S ALL GREAT. ANYTHING ELSE? I NEED TO KNOW EVERYTHING.
EVERYTHING?
YOU OKAY, ARCH?
I'M FINE. JUST INTER-ESTED.
OKAY. IF YOU SAY SO.
SO!
HER LITTLE SISTER, ***SIS***. THAT'S HER REAL NAME BY THE WAY...
I THINK I'VE GOT SOMETHING FOR YOU.

TO BE CONTINUED...

712

Archie® and Katy Keene™

STORY BY
MARIKO TAMAKI & KEVIN PANETTA

ART BY
LAURA BRAGA

LETTERING BY
JACK MORELLI

COLORS BY
MATT HERMS

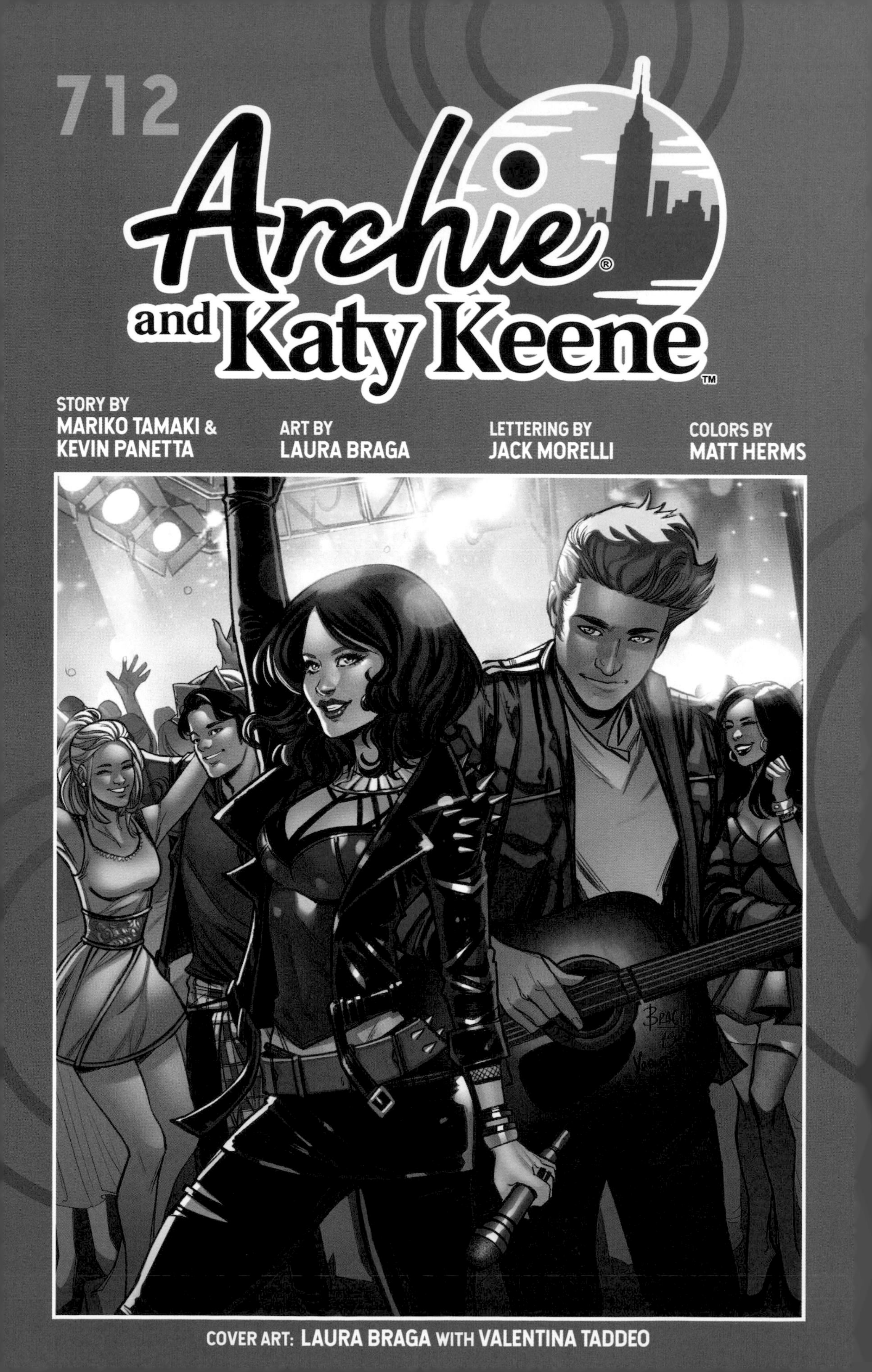

COVER ART: LAURA BRAGA WITH VALENTINA TADDEO

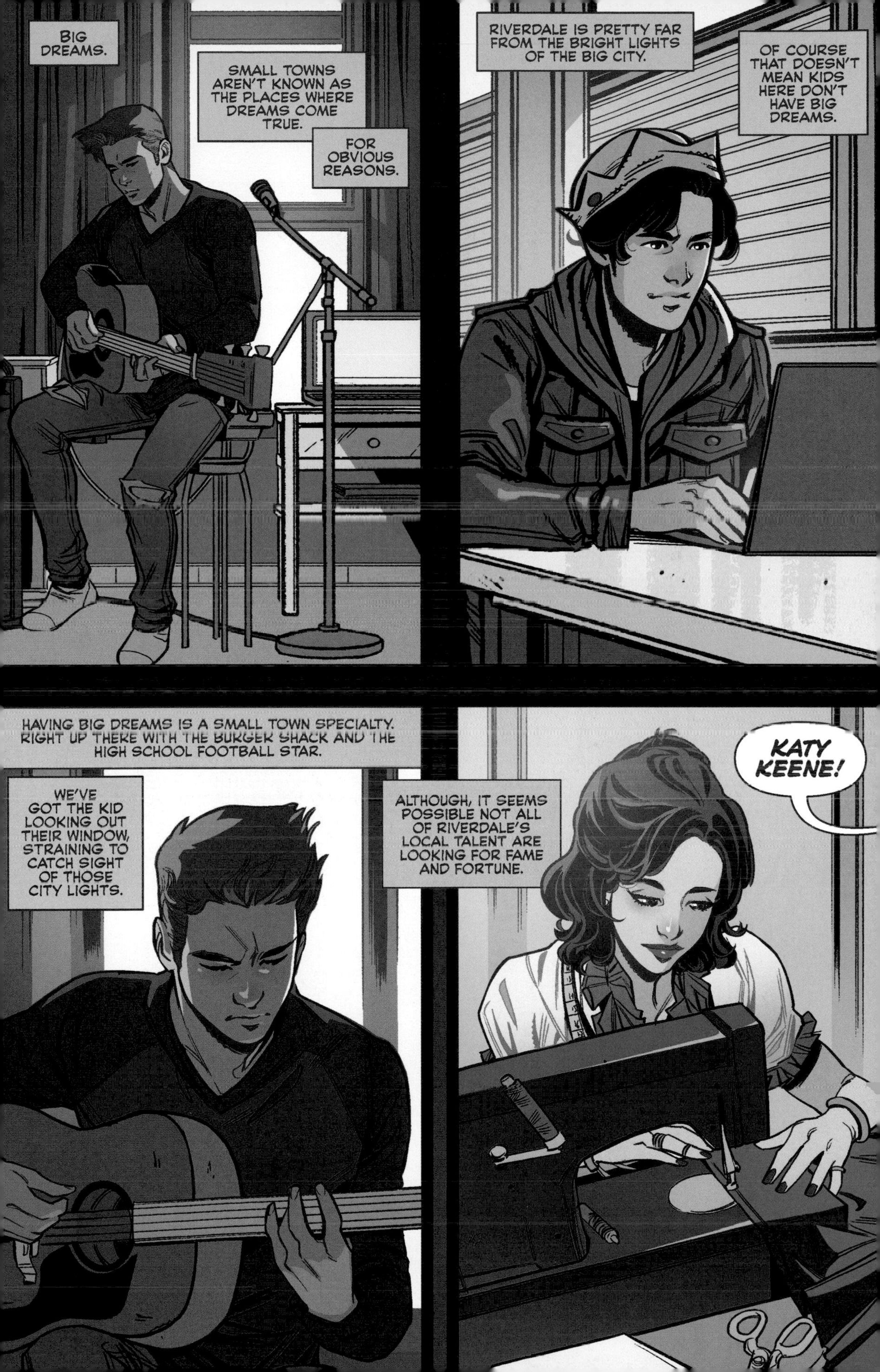

BIG DREAMS.
SMALL TOWNS AREN'T KNOWN AS THE PLACES WHERE DREAMS COME TRUE.
FOR OBVIOUS REASONS.
RIVERDALE IS PRETTY FAR FROM THE BRIGHT LIGHTS OF THE BIG CITY.
OF COURSE THAT DOESN'T MEAN KIDS HERE DON'T HAVE BIG DREAMS.
HAVING BIG DREAMS IS A SMALL TOWN SPECIALTY. RIGHT UP THERE WITH THE BURGER SHACK AND THE HIGH SCHOOL FOOTBALL STAR.
WE'VE GOT THE KID LOOKING OUT THEIR WINDOW, STRAINING TO CATCH SIGHT OF THOSE CITY LIGHTS.
ALTHOUGH, IT SEEMS POSSIBLE NOT ALL OF RIVERDALE'S LOCAL TALENT ARE LOOKING FOR FAME AND FORTUNE.
KATY KEENE!

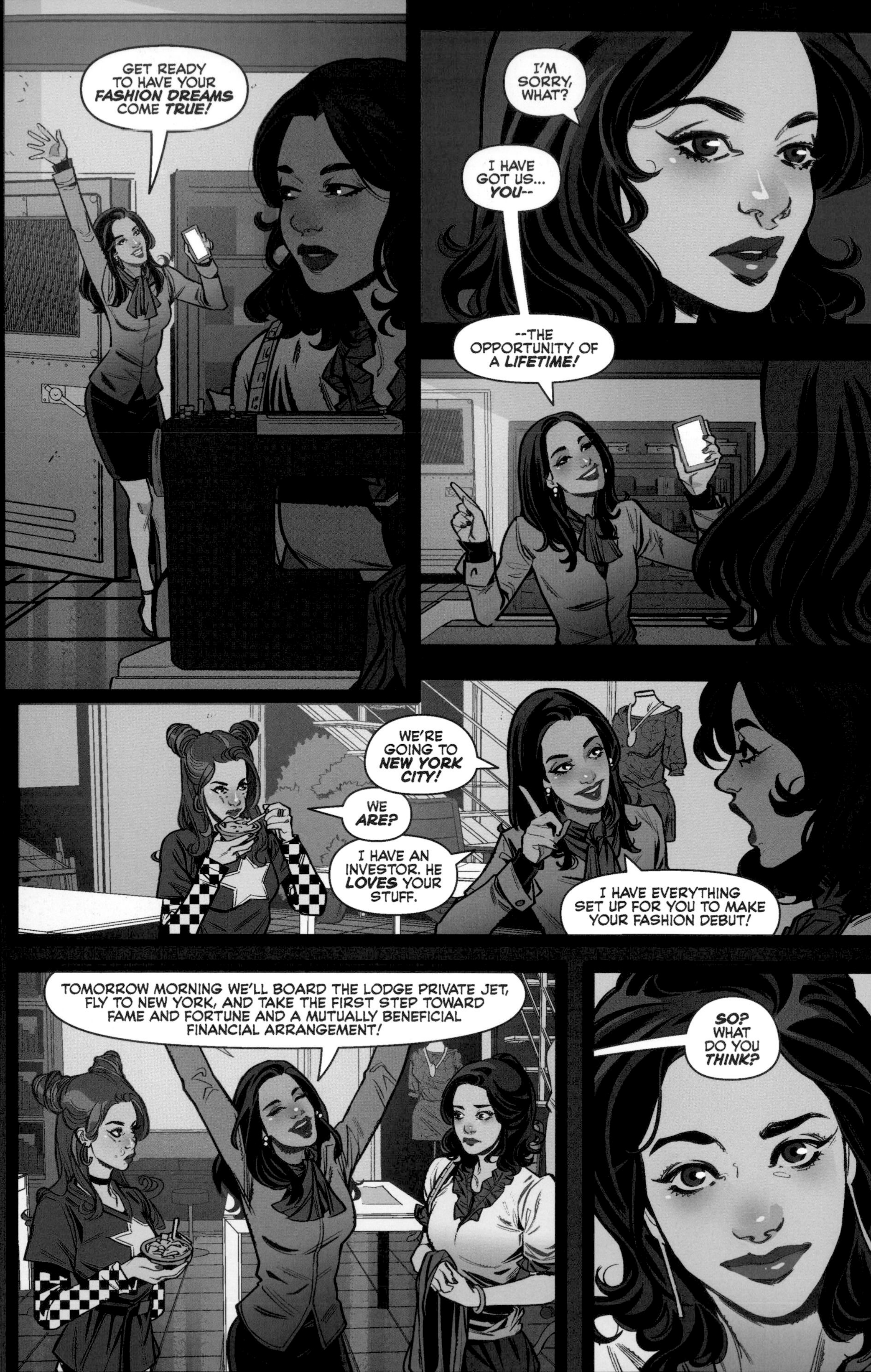
GET READY TO HAVE YOUR FASHION DREAMS COME TRUE!
I'M SORRY, WHAT?
I HAVE GOT US... YOU--
--THE OPPORTUNITY OF A LIFETIME!
WE'RE GOING TO NEW YORK CITY!
WE ARE?
I HAVE AN INVESTOR. HE LOVES YOUR STUFF.
I HAVE EVERYTHING SET UP FOR YOU TO MAKE YOUR FASHION DEBUT!
TOMORROW MORNING WE'LL BOARD THE LODGE PRIVATE JET, FLY TO NEW YORK, AND TAKE THE FIRST STEP TOWARD FAME AND FORTUNE AND A MUTUALLY BENEFICIAL FINANCIAL ARRANGEMENT!
SO? WHAT DO YOU THINK?

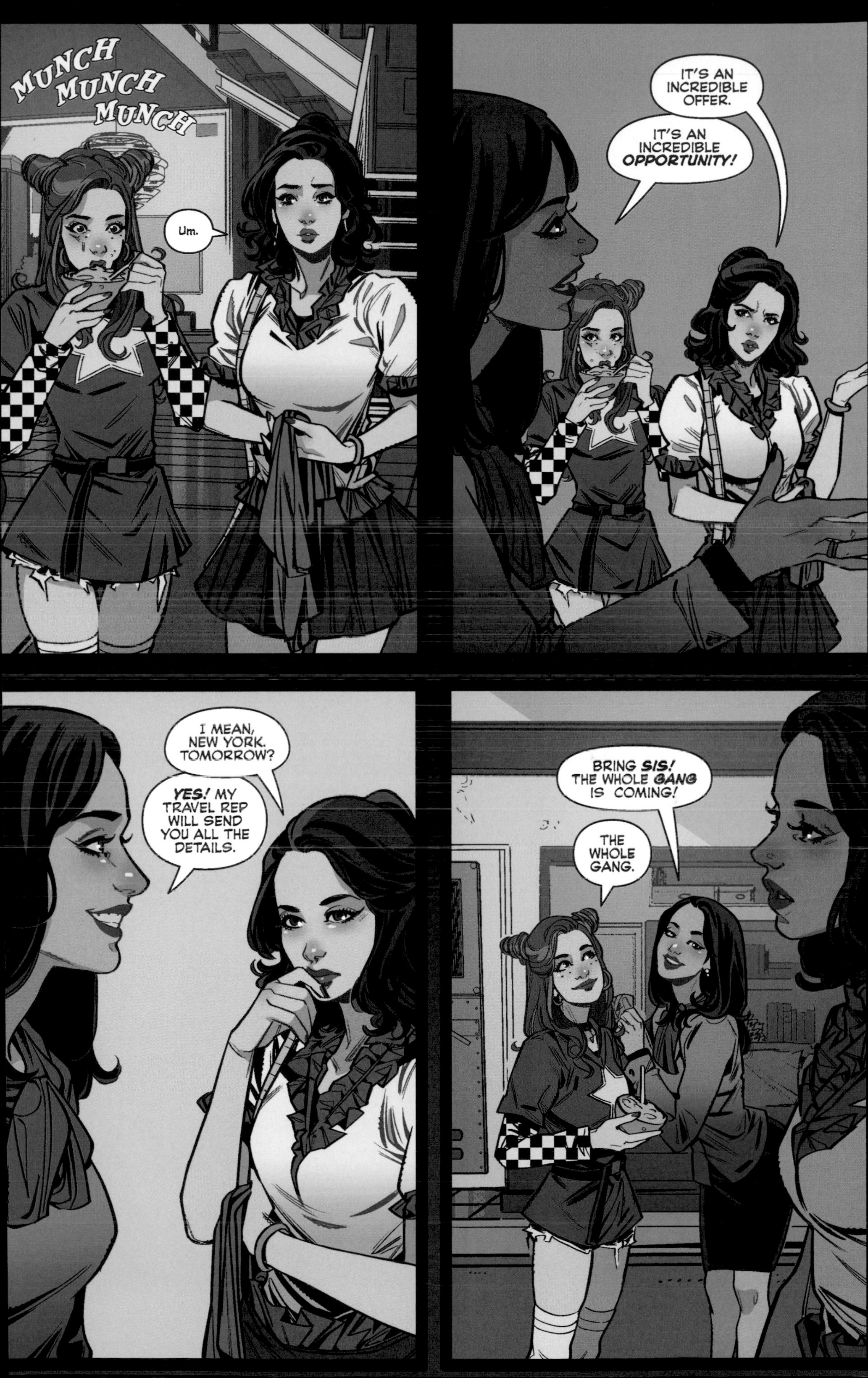
MUNCH MUNCH MUNCH
Um.
IT'S AN INCREDIBLE OFFER.
IT'S AN INCREDIBLE OPPORTUNITY!
I MEAN, NEW YORK. TOMORROW?
YES! MY TRAVEL REP WILL SEND YOU ALL THE DETAILS.
BRING SIS! THE WHOLE GANG IS COMING!
THE WHOLE GANG.

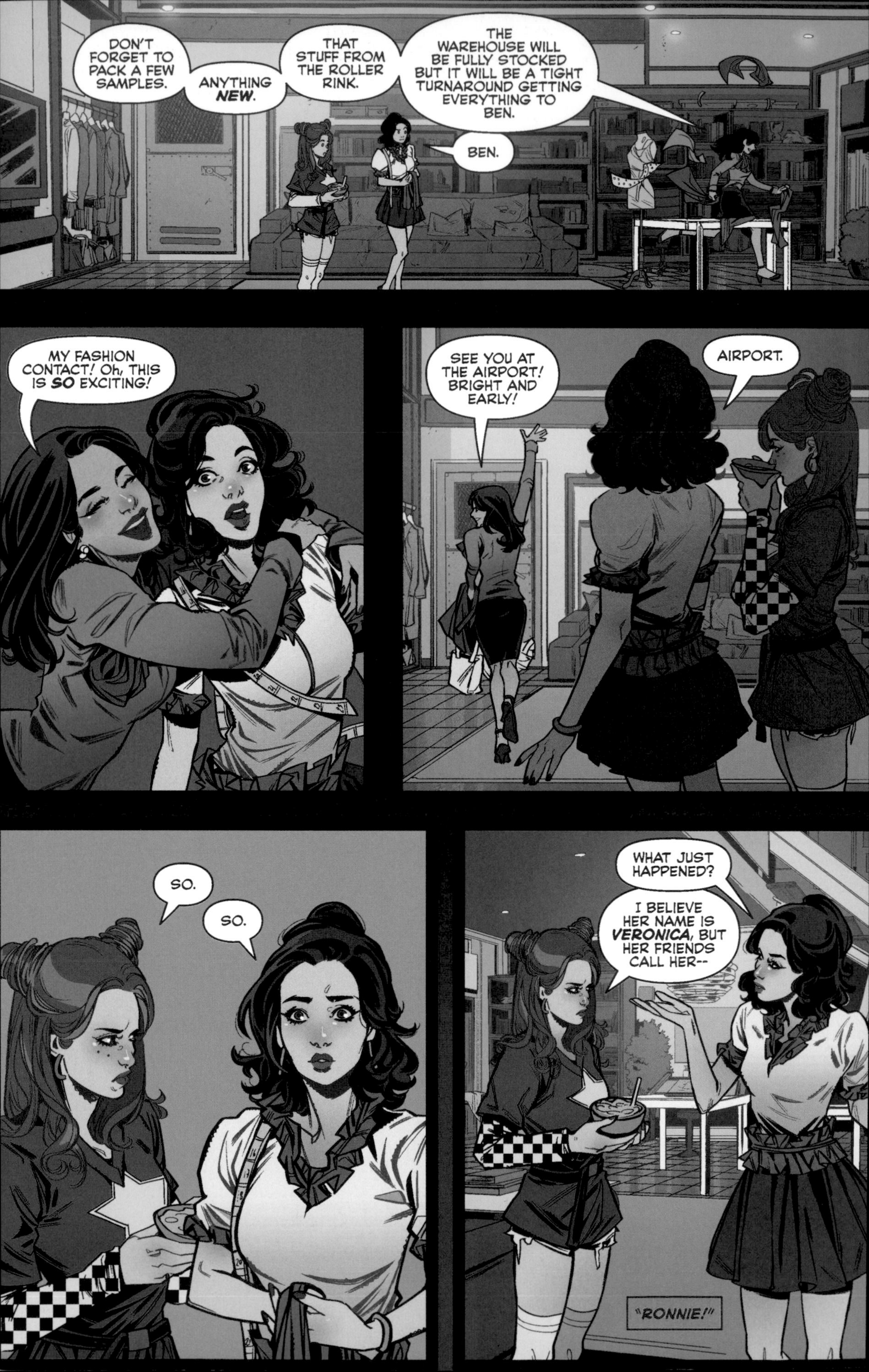
DON'T FORGET TO PACK A FEW SAMPLES.
ANYTHING NEW.
THAT STUFF FROM THE ROLLER RINK.
THE WAREHOUSE WILL BE FULLY STOCKED BUT IT WILL BE A TIGHT TURNAROUND GETTING EVERYTHING TO BEN.
BEN.
MY FASHION CONTACT! Oh, THIS IS SO EXCITING!
SEE YOU AT THE AIRPORT! BRIGHT AND EARLY!
AIRPORT.
SO.
SO.
WHAT JUST HAPPENED?
I BELIEVE HER NAME IS VERONICA, BUT HER FRIENDS CALL HER--
"RONNIE!"

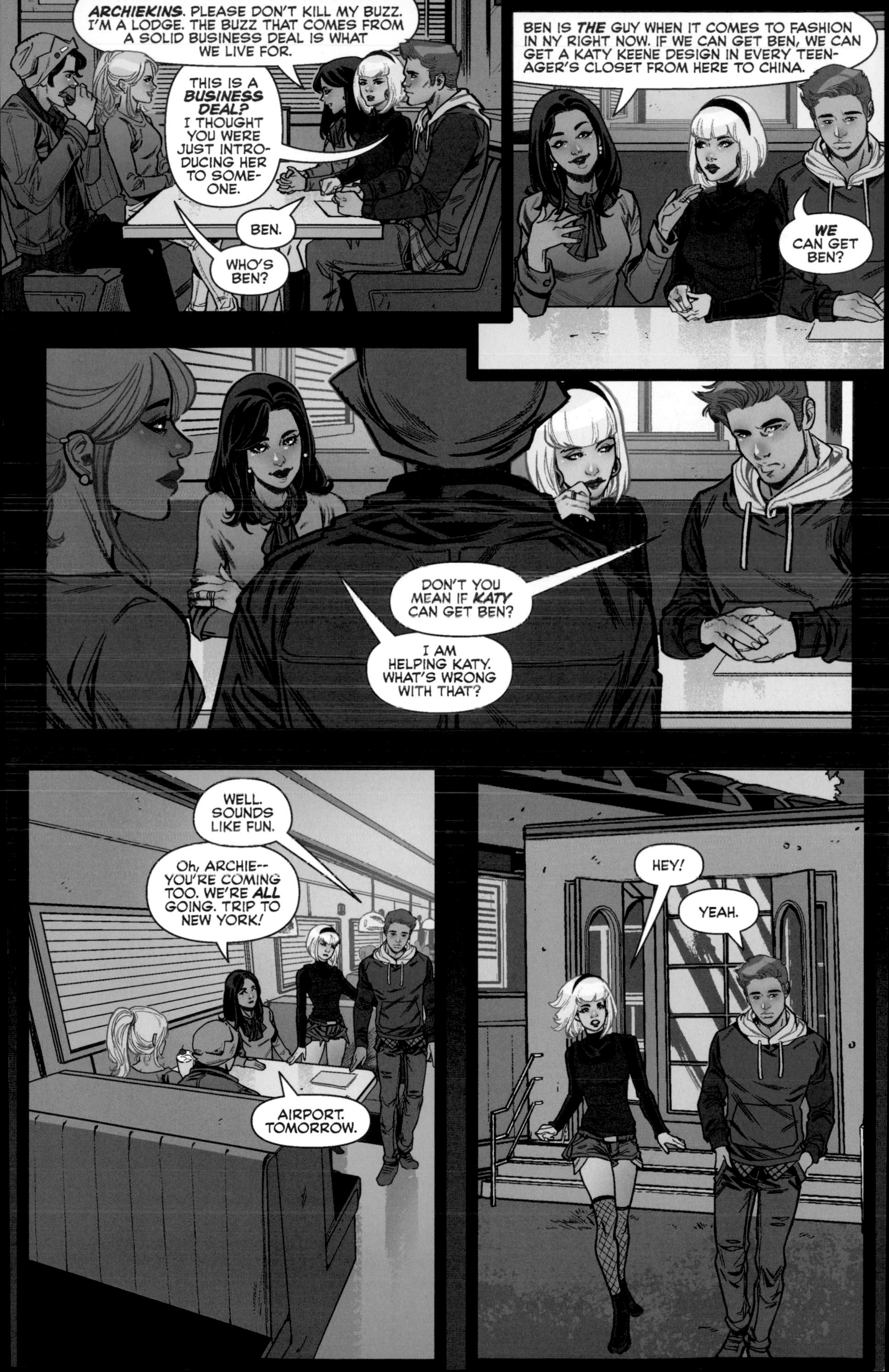
ARCHIEKINS. PLEASE DON'T KILL MY BUZZ. I'M A LODGE. THE BUZZ THAT COMES FROM A SOLID BUSINESS DEAL IS WHAT WE LIVE FOR.
THIS IS A BUSINESS DEAL? I THOUGHT YOU WERE JUST INTRODUCING HER TO SOMEONE.
BEN.
WHO'S BEN?
BEN IS THE GUY WHEN IT COMES TO FASHION IN NY RIGHT NOW. IF WE CAN GET BEN, WE CAN GET A KATY KEENE DESIGN IN EVERY TEENAGER'S CLOSET FROM HERE TO CHINA.
WE CAN GET BEN?
DON'T YOU MEAN IF KATY CAN GET BEN?
I AM HELPING KATY. WHAT'S WRONG WITH THAT?
WELL. SOUNDS LIKE FUN.
Oh, ARCHIE-- YOU'RE COMING TOO. WE'RE ALL GOING. TRIP TO NEW YORK!
AIRPORT. TOMORROW.
HEY!
YEAH.

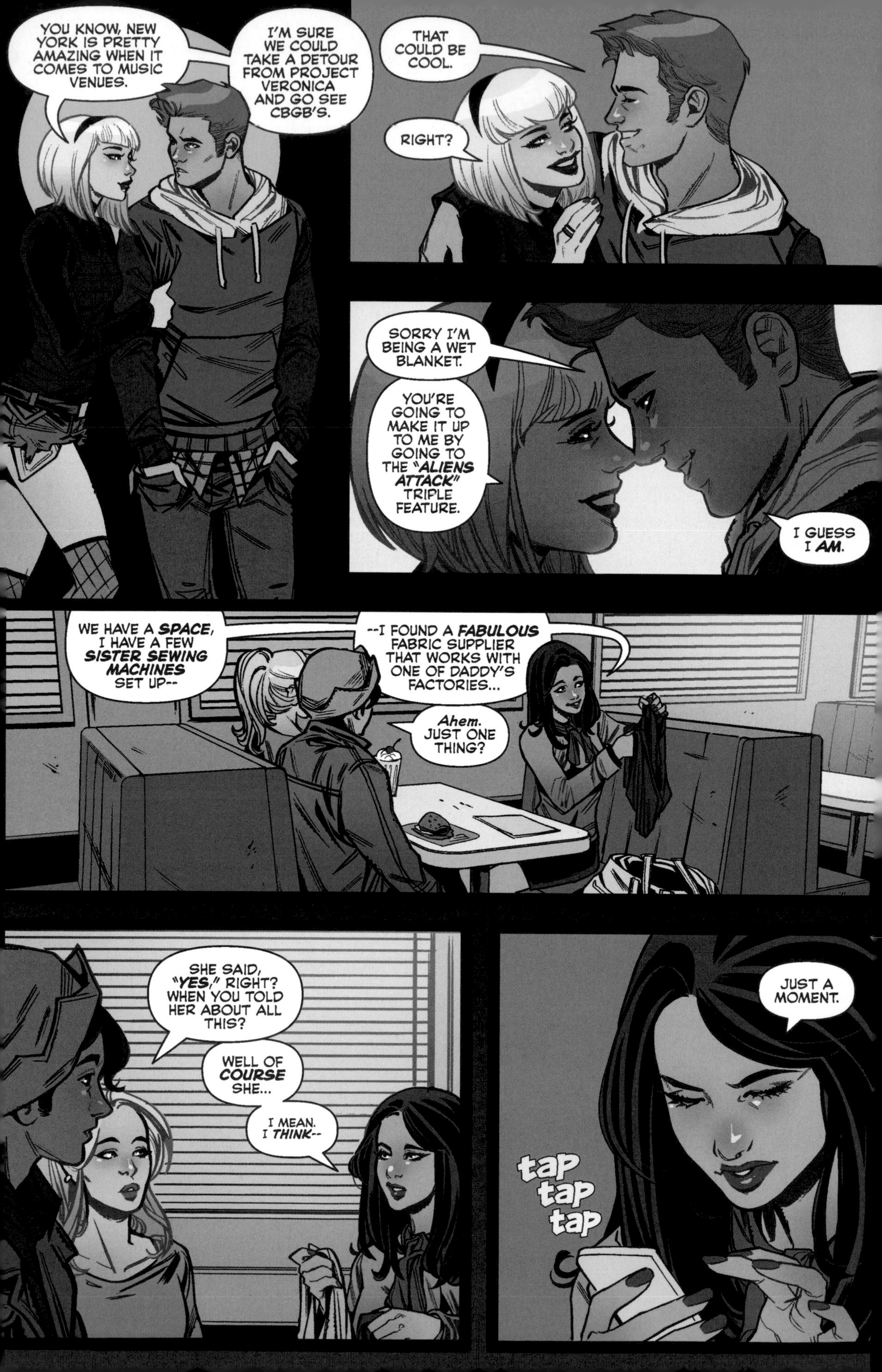
YOU KNOW, NEW YORK IS PRETTY AMAZING WHEN IT COMES TO MUSIC VENUES.
I'M SURE WE COULD TAKE A DETOUR FROM PROJECT VERONICA AND GO SEE CBGB'S.
THAT COULD BE COOL.
RIGHT?
SORRY I'M BEING A WET BLANKET.
YOU'RE GOING TO MAKE IT UP TO ME BY GOING TO THE *"ALIENS ATTACK"* TRIPLE FEATURE.
I GUESS I *AM*.
WE HAVE A *SPACE*, I HAVE A FEW *SISTER SEWING MACHINES* SET UP--
--I FOUND A *FABULOUS* FABRIC SUPPLIER THAT WORKS WITH ONE OF DADDY'S FACTORIES...
Ahem. JUST ONE THING?
SHE SAID, *"YES,"* RIGHT? WHEN YOU TOLD HER ABOUT ALL THIS?
WELL OF *COURSE* SHE...
I MEAN. I *THINK*--
JUST A MOMENT.
tap tap tap

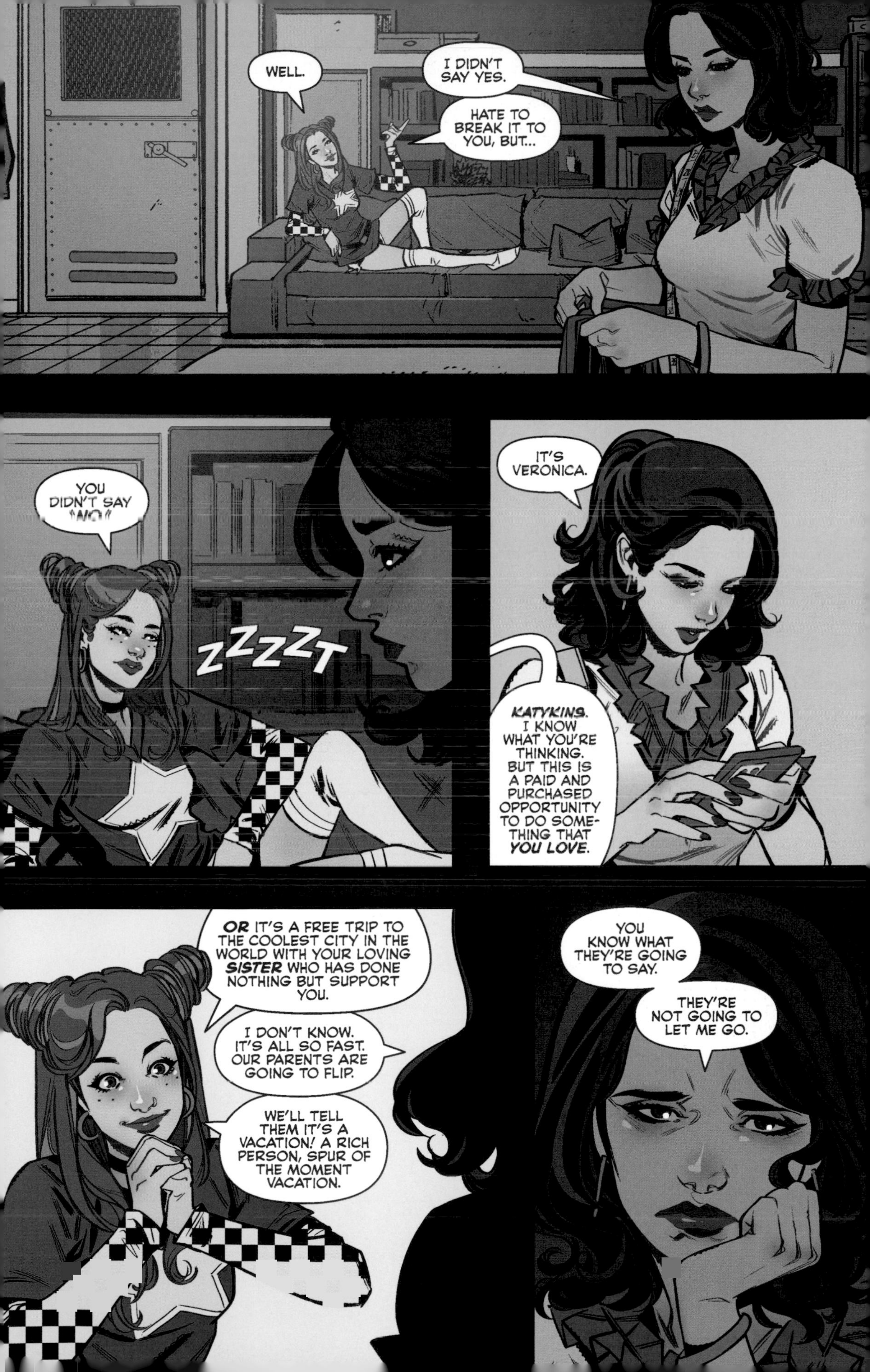
WELL.
I DIDN'T SAY YES.
HATE TO BREAK IT TO YOU, BUT...
YOU DIDN'T SAY NO!
ZZZZT
IT'S VERONICA.
KATYKINS. I KNOW WHAT YOU'RE THINKING. BUT THIS IS A PAID AND PURCHASED OPPORTUNITY TO DO SOMETHING THAT YOU LOVE.
OR IT'S A FREE TRIP TO THE COOLEST CITY IN THE WORLD WITH YOUR LOVING SISTER WHO HAS DONE NOTHING BUT SUPPORT YOU.
I DON'T KNOW. IT'S ALL SO FAST. OUR PARENTS ARE GOING TO FLIP.
WE'LL TELL THEM IT'S A VACATION! A RICH PERSON, SPUR OF THE MOMENT VACATION.
YOU KNOW WHAT THEY'RE GOING TO SAY.
THEY'RE NOT GOING TO LET ME GO.

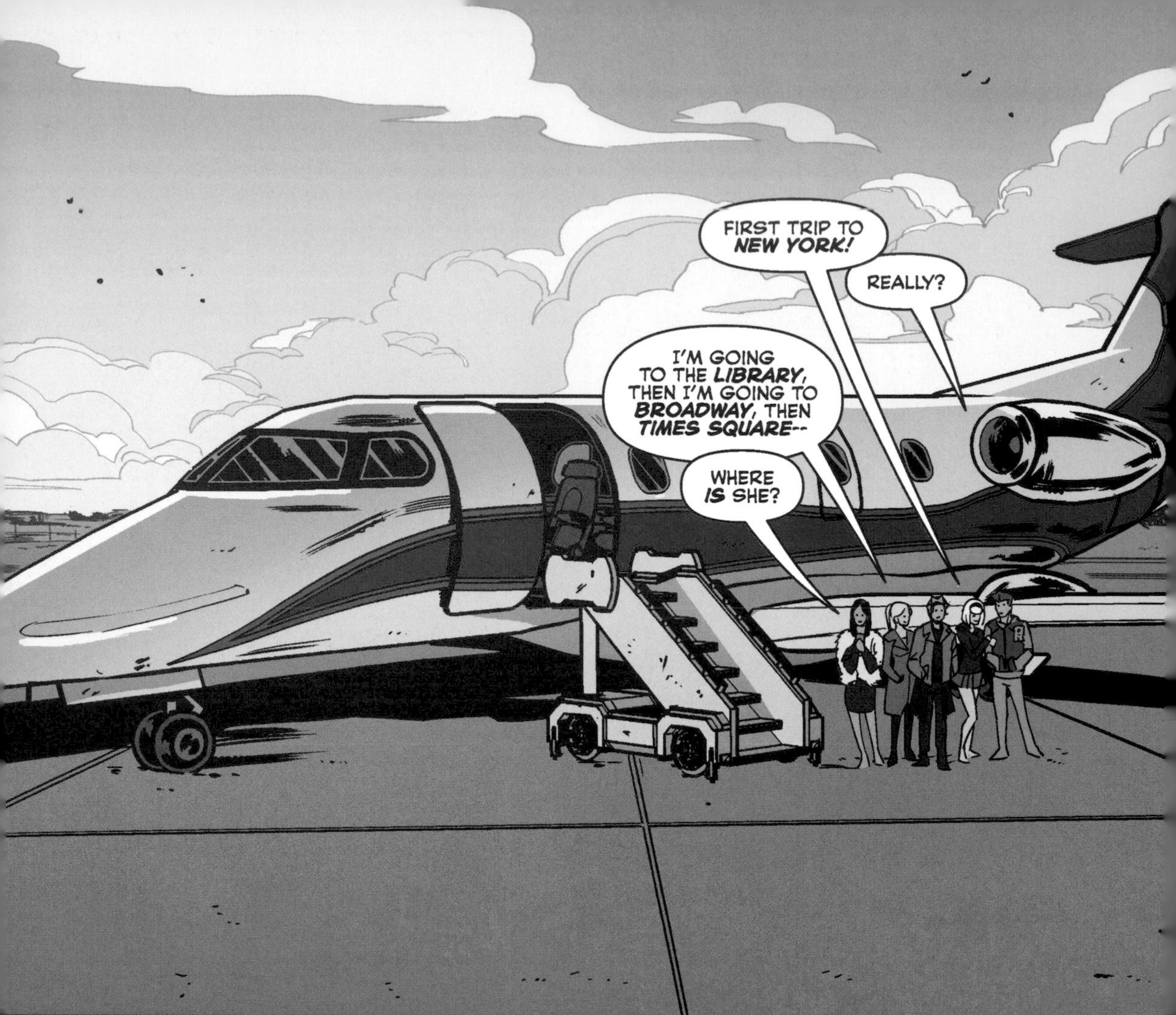
FIRST TRIP TO NEW YORK!
REALLY?
I'M GOING TO THE LIBRARY, THEN I'M GOING TO BROADWAY, THEN TIMES SQUARE--
WHERE IS SHE?

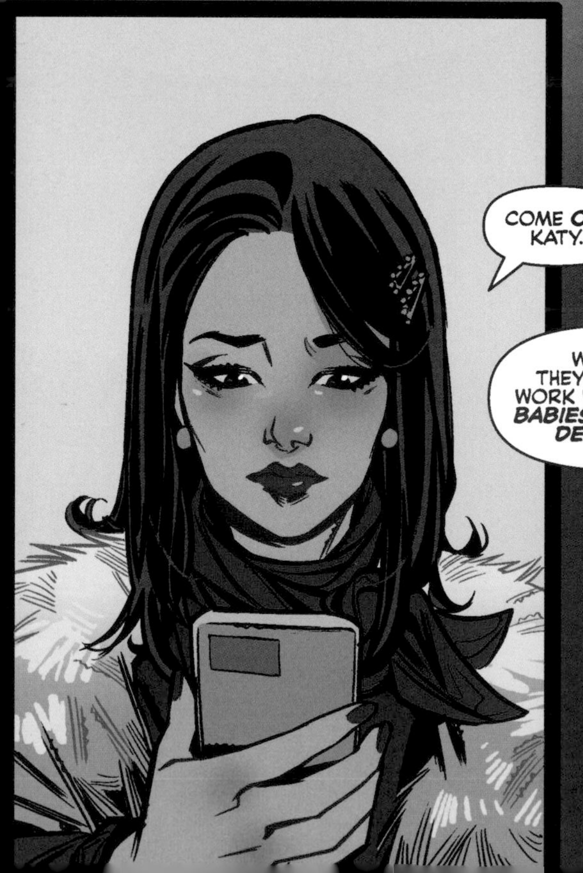
COME ON, KATY.

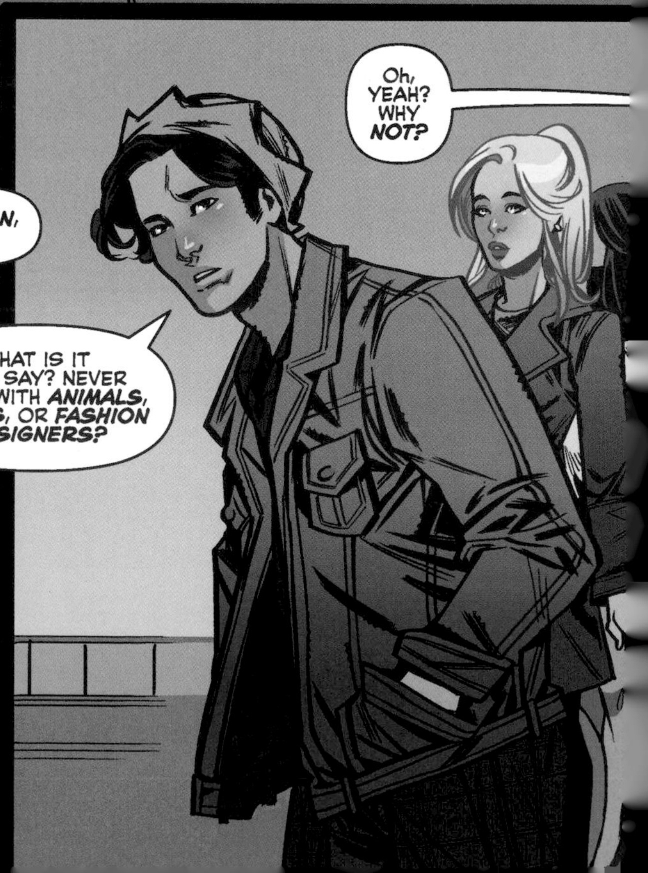
WHAT IS IT THEY SAY? NEVER WORK WITH ANIMALS, BABIES, OR FASHION DESIGNERS?
Oh, YEAH? WHY NOT?

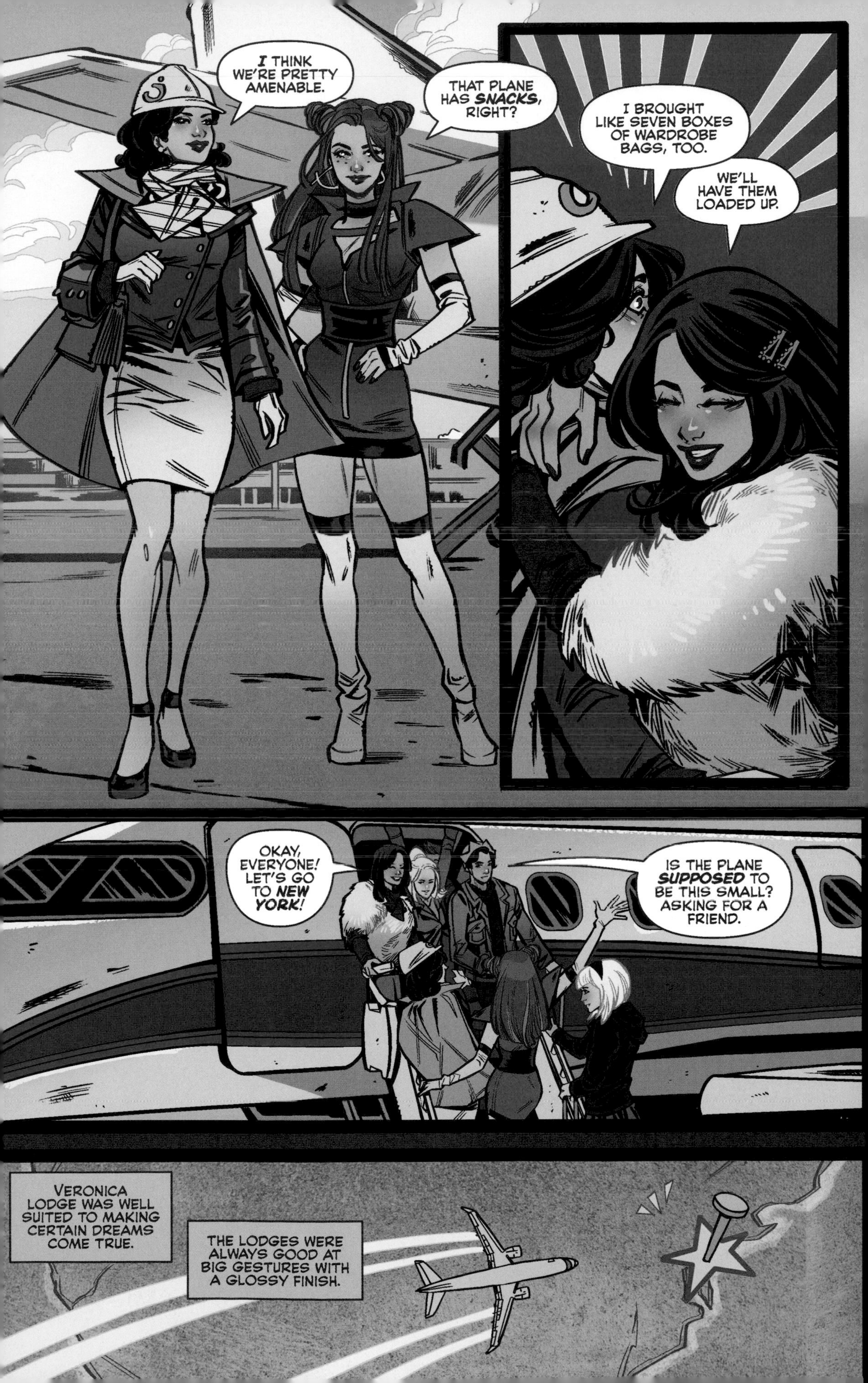

I THINK WE'RE PRETTY AMENABLE.
THAT PLANE HAS SNACKS, RIGHT?
I BROUGHT LIKE SEVEN BOXES OF WARDROBE BAGS, TOO.
WE'LL HAVE THEM LOADED UP.
OKAY, EVERYONE! LET'S GO TO NEW YORK!
IS THE PLANE SUPPOSED TO BE THIS SMALL? ASKING FOR A FRIEND.
VERONICA LODGE WAS WELL SUITED TO MAKING CERTAIN DREAMS COME TRUE.
THE LODGES WERE ALWAYS GOOD AT BIG GESTURES WITH A GLOSSY FINISH.

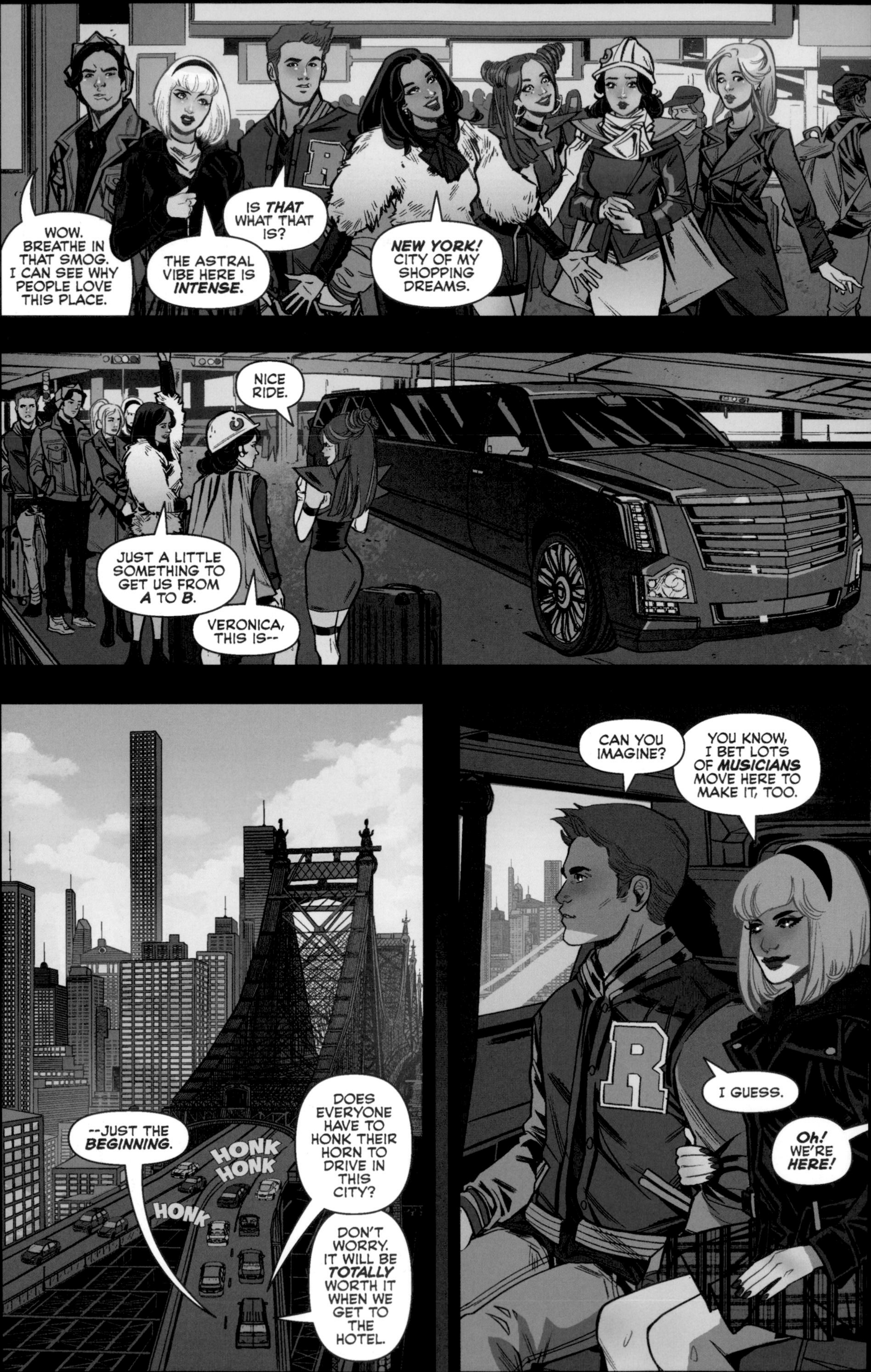
WOW. BREATHE IN THAT SMOG. I CAN SEE WHY PEOPLE LOVE THIS PLACE.
THE ASTRAL VIBE HERE IS *INTENSE*.
IS *THAT* WHAT THAT IS?
NEW YORK! CITY OF MY SHOPPING DREAMS.
NICE RIDE.
JUST A LITTLE SOMETHING TO GET US FROM *A* TO *B*.
VERONICA, THIS IS--
--JUST THE *BEGINNING*.
HONK HONK
HONK
DOES EVERYONE HAVE TO HONK THEIR HORN TO DRIVE IN THIS CITY?
DON'T WORRY. IT WILL BE *TOTALLY* WORTH IT WHEN WE GET TO THE HOTEL.
CAN YOU IMAGINE?
YOU KNOW, I BET LOTS OF *MUSICIANS* MOVE HERE TO MAKE IT, TOO.
I GUESS.
Oh! WE'RE *HERE!*

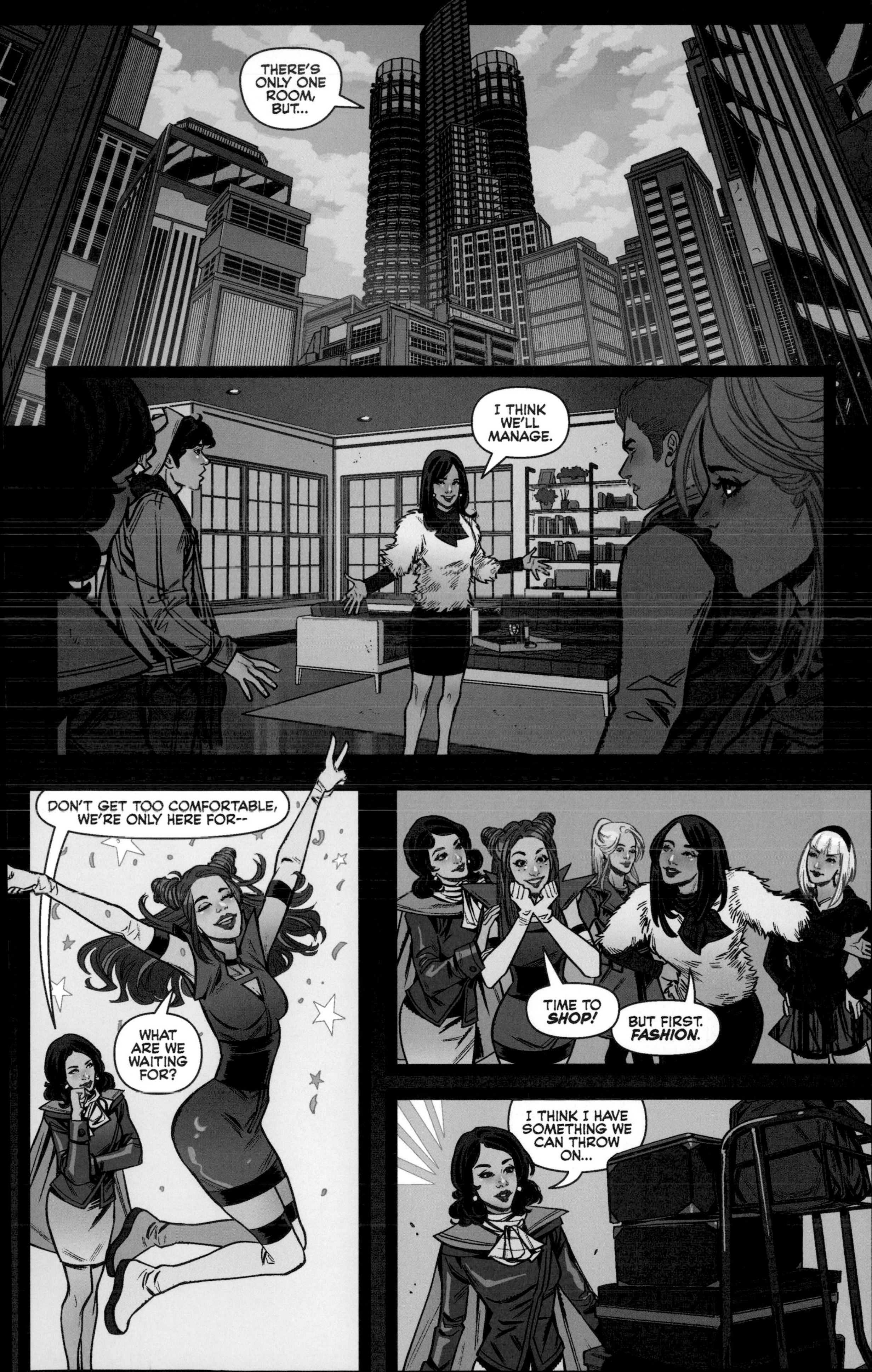
THERE'S ONLY ONE ROOM, BUT...
I THINK WE'LL MANAGE.
DON'T GET TOO COMFORTABLE, WE'RE ONLY HERE FOR--
WHAT ARE WE WAITING FOR?
TIME TO *SHOP!*
BUT FIRST. *FASHION.*
I THINK I HAVE SOMETHING WE CAN THROW ON...

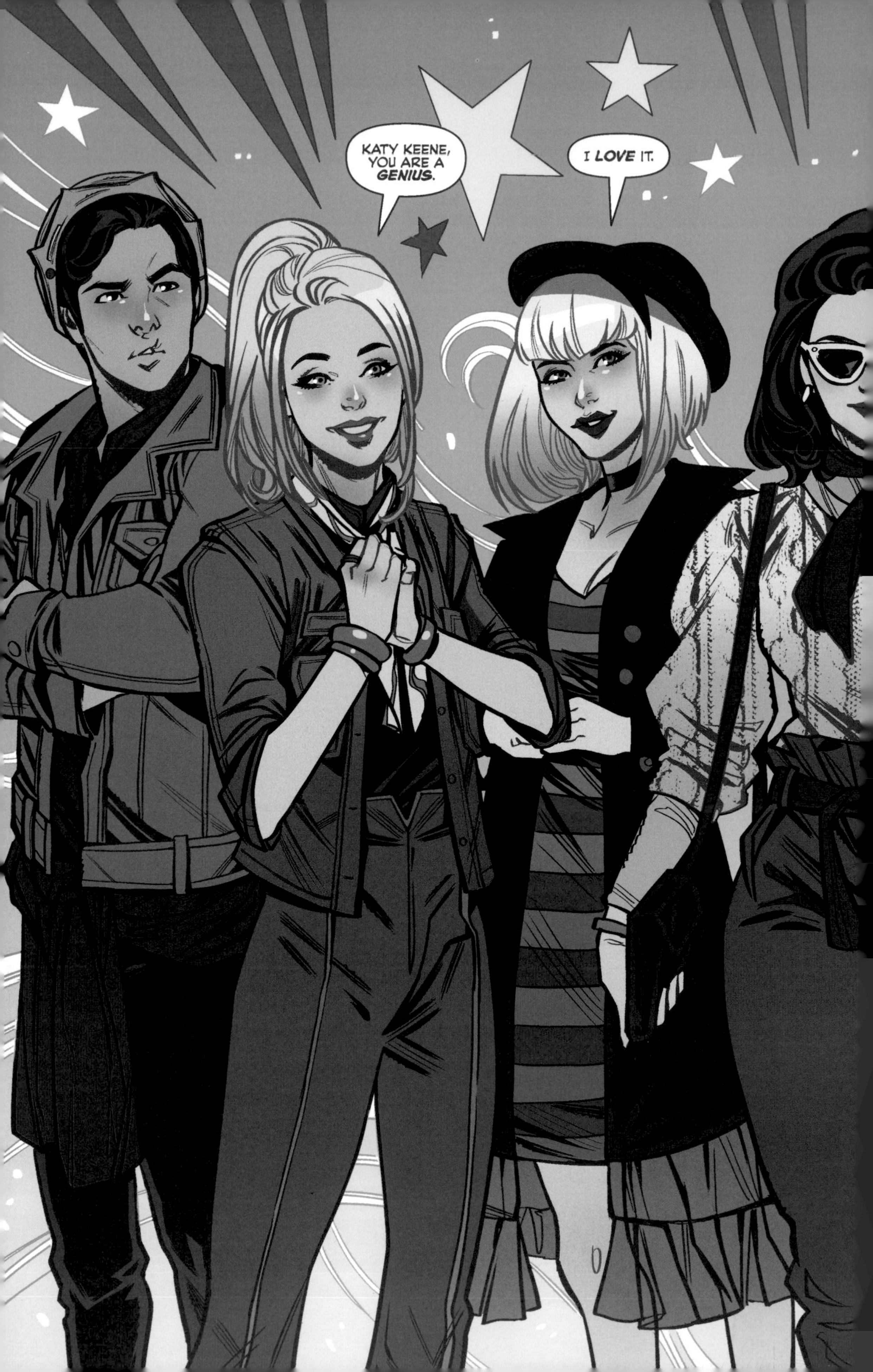
KATY KEENE, YOU ARE A GENIUS.
I LOVE IT.

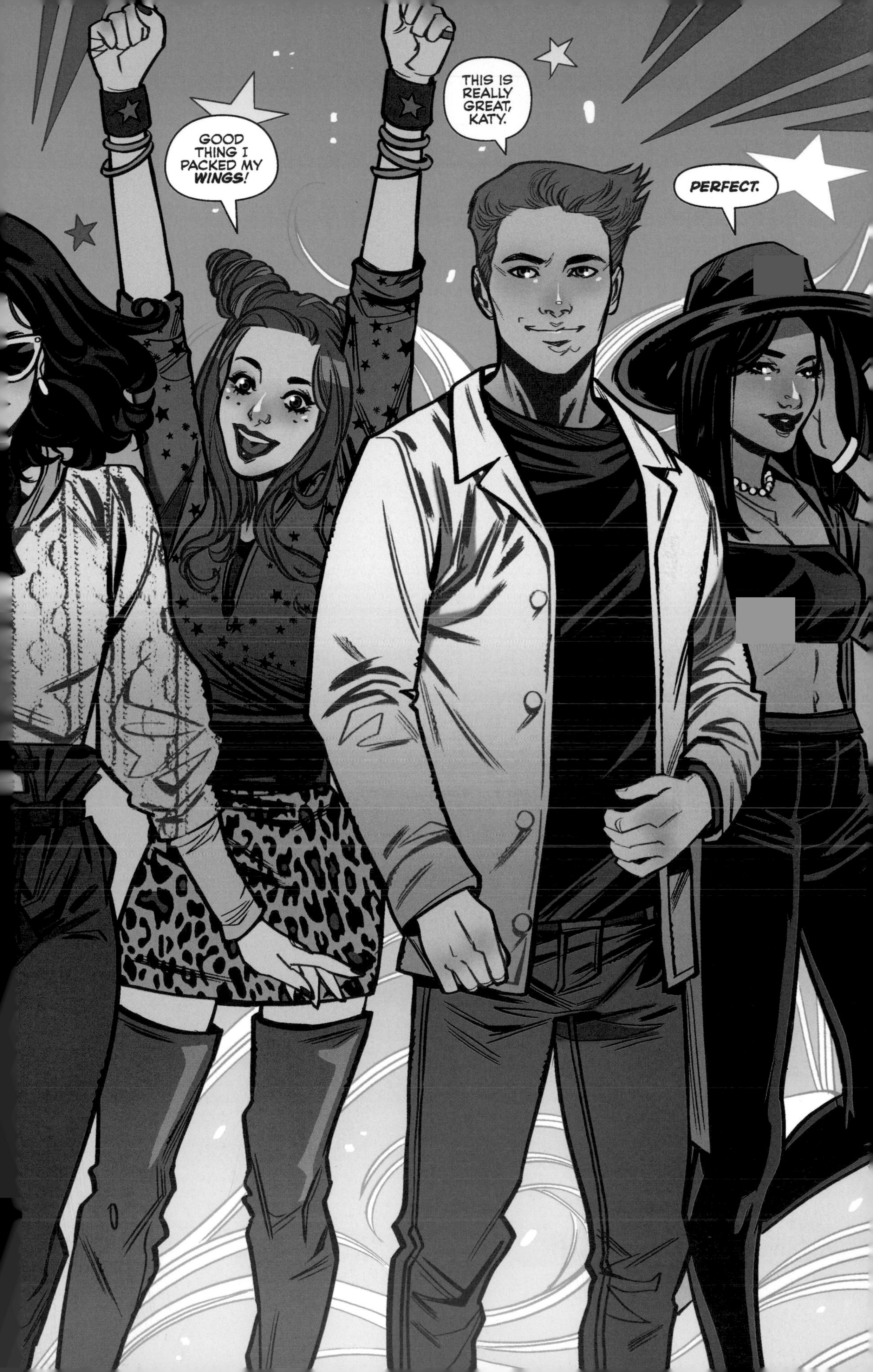
GOOD THING I PACKED MY WINGS!
THIS IS REALLY GREAT, KATY.
PERFECT.

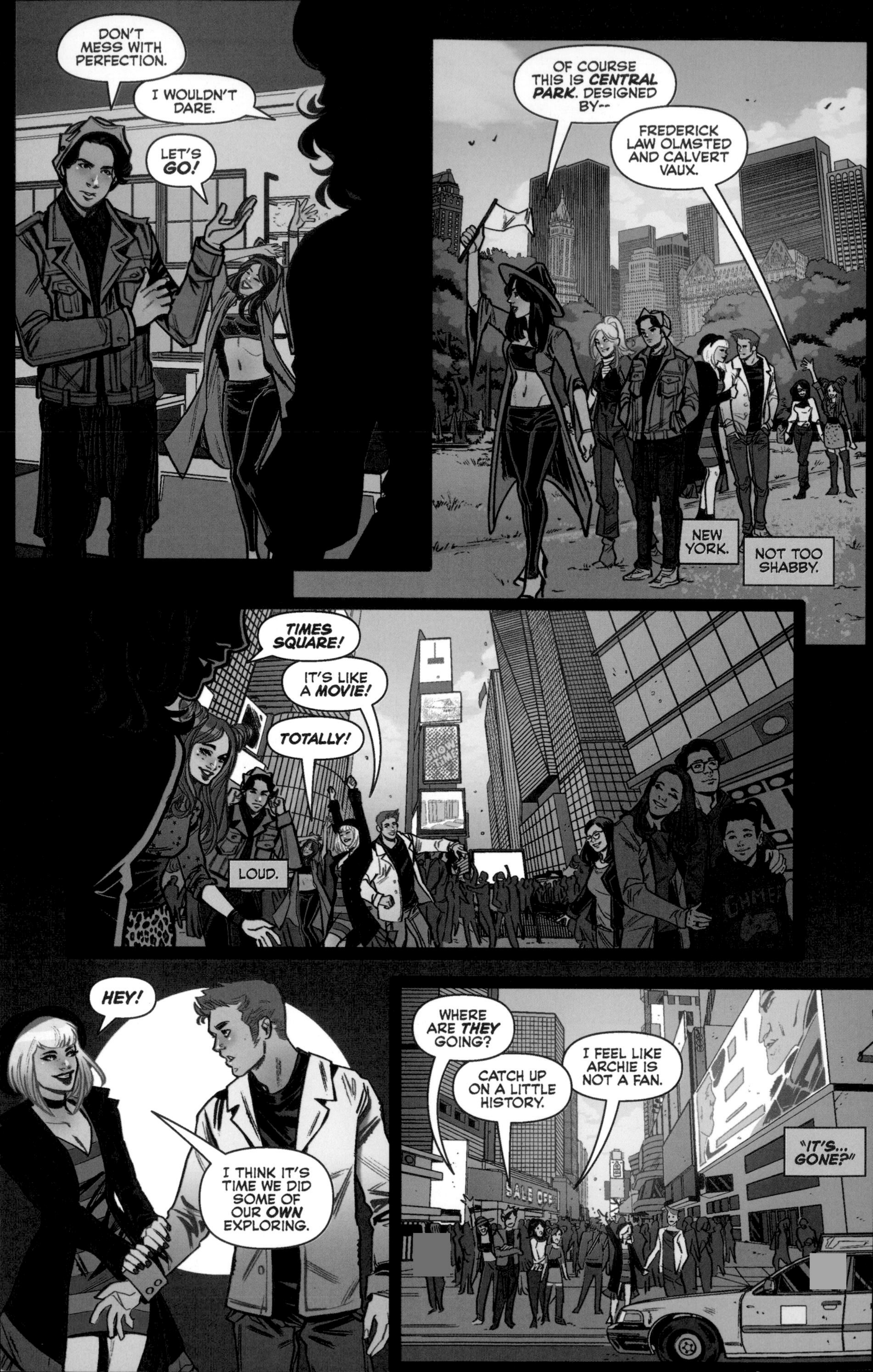
DON'T MESS WITH PERFECTION.
I WOULDN'T DARE.
LET'S GO!
OF COURSE THIS IS CENTRAL PARK. DESIGNED BY--
FREDERICK LAW OLMSTED AND CALVERT VAUX.
NEW YORK.
NOT TOO SHABBY.
TIMES SQUARE!
IT'S LIKE A MOVIE!
TOTALLY!
LOUD.
HEY!
I THINK IT'S TIME WE DID SOME OF OUR OWN EXPLORING.
WHERE ARE THEY GOING?
CATCH UP ON A LITTLE HISTORY.
I FEEL LIKE ARCHIE IS NOT A FAN.
"IT'S... GONE?"

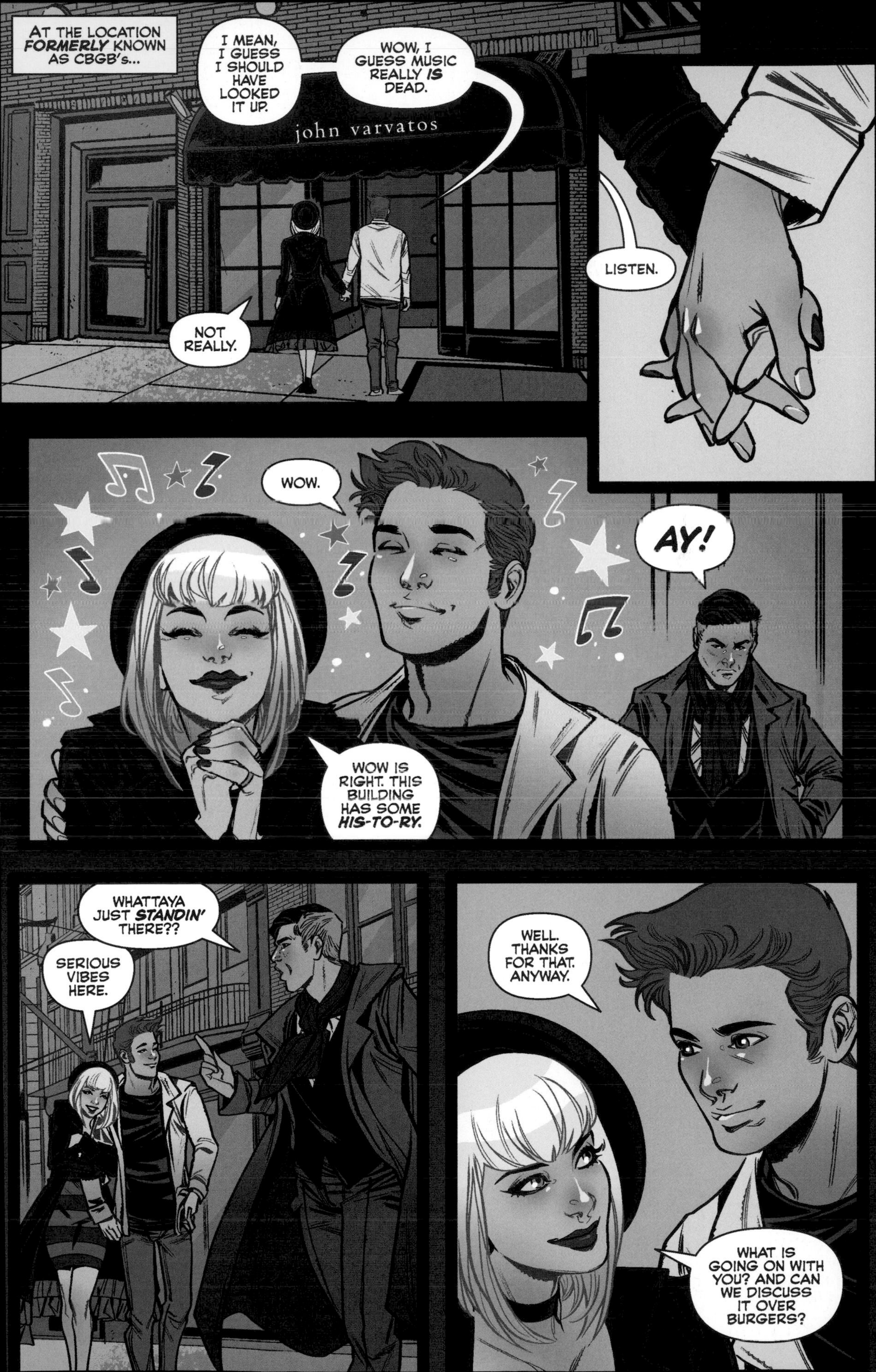
AT THE LOCATION FORMERLY KNOWN AS CBGB's...
I MEAN, I GUESS I SHOULD HAVE LOOKED IT UP.
WOW, I GUESS MUSIC REALLY IS DEAD.
john varvatos
NOT REALLY.
LISTEN.
WOW.
AY!
WOW IS RIGHT. THIS BUILDING HAS SOME HIS-TO-RY.
WHATTAYA JUST STANDIN' THERE??
SERIOUS VIBES HERE.
WELL. THANKS FOR THAT. ANYWAY.
WHAT IS GOING ON WITH YOU? AND CAN WE DISCUSS IT OVER BURGERS?

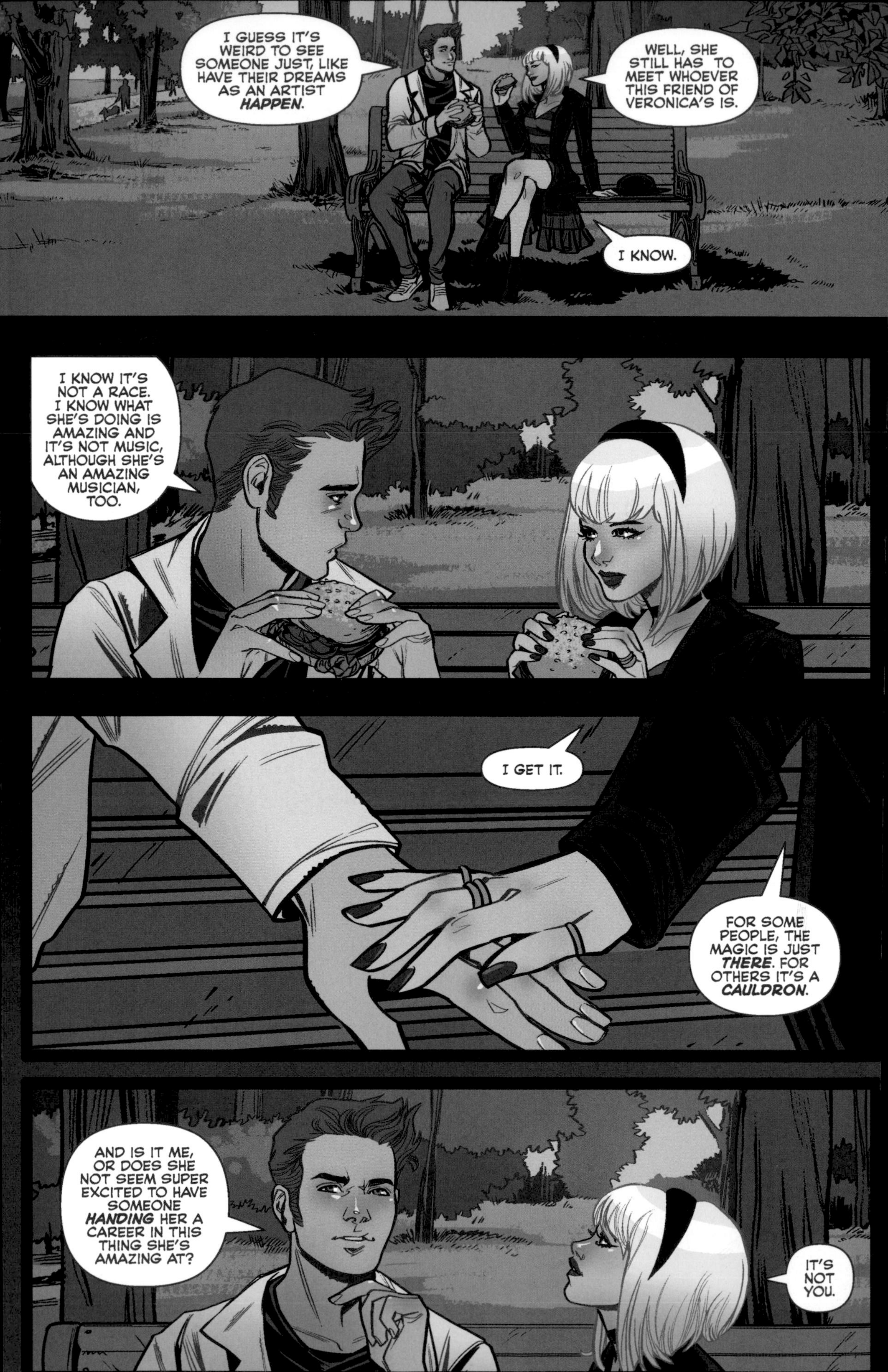
I GUESS IT'S WEIRD TO SEE SOMEONE JUST, LIKE HAVE THEIR DREAMS AS AN ARTIST ***HAPPEN***.
WELL, SHE STILL HAS TO MEET WHOEVER THIS FRIEND OF VERONICA'S IS.
I KNOW.
I KNOW IT'S NOT A RACE. I KNOW WHAT SHE'S DOING IS AMAZING AND IT'S NOT MUSIC, ALTHOUGH SHE'S AN AMAZING MUSICIAN, TOO.
I GET IT.
FOR SOME PEOPLE, THE MAGIC IS JUST ***THERE***. FOR OTHERS IT'S A ***CAULDRON***.
AND IS IT ME, OR DOES SHE NOT SEEM SUPER EXCITED TO HAVE SOMEONE ***HANDING*** HER A CAREER IN THIS THING SHE'S AMAZING AT?
IT'S NOT YOU.

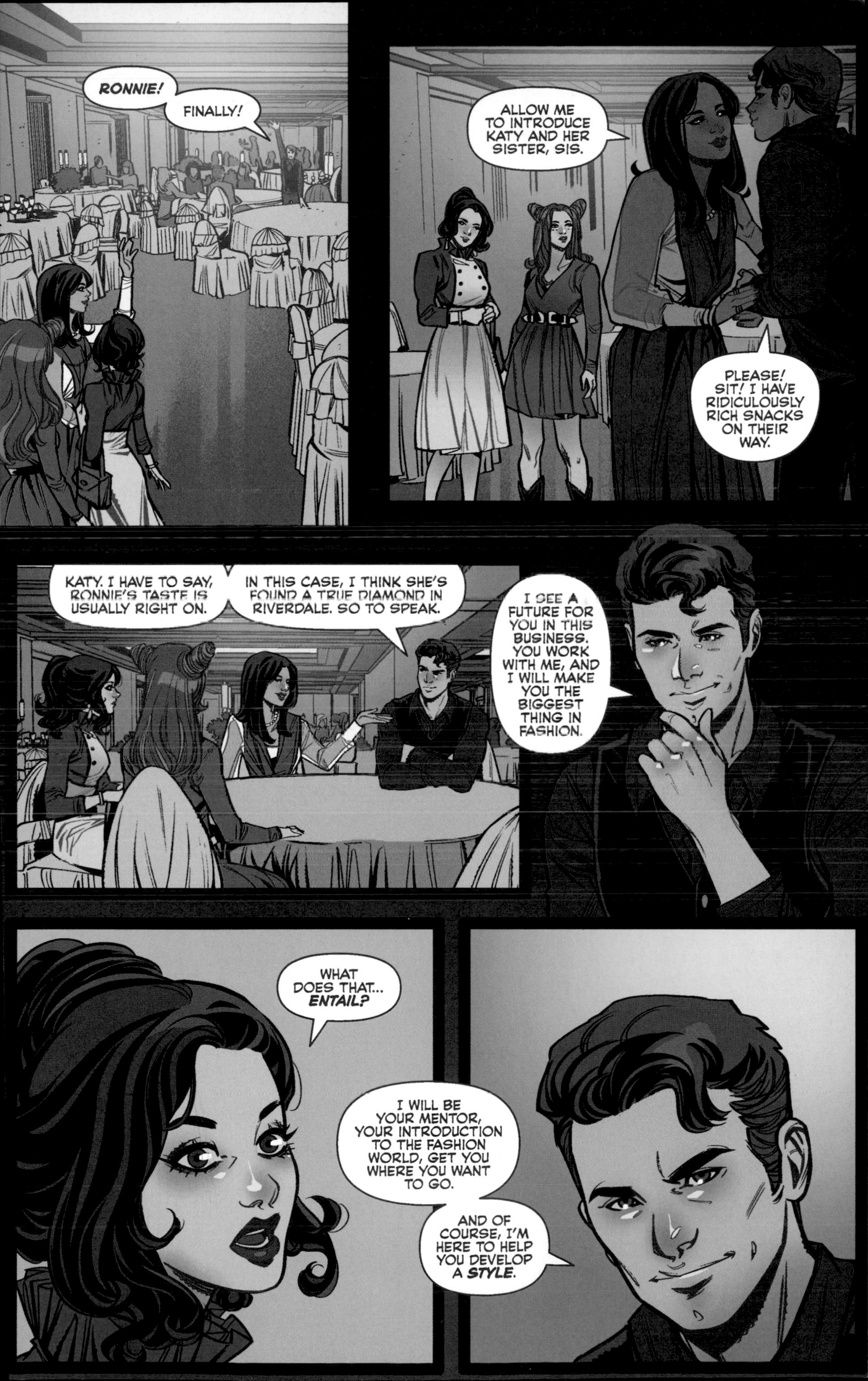
RONNIE!
FINALLY!
ALLOW ME TO INTRODUCE KATY AND HER SISTER, SIS.
PLEASE! SIT! I HAVE RIDICULOUSLY RICH SNACKS ON THEIR WAY.
KATY. I HAVE TO SAY, RONNIE'S TASTE IS USUALLY RIGHT ON.
IN THIS CASE, I THINK SHE'S FOUND A TRUE DIAMOND IN RIVERDALE. SO TO SPEAK.
I SEE A FUTURE FOR YOU IN THIS BUSINESS. YOU WORK WITH ME, AND I WILL MAKE YOU THE BIGGEST THING IN FASHION.
WHAT DOES THAT... ENTAIL?
I WILL BE YOUR MENTOR, YOUR INTRODUCTION TO THE FASHION WORLD, GET YOU WHERE YOU WANT TO GO.
AND OF COURSE, I'M HERE TO HELP YOU DEVELOP A STYLE.

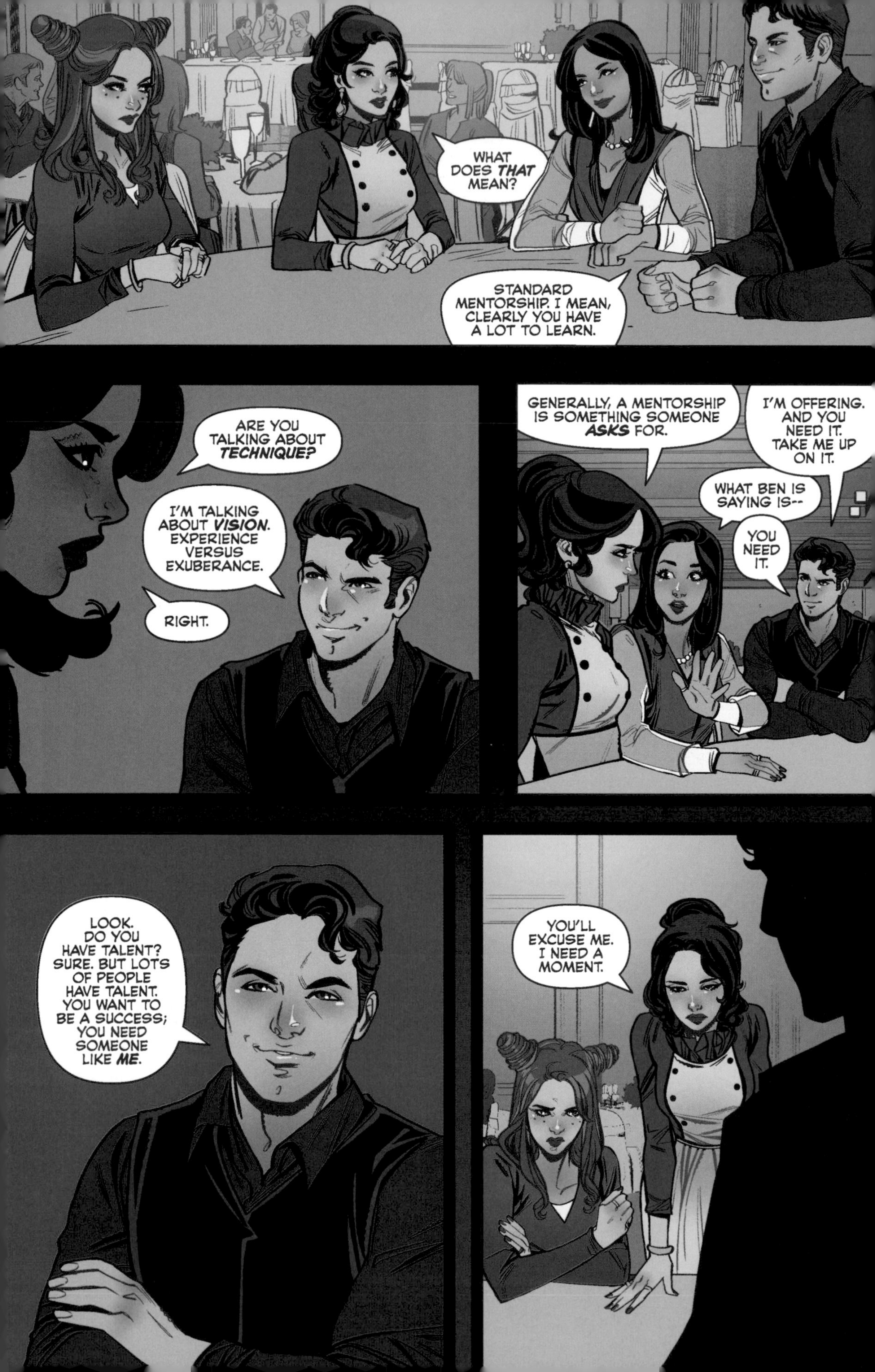
WHAT DOES THAT MEAN?
STANDARD MENTORSHIP. I MEAN, CLEARLY YOU HAVE A LOT TO LEARN.
ARE YOU TALKING ABOUT TECHNIQUE?
I'M TALKING ABOUT VISION. EXPERIENCE VERSUS EXUBERANCE.
RIGHT.
GENERALLY, A MENTORSHIP IS SOMETHING SOMEONE ASKS FOR.
I'M OFFERING. AND YOU NEED IT. TAKE ME UP ON IT.
WHAT BEN IS SAYING IS--
YOU NEED IT.
LOOK. DO YOU HAVE TALENT? SURE. BUT LOTS OF PEOPLE HAVE TALENT. YOU WANT TO BE A SUCCESS; YOU NEED SOMEONE LIKE ME.
YOU'LL EXCUSE ME. I NEED A MOMENT.

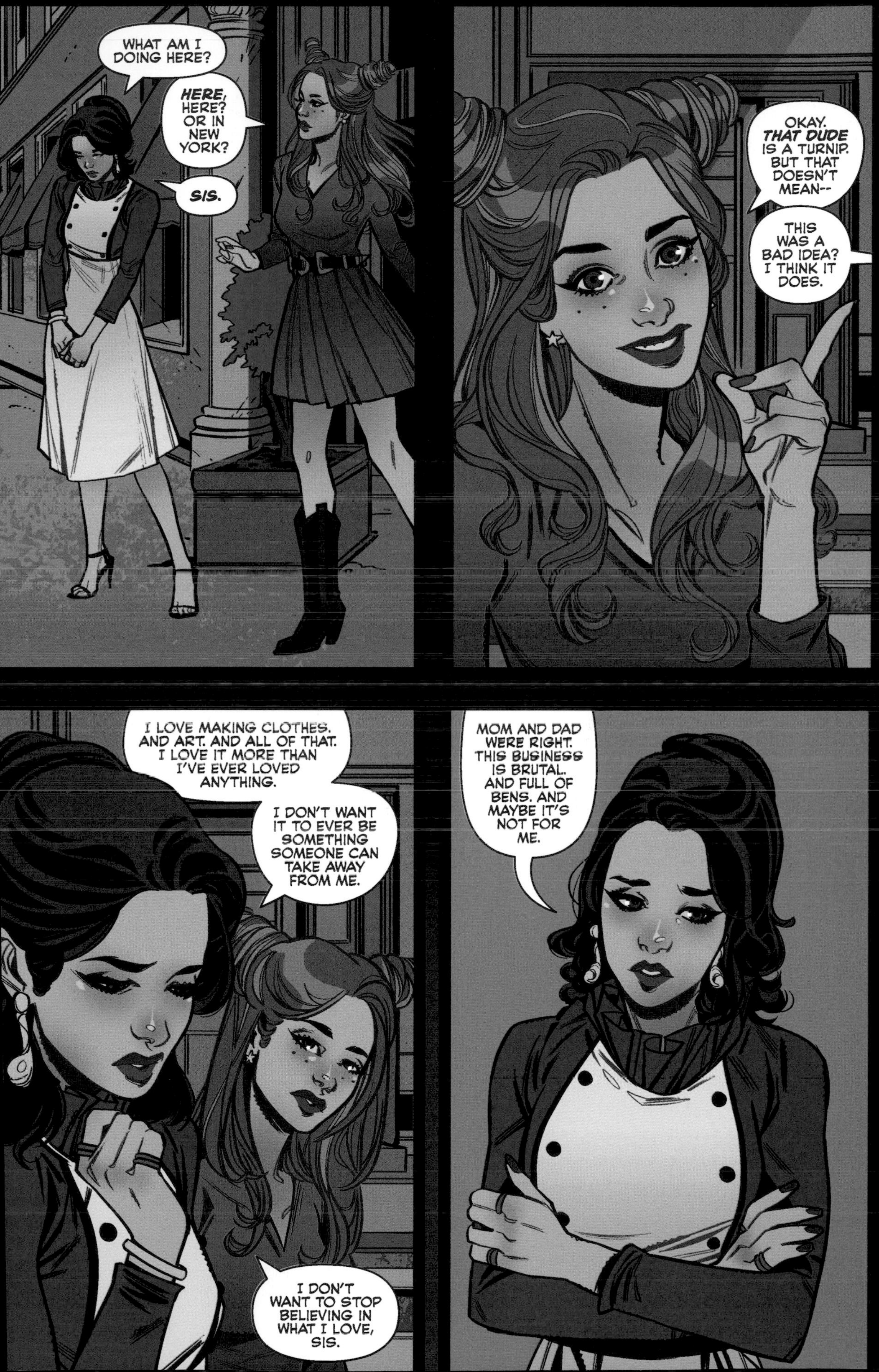
WHAT AM I DOING HERE?
HERE, HERE? OR IN NEW YORK?
SIS.
OKAY. *THAT DUDE* IS A TURNIP. BUT THAT DOESN'T MEAN--
THIS WAS A BAD IDEA? I THINK IT DOES.
I LOVE MAKING CLOTHES. AND ART. AND ALL OF THAT. I LOVE IT MORE THAN I'VE EVER LOVED ANYTHING.
I DON'T WANT IT TO EVER BE SOMETHING SOMEONE CAN TAKE AWAY FROM ME.
I DON'T WANT TO STOP BELIEVING IN WHAT I LOVE, SIS.
MOM AND DAD WERE RIGHT. THIS BUSINESS IS BRUTAL. AND FULL OF BENS. AND MAYBE IT'S NOT FOR ME.

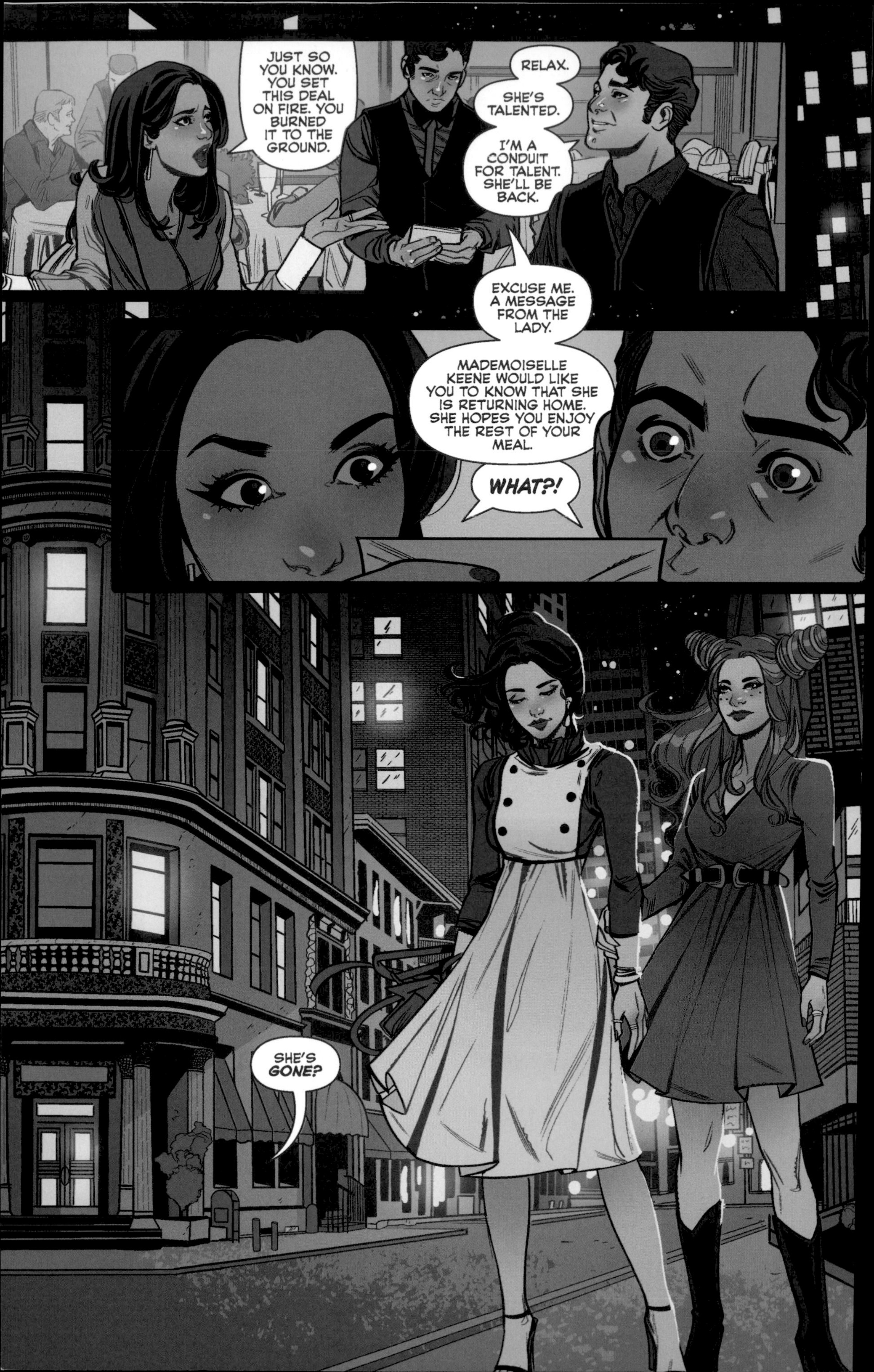
JUST SO YOU KNOW. YOU SET THIS DEAL ON FIRE. YOU BURNED IT TO THE GROUND.
RELAX.
SHE'S TALENTED.
I'M A CONDUIT FOR TALENT. SHE'LL BE BACK.
EXCUSE ME. A MESSAGE FROM THE LADY.
MADEMOISELLE KEENE WOULD LIKE YOU TO KNOW THAT SHE IS RETURNING HOME. SHE HOPES YOU ENJOY THE REST OF YOUR MEAL.
WHAT?!
SHE'S GONE?

TO BE CONTINUED...

713

Archie® and Katy Keene™

STORY BY
MARIKO TAMAKI &
KEVIN PANETTA

ART BY
LAURA BRAGA

LETTERING BY
JACK MORELLI

COLORS BY
MATT HERMS

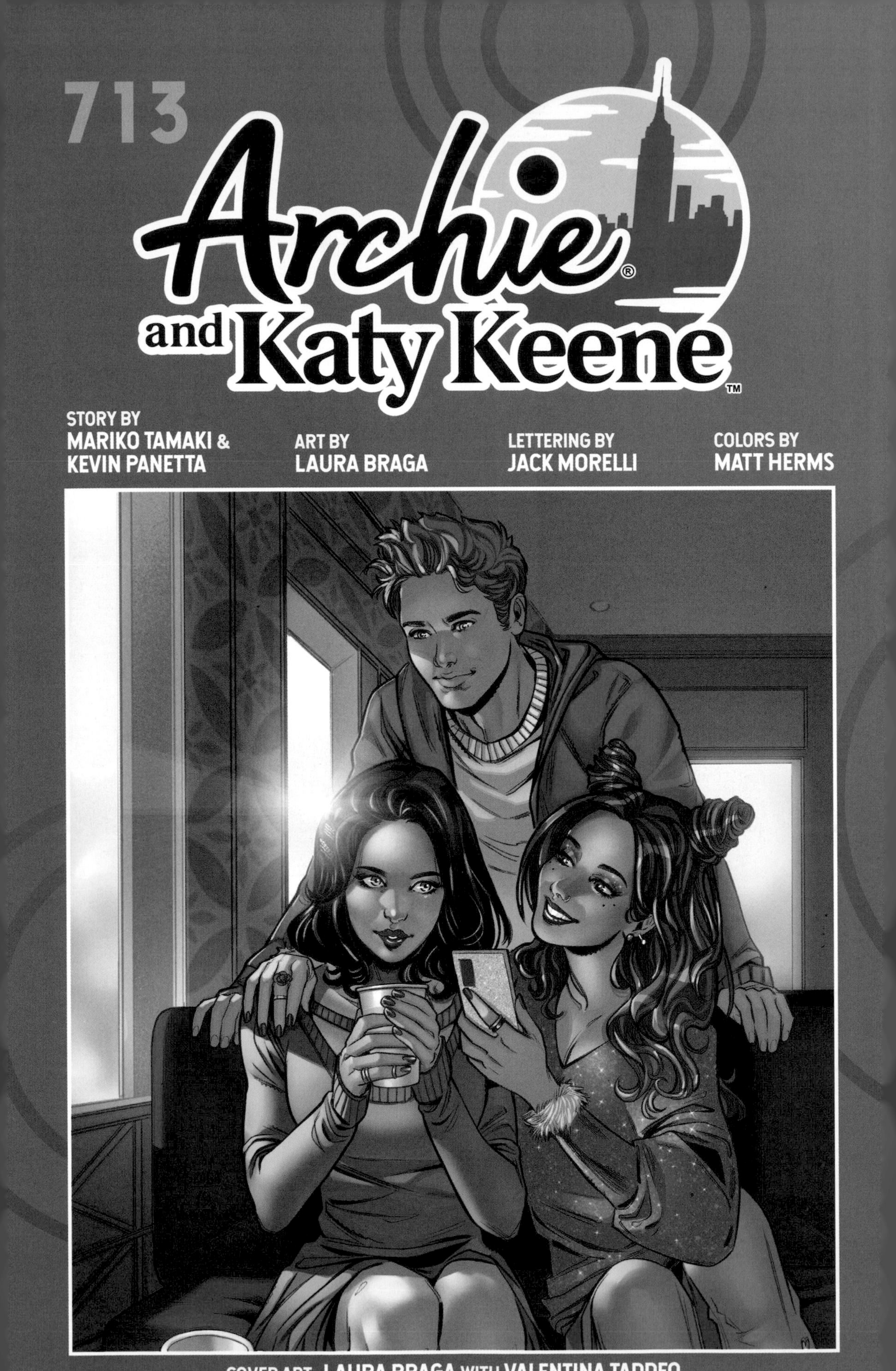

COVER ART: LAURA BRAGA WITH VALENTINA TADDEO

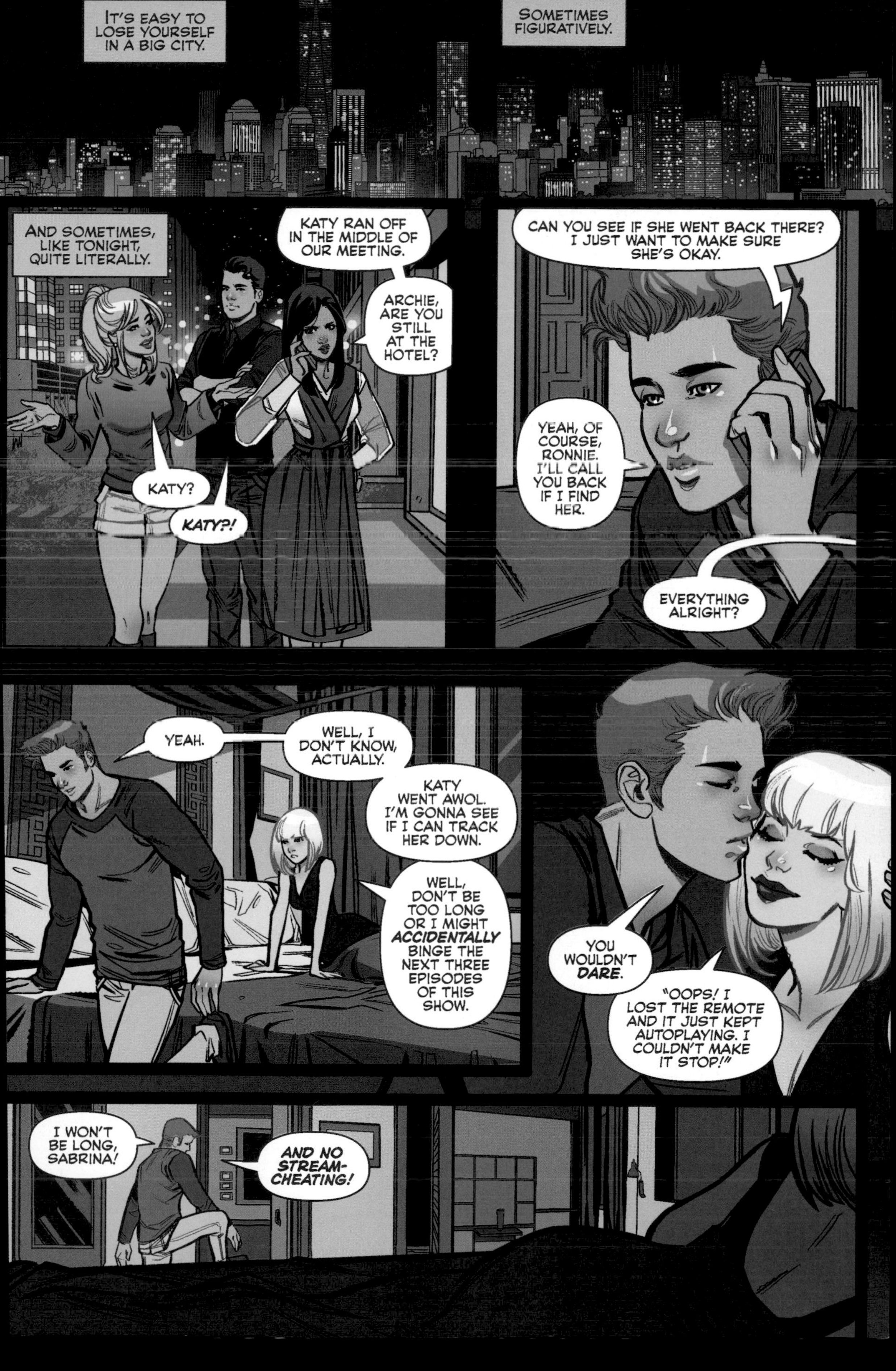
IT'S EASY TO LOSE YOURSELF IN A BIG CITY.
SOMETIMES FIGURATIVELY.
AND SOMETIMES, LIKE TONIGHT, QUITE LITERALLY.
KATY RAN OFF IN THE MIDDLE OF OUR MEETING.
ARCHIE, ARE YOU STILL AT THE HOTEL?
KATY?
KATY?!
CAN YOU SEE IF SHE WENT BACK THERE? I JUST WANT TO MAKE SURE SHE'S OKAY.
YEAH, OF COURSE, RONNIE. I'LL CALL YOU BACK IF I FIND HER.
EVERYTHING ALRIGHT?
YEAH.
WELL, I DON'T KNOW, ACTUALLY.
KATY WENT AWOL. I'M GONNA SEE IF I CAN TRACK HER DOWN.
WELL, DON'T BE TOO LONG OR I MIGHT ACCIDENTALLY BINGE THE NEXT THREE EPISODES OF THIS SHOW.
YOU WOULDN'T DARE.
"OOPS! I LOST THE REMOTE AND IT JUST KEPT AUTOPLAYING. I COULDN'T MAKE IT STOP!"
I WON'T BE LONG, SABRINA!
AND NO STREAM-CHEATING!

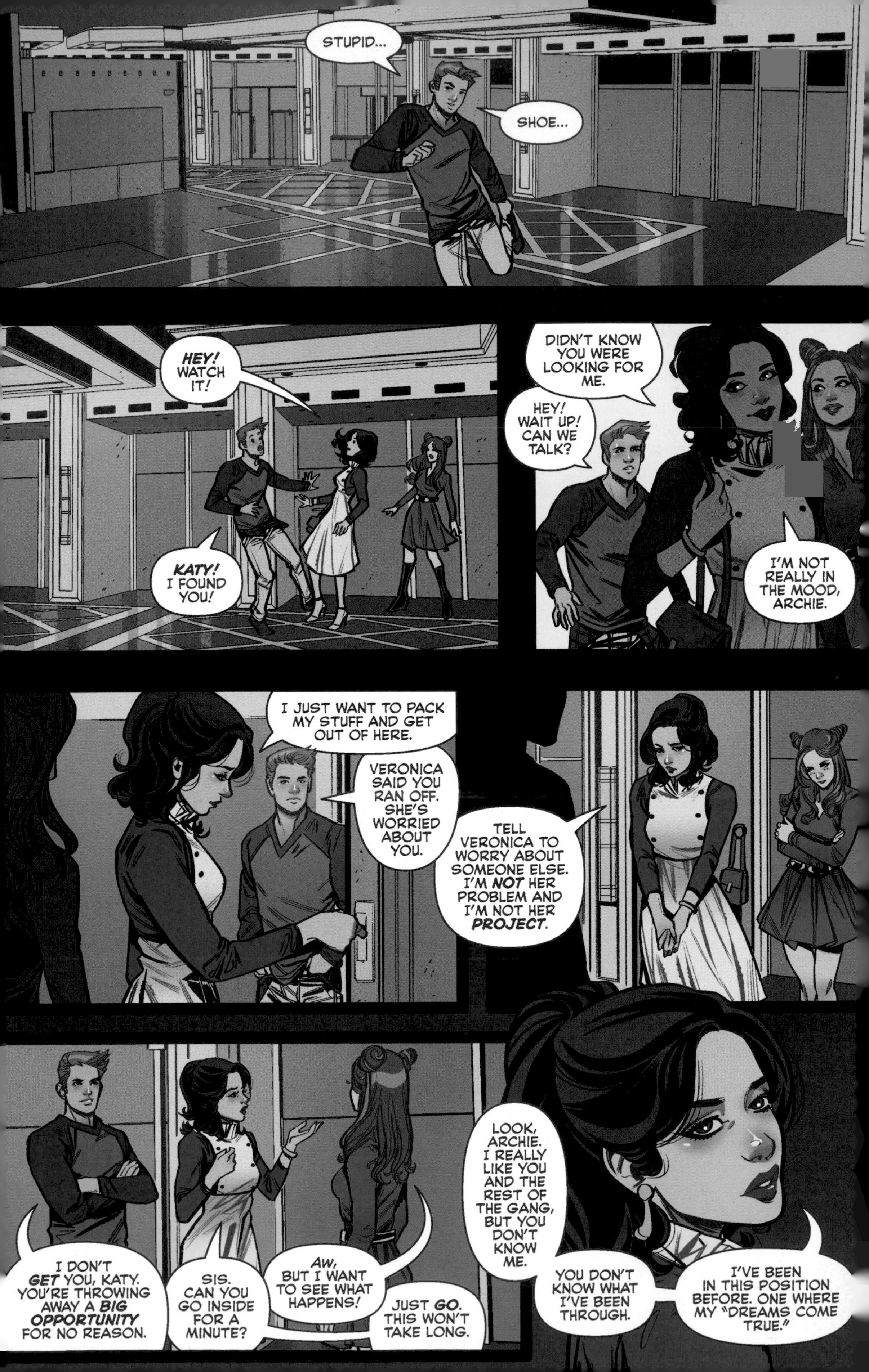
STUPID...
SHOE...
HEY! WATCH IT!
KATY! I FOUND YOU!
DIDN'T KNOW YOU WERE LOOKING FOR ME.
HEY! WAIT UP! CAN WE TALK?
I'M NOT REALLY IN THE MOOD, ARCHIE.
I JUST WANT TO PACK MY STUFF AND GET OUT OF HERE.
VERONICA SAID YOU RAN OFF. SHE'S WORRIED ABOUT YOU.
TELL VERONICA TO WORRY ABOUT SOMEONE ELSE. I'M NOT HER PROBLEM AND I'M NOT HER PROJECT.
I DON'T GET YOU, KATY. YOU'RE THROWING AWAY A BIG OPPORTUNITY FOR NO REASON.
SIS. CAN YOU GO INSIDE FOR A MINUTE?
AW, BUT I WANT TO SEE WHAT HAPPENS!
JUST GO. THIS WON'T TAKE LONG.
LOOK, ARCHIE. I REALLY LIKE YOU AND THE REST OF THE GANG, BUT YOU DON'T KNOW ME.
YOU DON'T KNOW WHAT I'VE BEEN THROUGH.
I'VE BEEN IN THIS POSITION BEFORE. ONE WHERE MY "DREAMS COME TRUE."

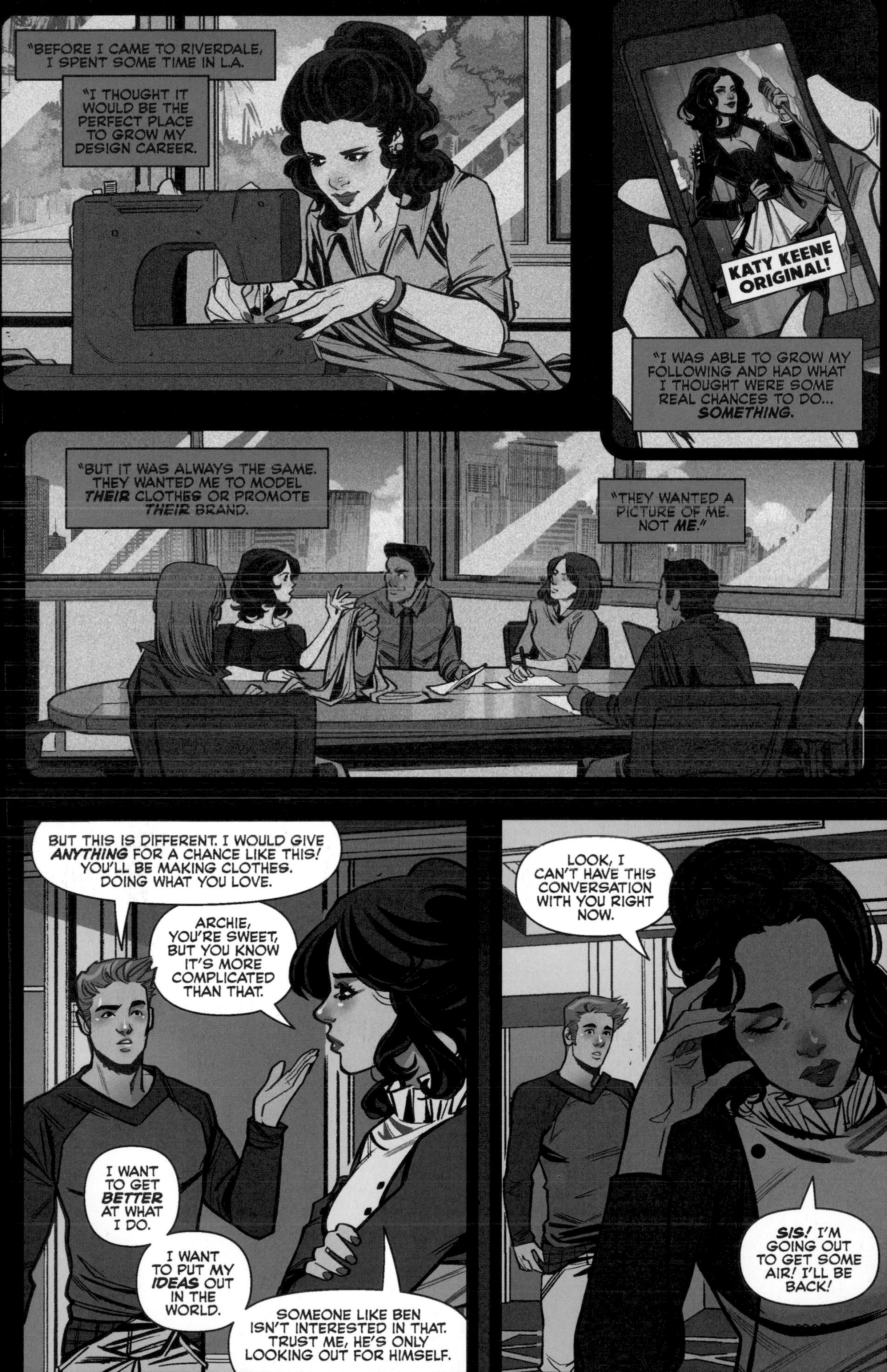
"BEFORE I CAME TO RIVERDALE, I SPENT SOME TIME IN L.A.
"I THOUGHT IT WOULD BE THE PERFECT PLACE TO GROW MY DESIGN CAREER.
KATY KEENE ORIGINAL!
"I WAS ABLE TO GROW MY FOLLOWING AND HAD WHAT I THOUGHT WERE SOME REAL CHANCES TO DO... SOMETHING.
"BUT IT WAS ALWAYS THE SAME. THEY WANTED ME TO MODEL THEIR CLOTHES OR PROMOTE THEIR BRAND.
"THEY WANTED A PICTURE OF ME. NOT ME."
BUT THIS IS DIFFERENT. I WOULD GIVE ANYTHING FOR A CHANCE LIKE THIS! YOU'LL BE MAKING CLOTHES. DOING WHAT YOU LOVE.
ARCHIE, YOU'RE SWEET, BUT YOU KNOW IT'S MORE COMPLICATED THAN THAT.
I WANT TO GET BETTER AT WHAT I DO.
I WANT TO PUT MY IDEAS OUT IN THE WORLD.
SOMEONE LIKE BEN ISN'T INTERESTED IN THAT. TRUST ME, HE'S ONLY LOOKING OUT FOR HIMSELF.
LOOK, I CAN'T HAVE THIS CONVERSATION WITH YOU RIGHT NOW.
SIS! I'M GOING OUT TO GET SOME AIR! I'LL BE BACK!

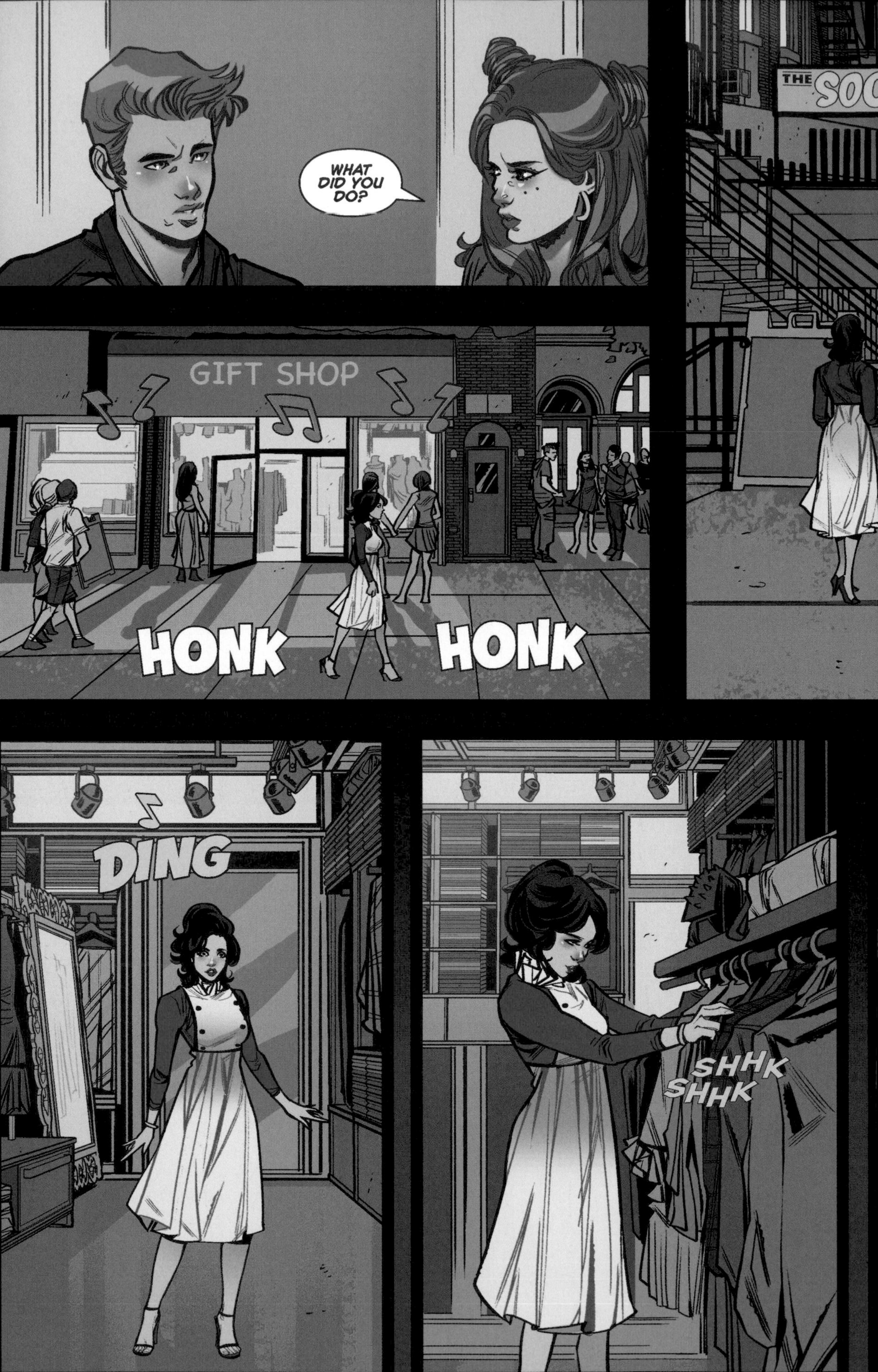
WHAT DID YOU DO?
THE SOC
GIFT SHOP
HONK
HONK
DING
SHHK
SHHK

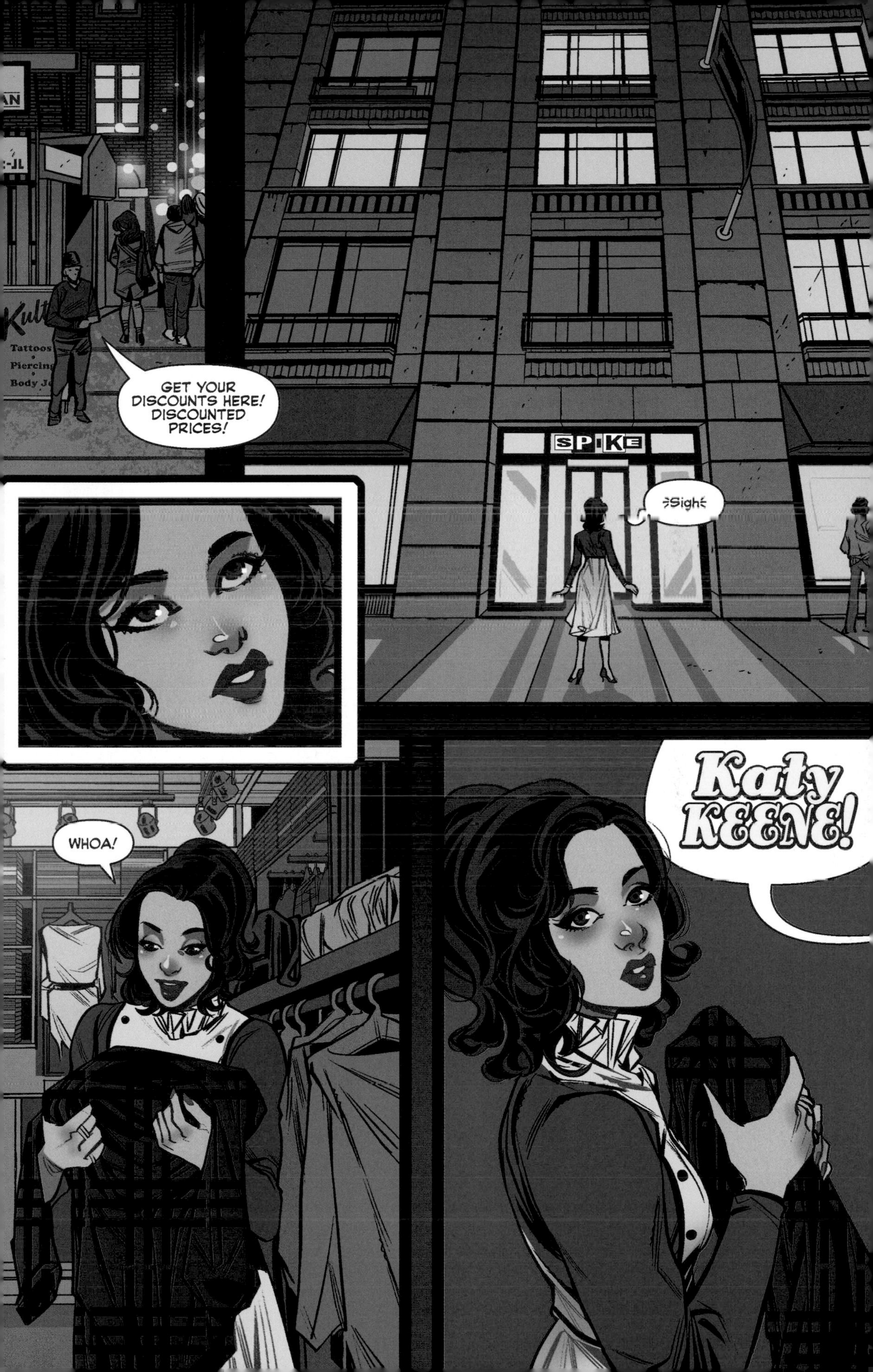
Kult
Tattoos
Piercing
Body J
GET YOUR DISCOUNTS HERE! DISCOUNTED PRICES!
SPIKE
Sigh
WHOA!
Katy KEENE!

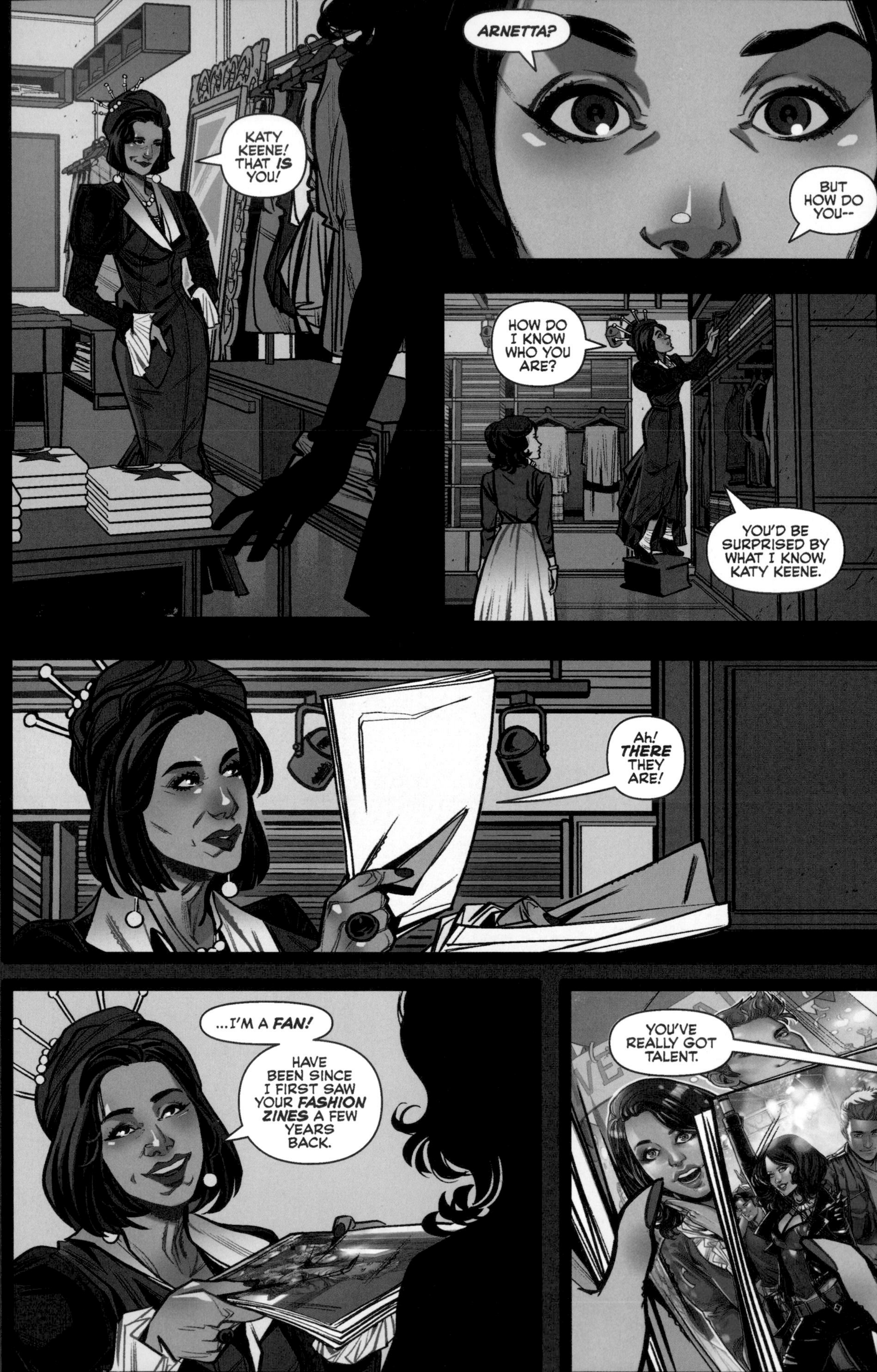
KATY KEENE! THAT IS YOU!
ARNETTA?
BUT HOW DO YOU--
HOW DO I KNOW WHO YOU ARE?
YOU'D BE SURPRISED BY WHAT I KNOW, KATY KEENE.
Ah! THERE THEY ARE!
...I'M A FAN!
HAVE BEEN SINCE I FIRST SAW YOUR FASHION ZINES A FEW YEARS BACK.
YOU'VE REALLY GOT TALENT.

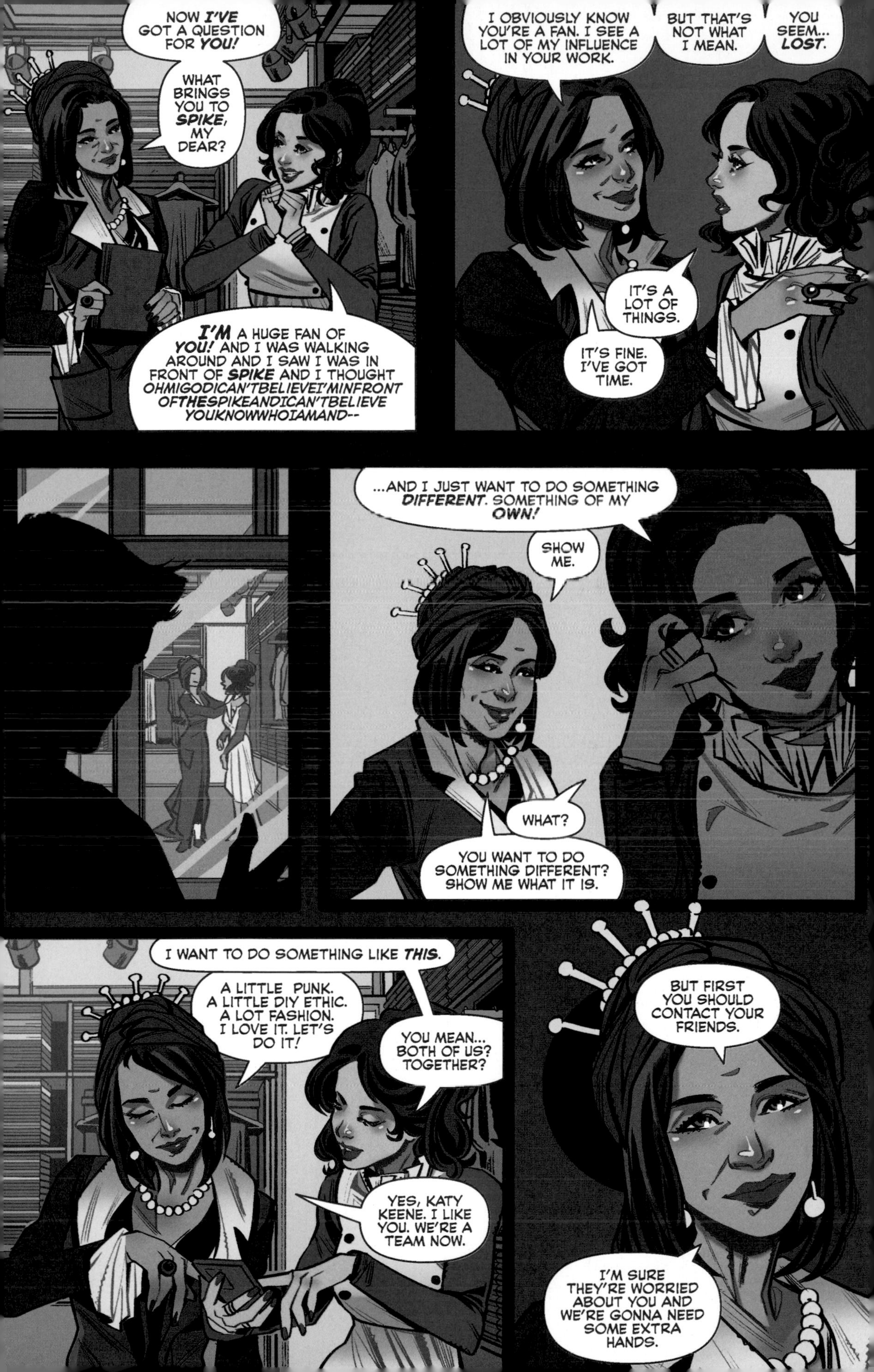

NOW I'VE GOT A QUESTION FOR YOU!
WHAT BRINGS YOU TO SPIKE, MY DEAR?
I'M A HUGE FAN OF YOU! AND I WAS WALKING AROUND AND I SAW I WAS IN FRONT OF SPIKE AND I THOUGHT OHMIGODICAN'TBELIEVEI'MINFRONT OFTHESPIKEANDICAN'TBELIEVE YOUKNOWWHOIAMAND--
I OBVIOUSLY KNOW YOU'RE A FAN. I SEE A LOT OF MY INFLUENCE IN YOUR WORK.
BUT THAT'S NOT WHAT I MEAN.
YOU SEEM... LOST.
IT'S A LOT OF THINGS.
IT'S FINE. I'VE GOT TIME.
...AND I JUST WANT TO DO SOMETHING DIFFERENT. SOMETHING OF MY OWN!
SHOW ME.
WHAT?
YOU WANT TO DO SOMETHING DIFFERENT? SHOW ME WHAT IT IS.
I WANT TO DO SOMETHING LIKE THIS.
A LITTLE PUNK. A LITTLE DIY ETHIC. A LOT FASHION. I LOVE IT. LET'S DO IT!
YOU MEAN... BOTH OF US? TOGETHER?
YES, KATY KEENE. I LIKE YOU. WE'RE A TEAM NOW.
BUT FIRST YOU SHOULD CONTACT YOUR FRIENDS.
I'M SURE THEY'RE WORRIED ABOUT YOU AND WE'RE GONNA NEED SOME EXTRA HANDS.

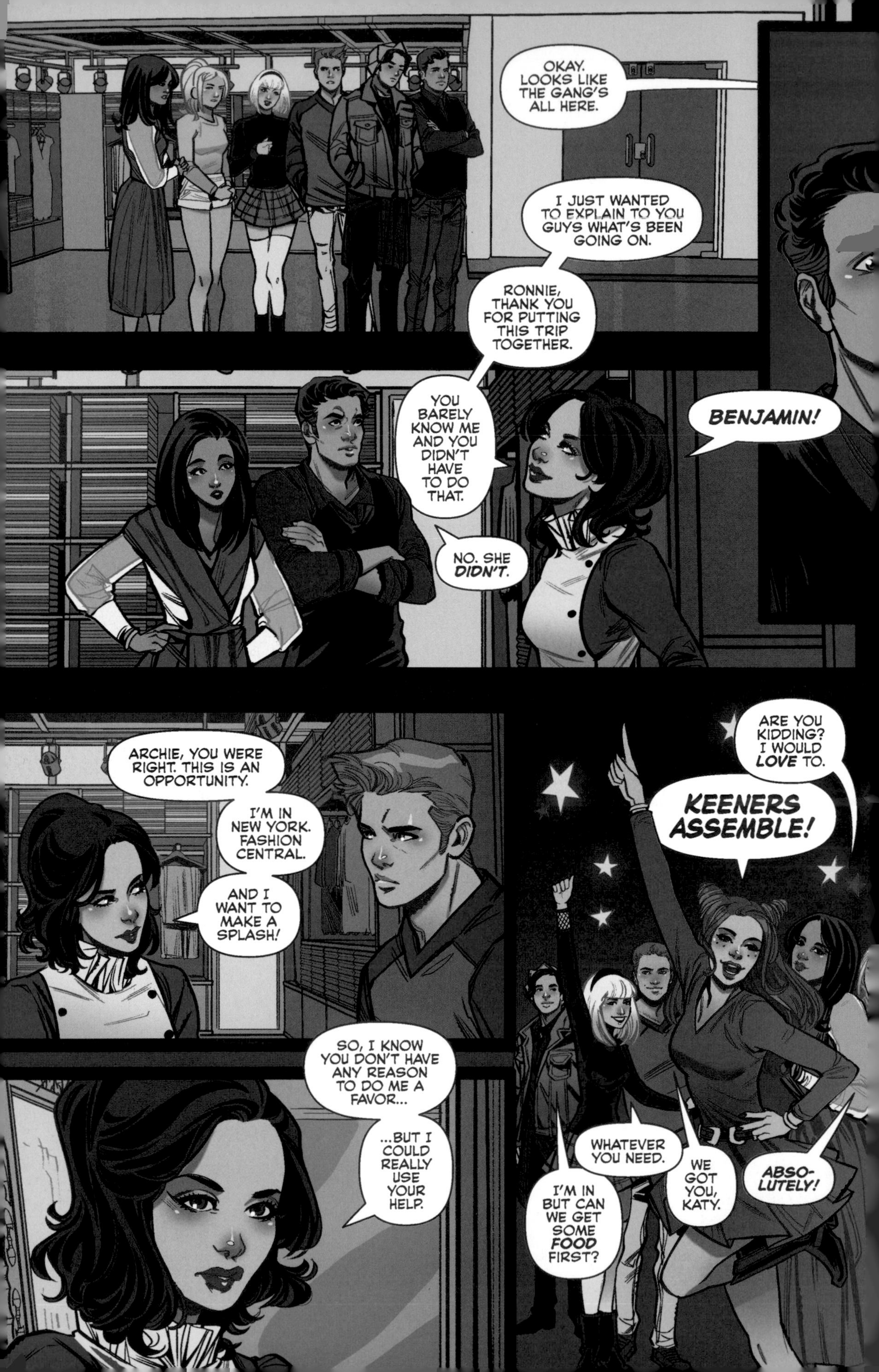
OKAY. LOOKS LIKE THE GANG'S ALL HERE.
I JUST WANTED TO EXPLAIN TO YOU GUYS WHAT'S BEEN GOING ON.
RONNIE, THANK YOU FOR PUTTING THIS TRIP TOGETHER.
YOU BARELY KNOW ME AND YOU DIDN'T HAVE TO DO THAT.
NO. SHE *DIDN'T*.
BENJAMIN!
ARCHIE, YOU WERE RIGHT. THIS IS AN OPPORTUNITY.
I'M IN NEW YORK. FASHION CENTRAL.
AND I WANT TO MAKE A SPLASH!
SO, I KNOW YOU DON'T HAVE ANY REASON TO DO ME A FAVOR...
...BUT I COULD REALLY USE YOUR HELP.
ARE YOU KIDDING? I WOULD **LOVE** TO.
KEENERS ASSEMBLE!
WHATEVER YOU NEED.
I'M IN BUT CAN WE GET SOME **FOOD** FIRST?
WE GOT YOU, KATY.
ABSO-LUTELY!

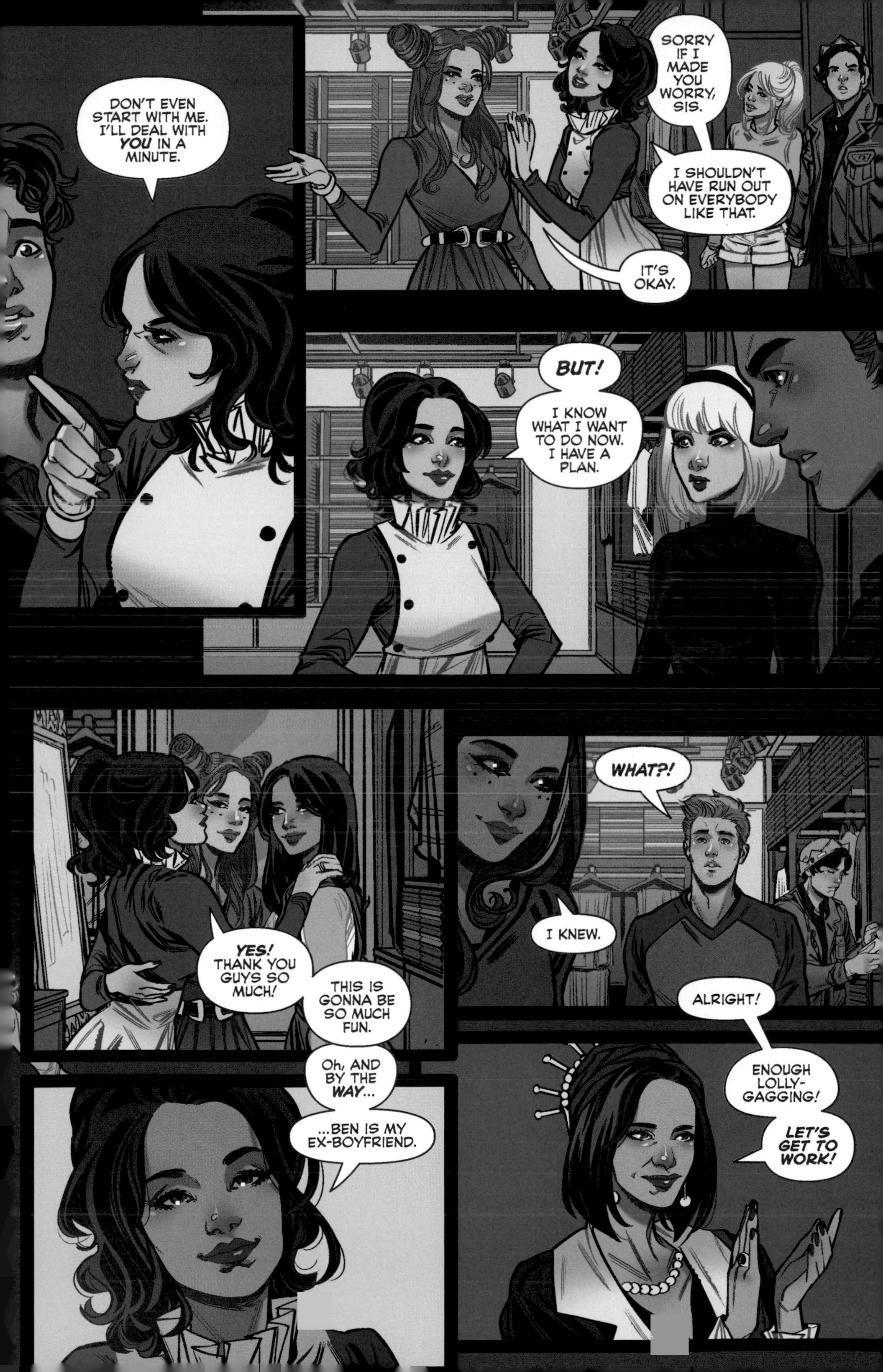

DON'T EVEN START WITH ME. I'LL DEAL WITH *YOU* IN A MINUTE.
SORRY IF I MADE YOU WORRY, SIS.
I SHOULDN'T HAVE RUN OUT ON EVERYBODY LIKE THAT.
IT'S OKAY.
BUT!
I KNOW WHAT I WANT TO DO NOW. I HAVE A PLAN.
YES! THANK YOU GUYS SO MUCH!
THIS IS GONNA BE SO MUCH FUN.
WHAT?!
I KNEW.
ALRIGHT!
Oh, AND BY THE *WAY*...
...BEN IS MY EX-BOYFRIEND.
ENOUGH LOLLY-GAGGING!
LET'S GET TO WORK!

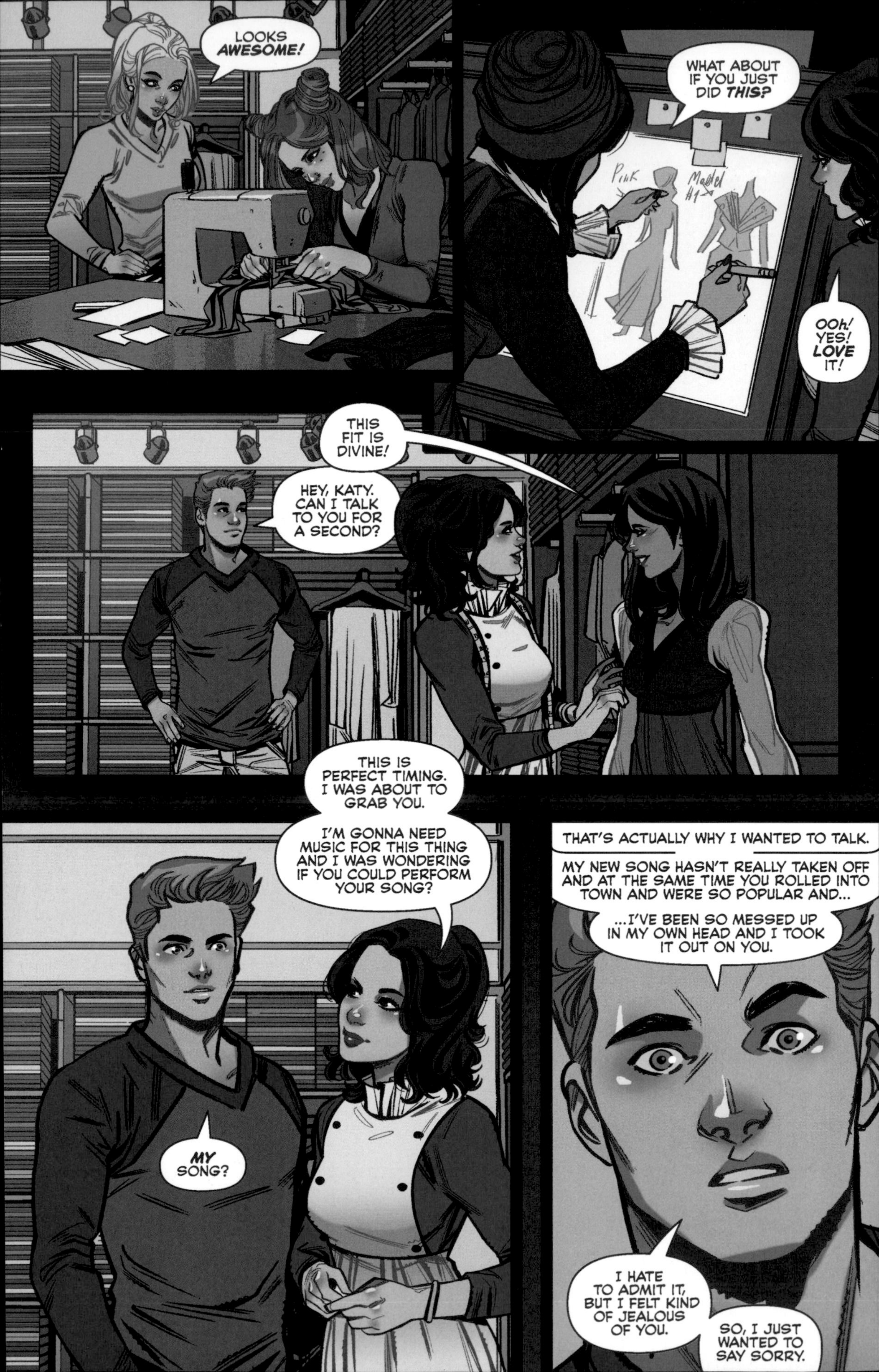
LOOKS AWESOME!
WHAT ABOUT IF YOU JUST DID THIS?
Pink
Model #1
OOH! YES! LOVE IT!
THIS FIT IS DIVINE!
HEY, KATY. CAN I TALK TO YOU FOR A SECOND?
THIS IS PERFECT TIMING. I WAS ABOUT TO GRAB YOU.
I'M GONNA NEED MUSIC FOR THIS THING AND I WAS WONDERING IF YOU COULD PERFORM YOUR SONG?
MY SONG?
THAT'S ACTUALLY WHY I WANTED TO TALK.
MY NEW SONG HASN'T REALLY TAKEN OFF AND AT THE SAME TIME YOU ROLLED INTO TOWN AND WERE SO POPULAR AND...
...I'VE BEEN SO MESSED UP IN MY OWN HEAD AND I TOOK IT OUT ON YOU.
I HATE TO ADMIT IT, BUT I FELT KIND OF JEALOUS OF YOU.
SO, I JUST WANTED TO SAY SORRY.

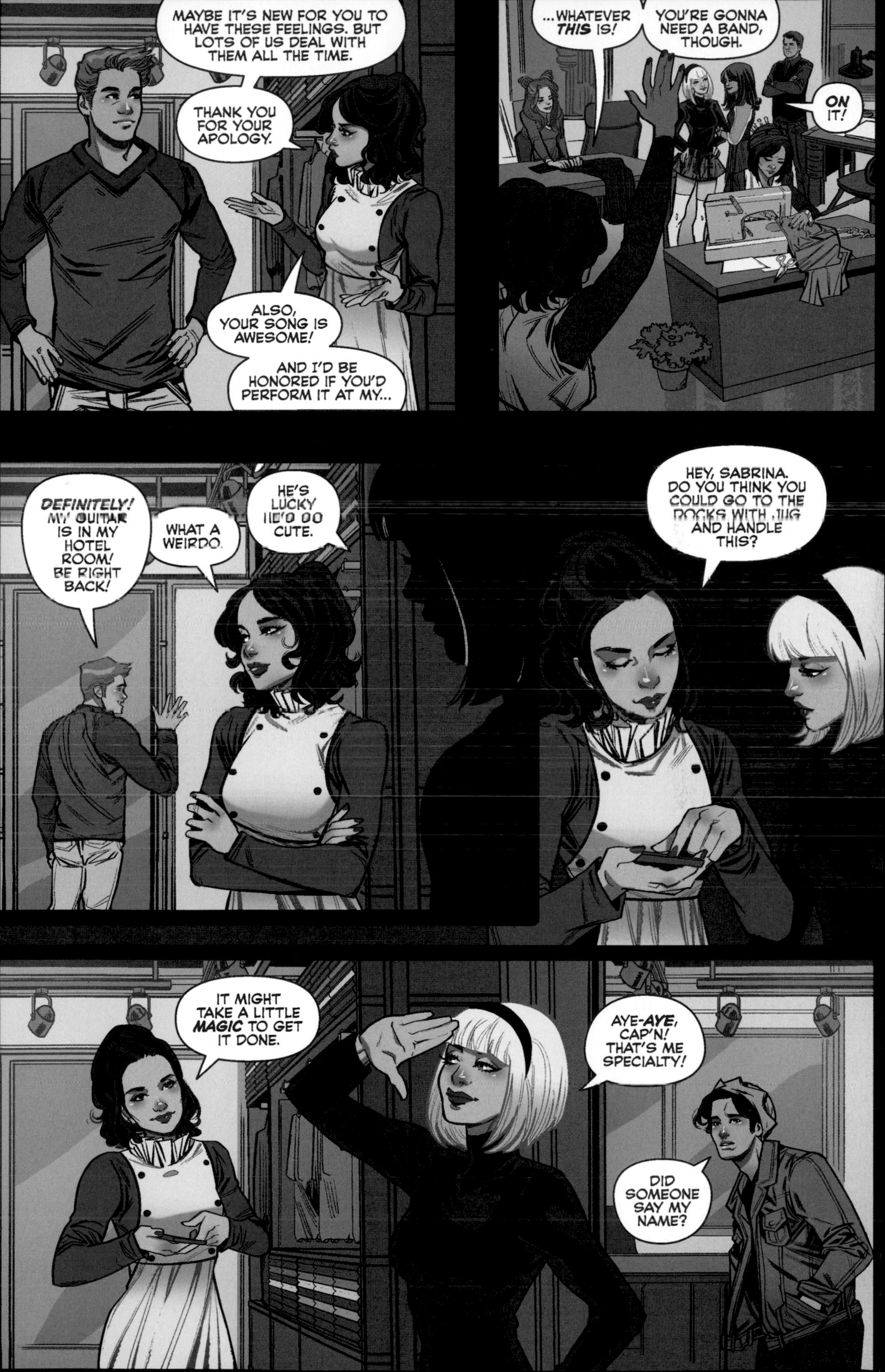
MAYBE IT'S NEW FOR YOU TO HAVE THESE FEELINGS. BUT LOTS OF US DEAL WITH THEM ALL THE TIME.
THANK YOU FOR YOUR APOLOGY.
ALSO, YOUR SONG IS AWESOME!
AND I'D BE HONORED IF YOU'D PERFORM IT AT MY...
...WHATEVER *THIS* IS!
YOU'RE GONNA NEED A BAND, THOUGH.
ON IT!
DEFINITELY! MY GUITAR IS IN MY HOTEL ROOM! BE RIGHT BACK!
WHAT A WEIRDO.
HE'S LUCKY HE'S SO CUTE.
HEY, SABRINA. DO YOU THINK YOU COULD GO TO THE DOCKS WITH JUG AND HANDLE THIS?
IT MIGHT TAKE A LITTLE *MAGIC* TO GET IT DONE.
AYE-*AYE*, CAP'N! THAT'S ME SPECIALTY!
DID SOMEONE SAY MY NAME?

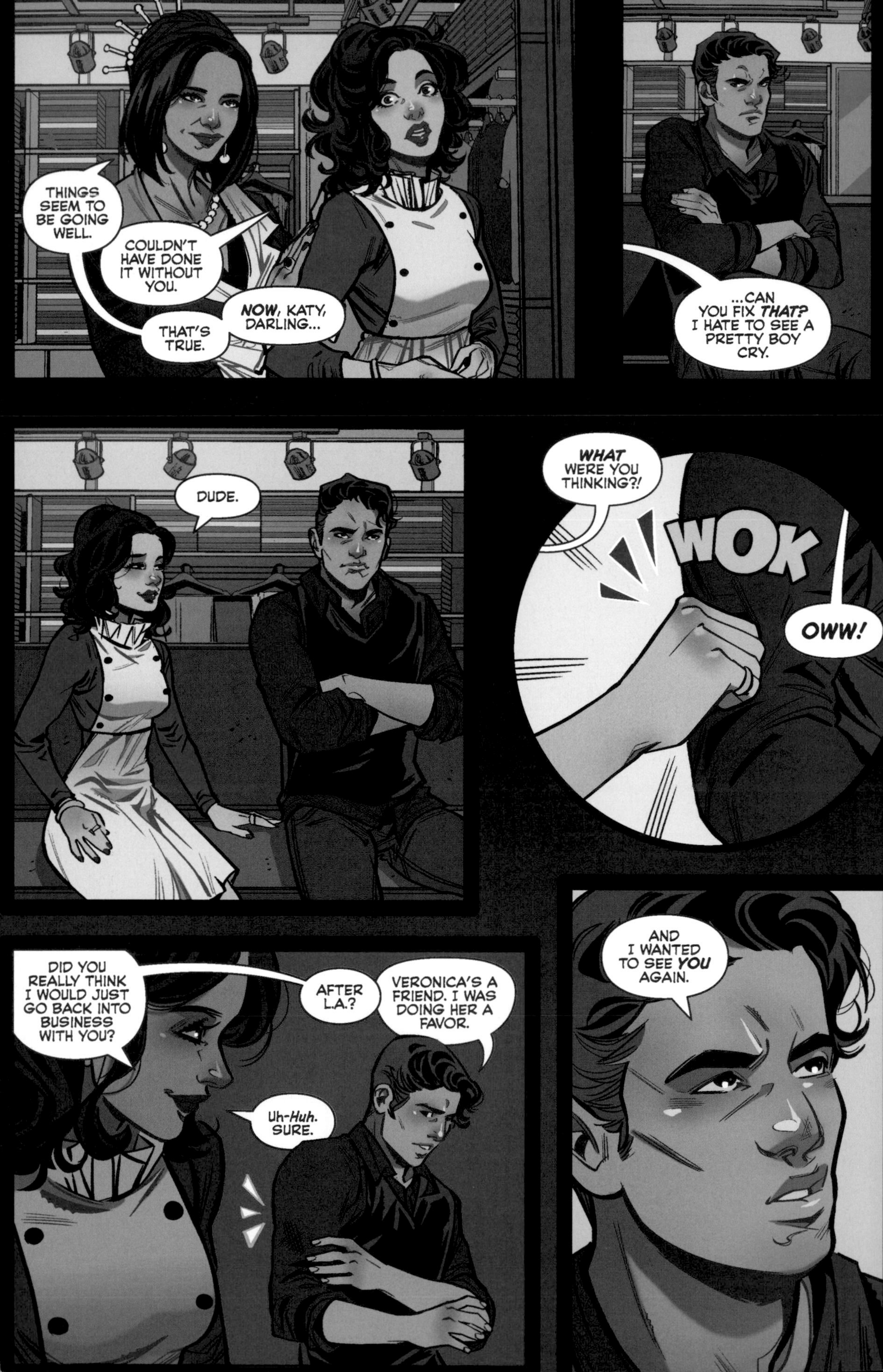
THINGS SEEM TO BE GOING WELL.
COULDN'T HAVE DONE IT WITHOUT YOU.
THAT'S TRUE.
NOW, KATY, DARLING...
...CAN YOU FIX THAT? I HATE TO SEE A PRETTY BOY CRY.
DUDE.
WHAT WERE YOU THINKING?!
WOK
OWW!
DID YOU REALLY THINK I WOULD JUST GO BACK INTO BUSINESS WITH YOU?
AFTER L.A.?
VERONICA'S A FRIEND. I WAS DOING HER A FAVOR.
Uh-Huh. SURE.
AND I WANTED TO SEE YOU AGAIN.

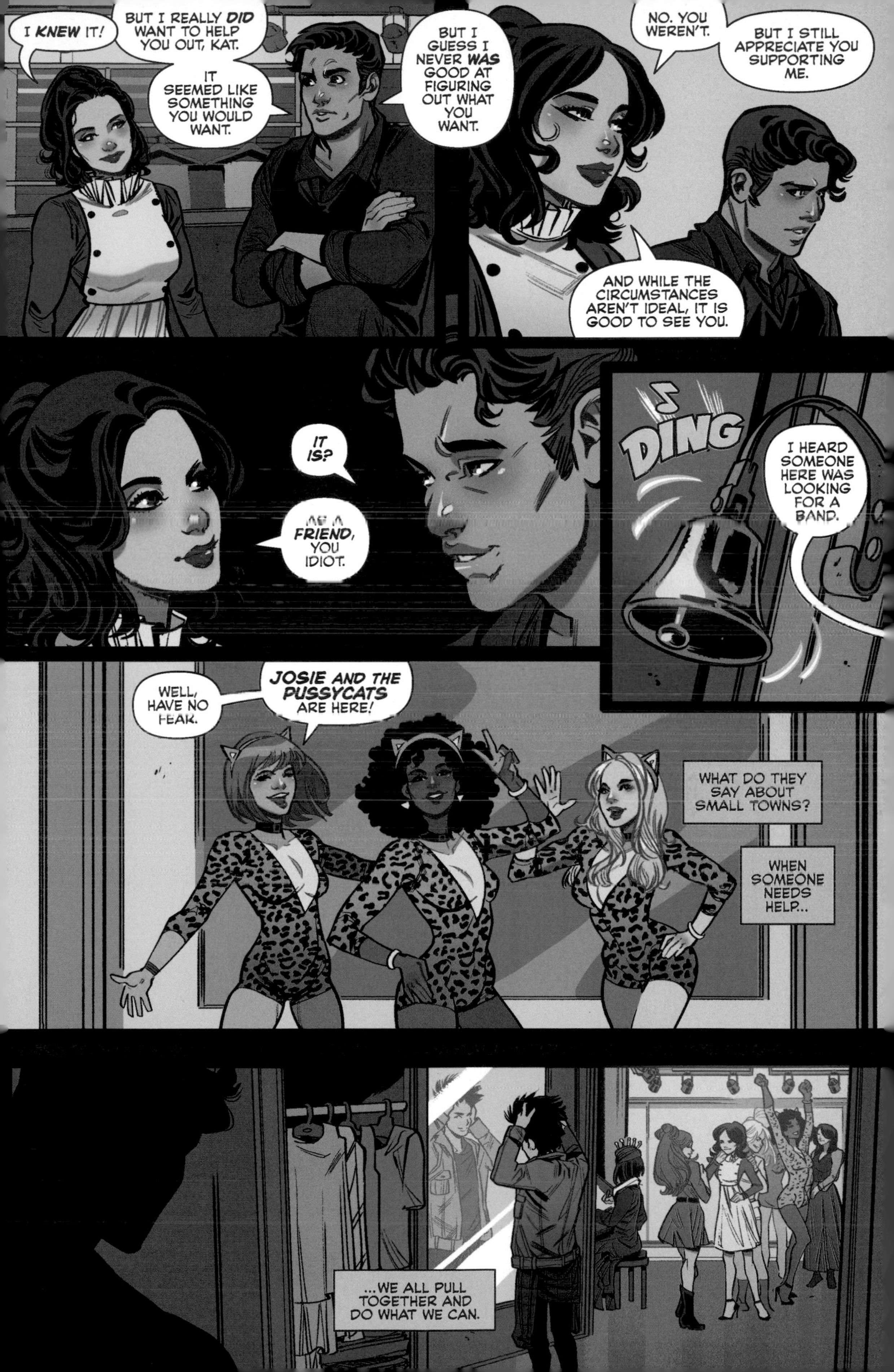
I **KNEW** IT!
BUT I REALLY **DID** WANT TO HELP YOU OUT, KAT.
IT SEEMED LIKE SOMETHING YOU WOULD WANT.
BUT I GUESS I NEVER **WAS** GOOD AT FIGURING OUT WHAT YOU WANT.
NO. YOU WEREN'T.
BUT I STILL APPRECIATE YOU SUPPORTING ME.
AND WHILE THE CIRCUMSTANCES AREN'T IDEAL, IT IS GOOD TO SEE YOU.
IT IS?
AS A **FRIEND**, YOU IDIOT.
DING
I HEARD SOMEONE HERE WAS LOOKING FOR A BAND.
WELL, HAVE NO FEAR.
JOSIE AND THE PUSSYCATS ARE HERE!
WHAT DO THEY SAY ABOUT SMALL TOWNS?
WHEN SOMEONE NEEDS HELP...
...WE ALL PULL TOGETHER AND DO WHAT WE CAN.

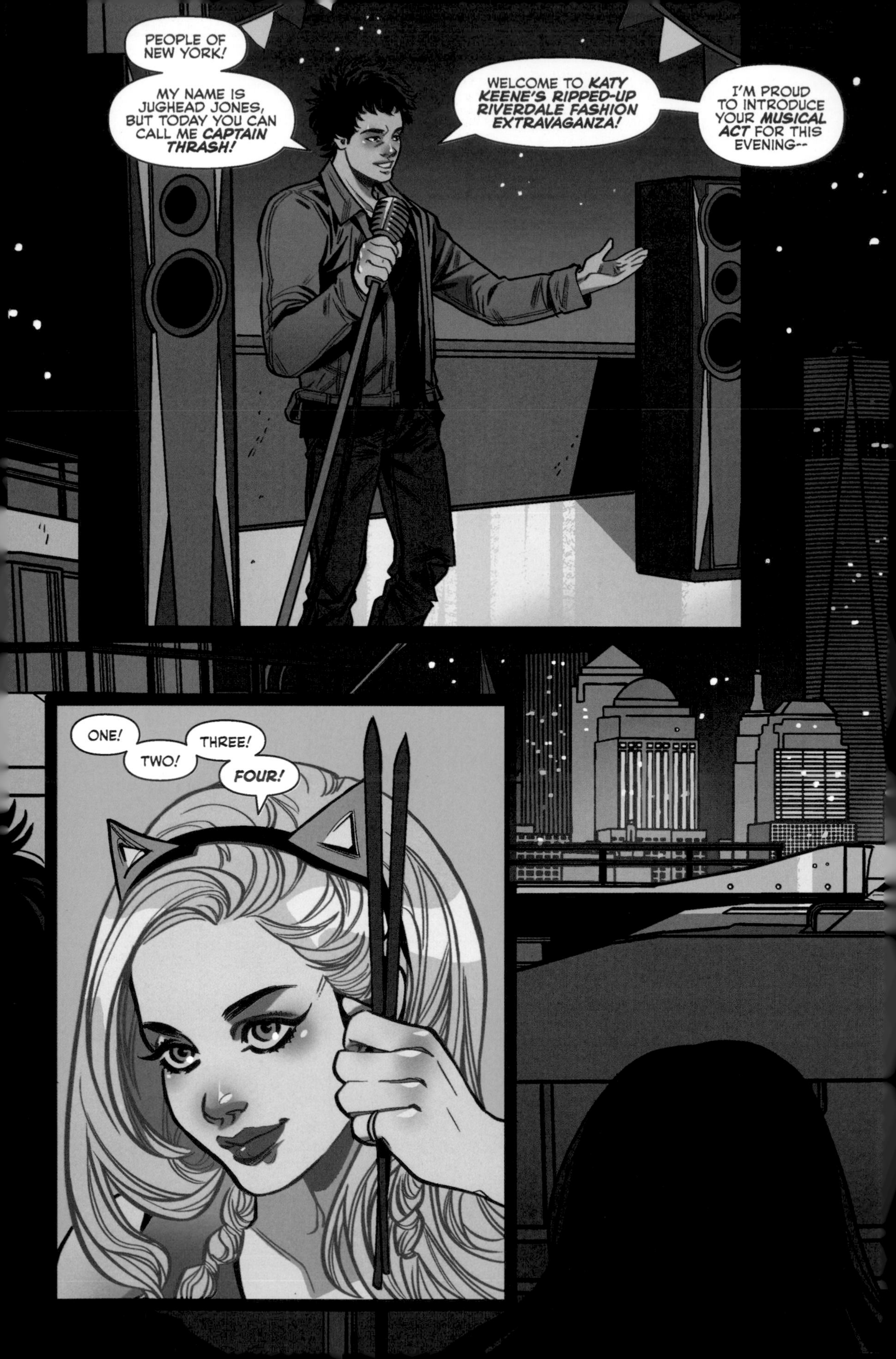

PEOPLE OF NEW YORK!
MY NAME IS JUGHEAD JONES, BUT TODAY YOU CAN CALL ME *CAPTAIN THRASH!*
WELCOME TO *KATY KEENE'S RIPPED-UP RIVERDALE FASHION EXTRAVAGANZA!*
I'M PROUD TO INTRODUCE YOUR *MUSICAL ACT* FOR THIS EVENING--
ONE!
TWO!
THREE!
FOUR!

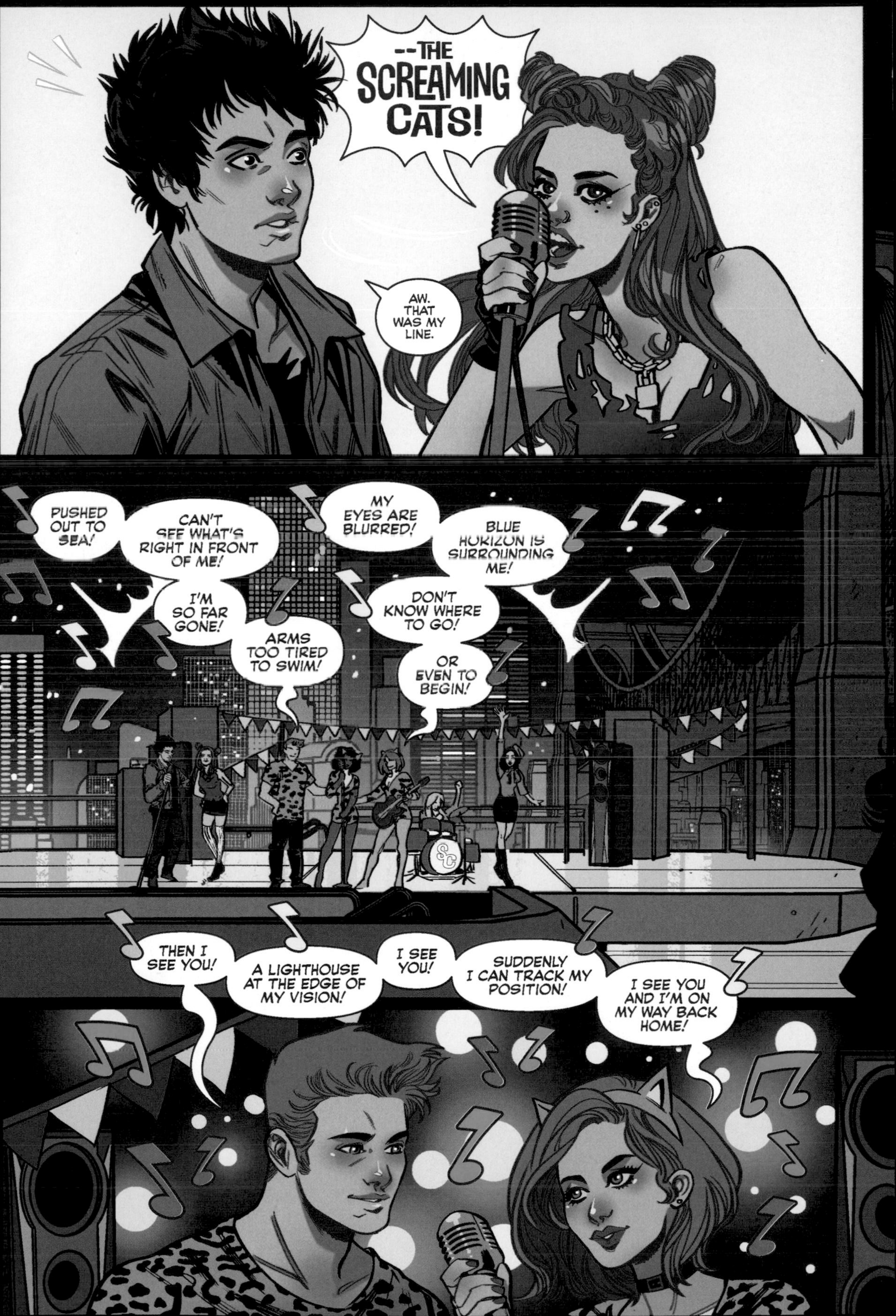
--THE SCREAMING CATS!
AW. THAT WAS MY LINE.
PUSHED OUT TO SEA!
CAN'T SEE WHAT'S RIGHT IN FRONT OF ME!
I'M SO FAR GONE!
ARMS TOO TIRED TO SWIM!
MY EYES ARE BLURRED!
BLUE HORIZON IS SURROUNDING ME!
DON'T KNOW WHERE TO GO!
OR EVEN TO BEGIN!
SC
THEN I SEE YOU!
A LIGHTHOUSE AT THE EDGE OF MY VISION!
I SEE YOU!
SUDDENLY I CAN TRACK MY POSITION!
I SEE YOU AND I'M ON MY WAY BACK HOME!

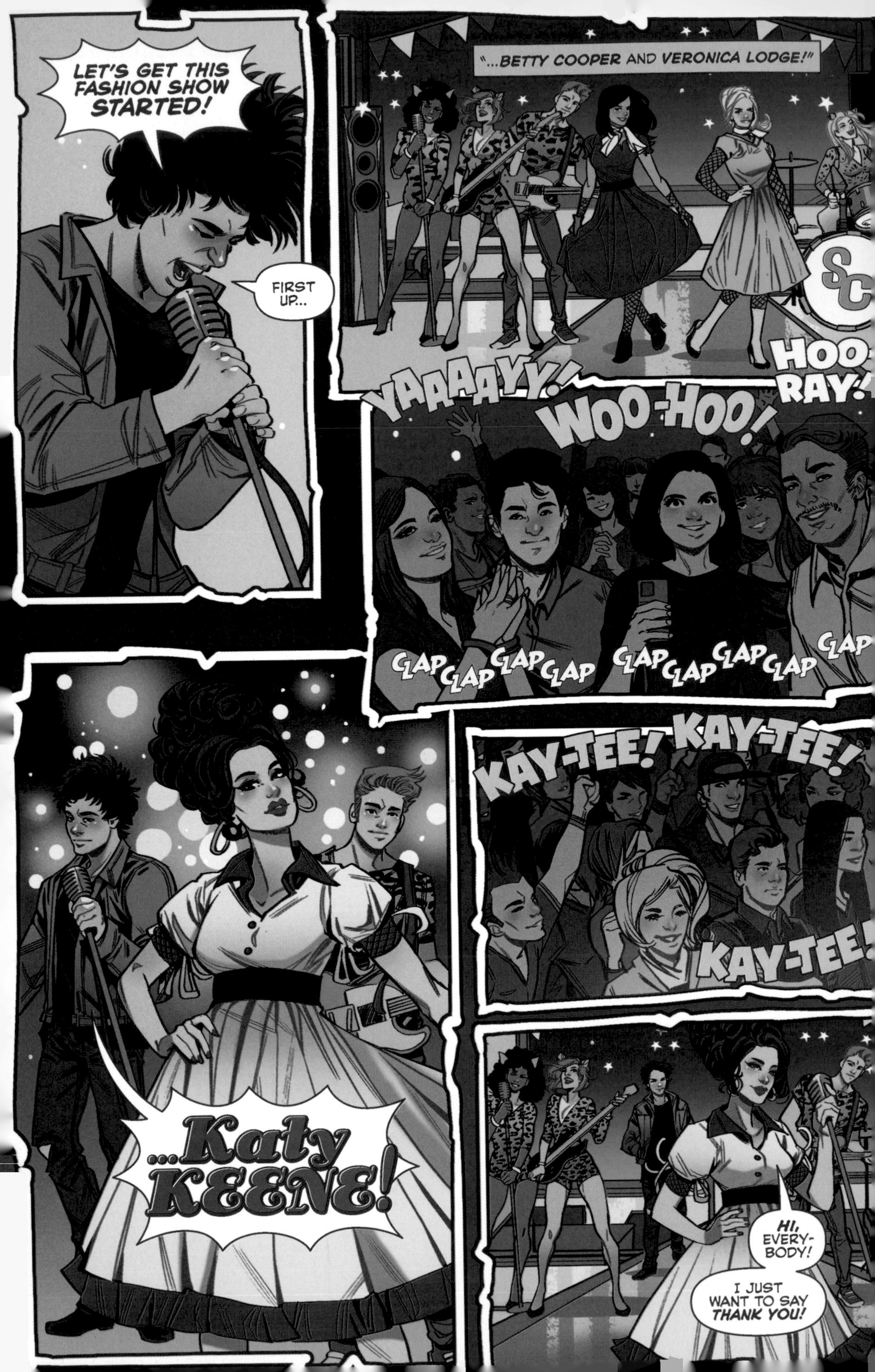
LET'S GET THIS FASHION SHOW STARTED!
FIRST UP...
"...BETTY COOPER AND VERONICA LODGE!"
HOO-RAY!
YAAAAYY!
WOO-HOO!
CLAP CLAP CLAP CLAP CLAP CLAP CLAP CLAP CLAP
...Katy KEENE!
KAY-TEE! KAY-TEE!
KAY-TEE!
HI, EVERY-BODY!
I JUST WANT TO SAY THANK YOU!

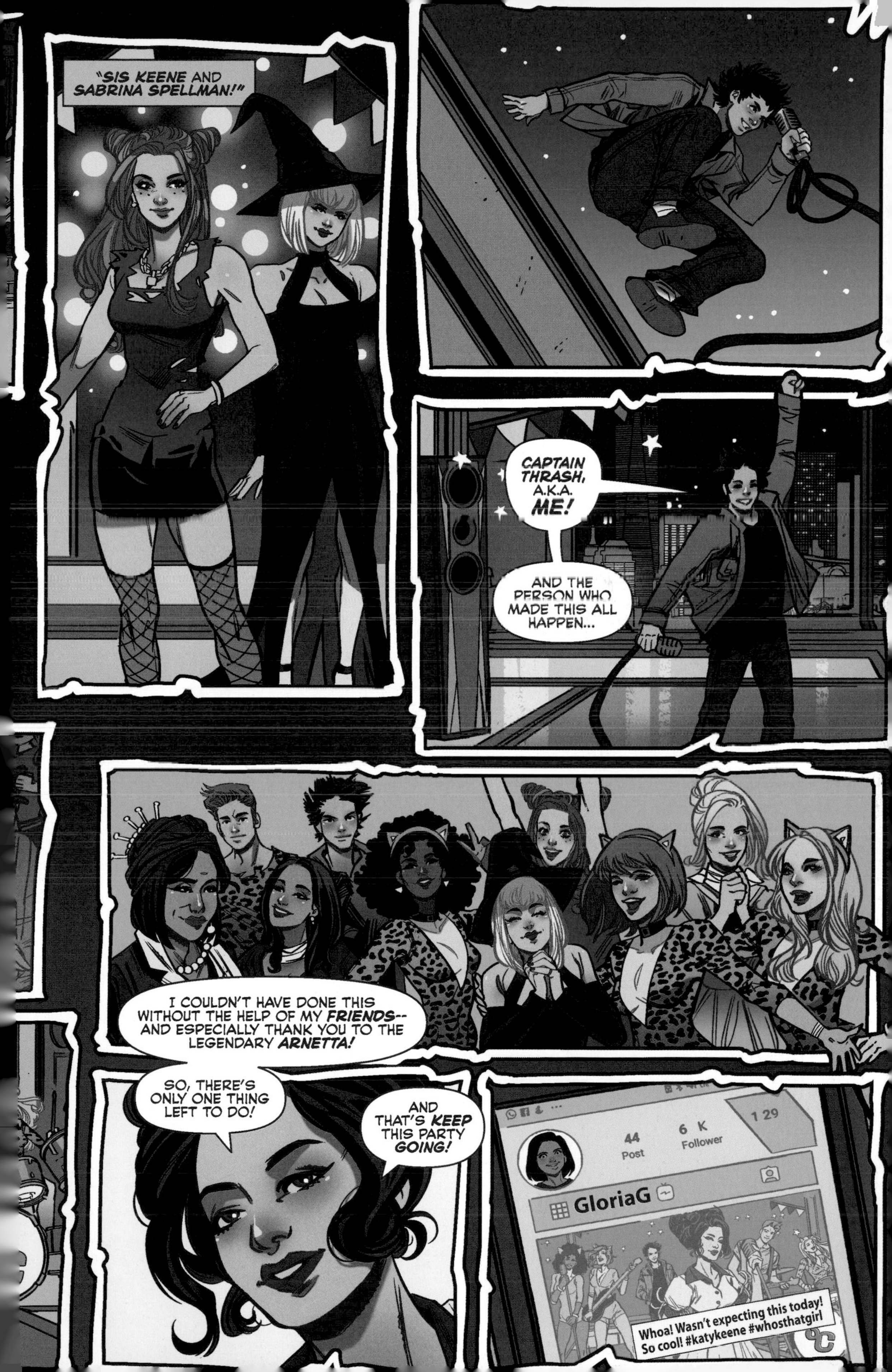
"SIS KEENE AND SABRINA SPELLMAN!"
CAPTAIN THRASH, A.K.A. ME!
AND THE PERSON WHO MADE THIS ALL HAPPEN...
I COULDN'T HAVE DONE THIS WITHOUT THE HELP OF MY FRIENDS-- AND ESPECIALLY THANK YOU TO THE LEGENDARY ARNETTA!
SO, THERE'S ONLY ONE THING LEFT TO DO!
AND THAT'S KEEP THIS PARTY GOING!
44
Post
6 K
Follower
1 29
GloriaG
Whoa! Wasn't expecting this today!
So cool! #katykeene #whosthatgirl

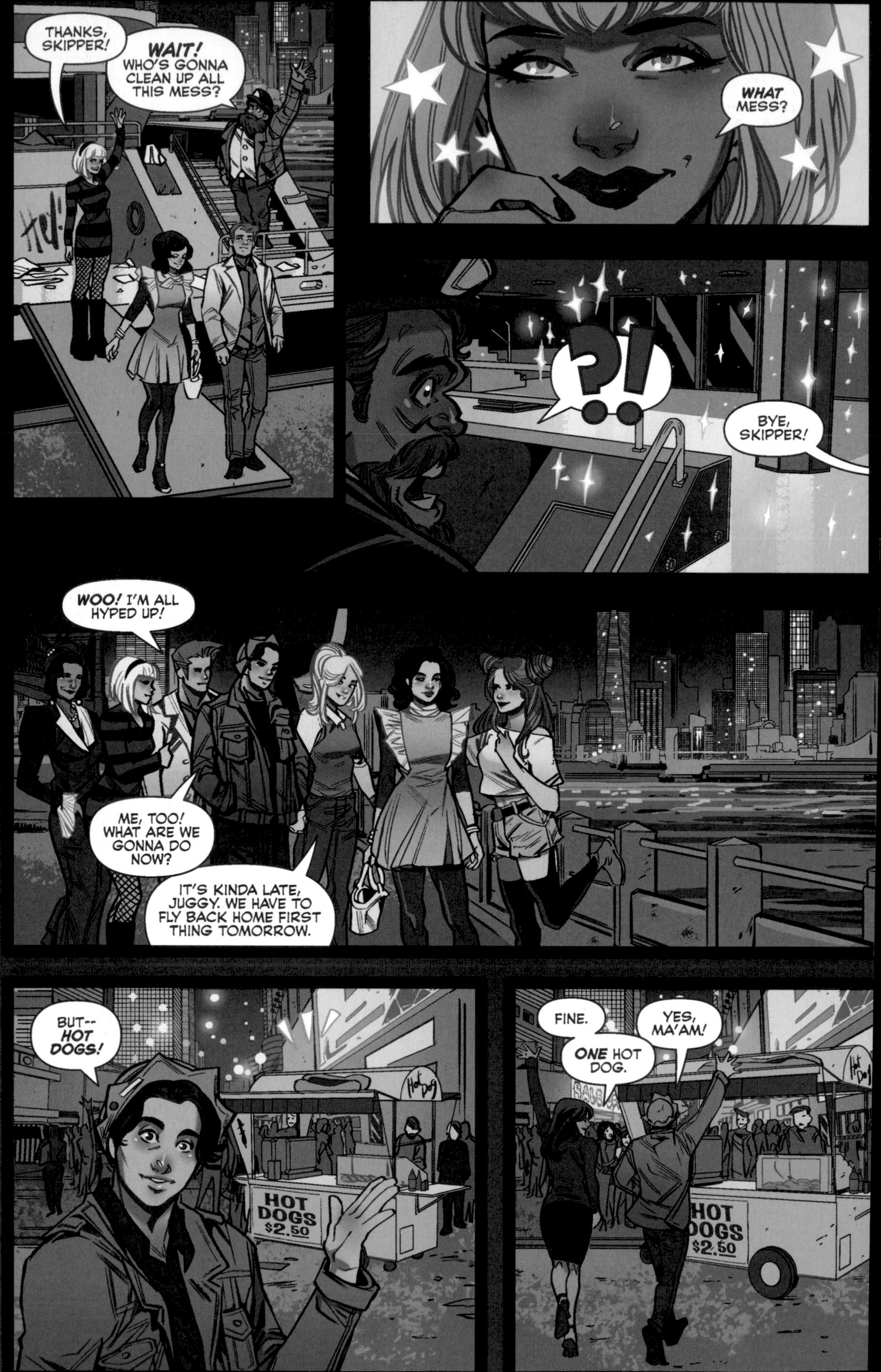
THANKS, SKIPPER!
WAIT! WHO'S GONNA CLEAN UP ALL THIS MESS?
WHAT MESS?
?!
BYE, SKIPPER!
WOO! I'M ALL HYPED UP!
ME, TOO! WHAT ARE WE GONNA DO NOW?
IT'S KINDA LATE, JUGGY. WE HAVE TO FLY BACK HOME FIRST THING TOMORROW.
BUT-- HOT DOGS!
HOT DOGS $2.50
FINE.
ONE HOT DOG.
YES, MA'AM!
HOT DOGS $2.50

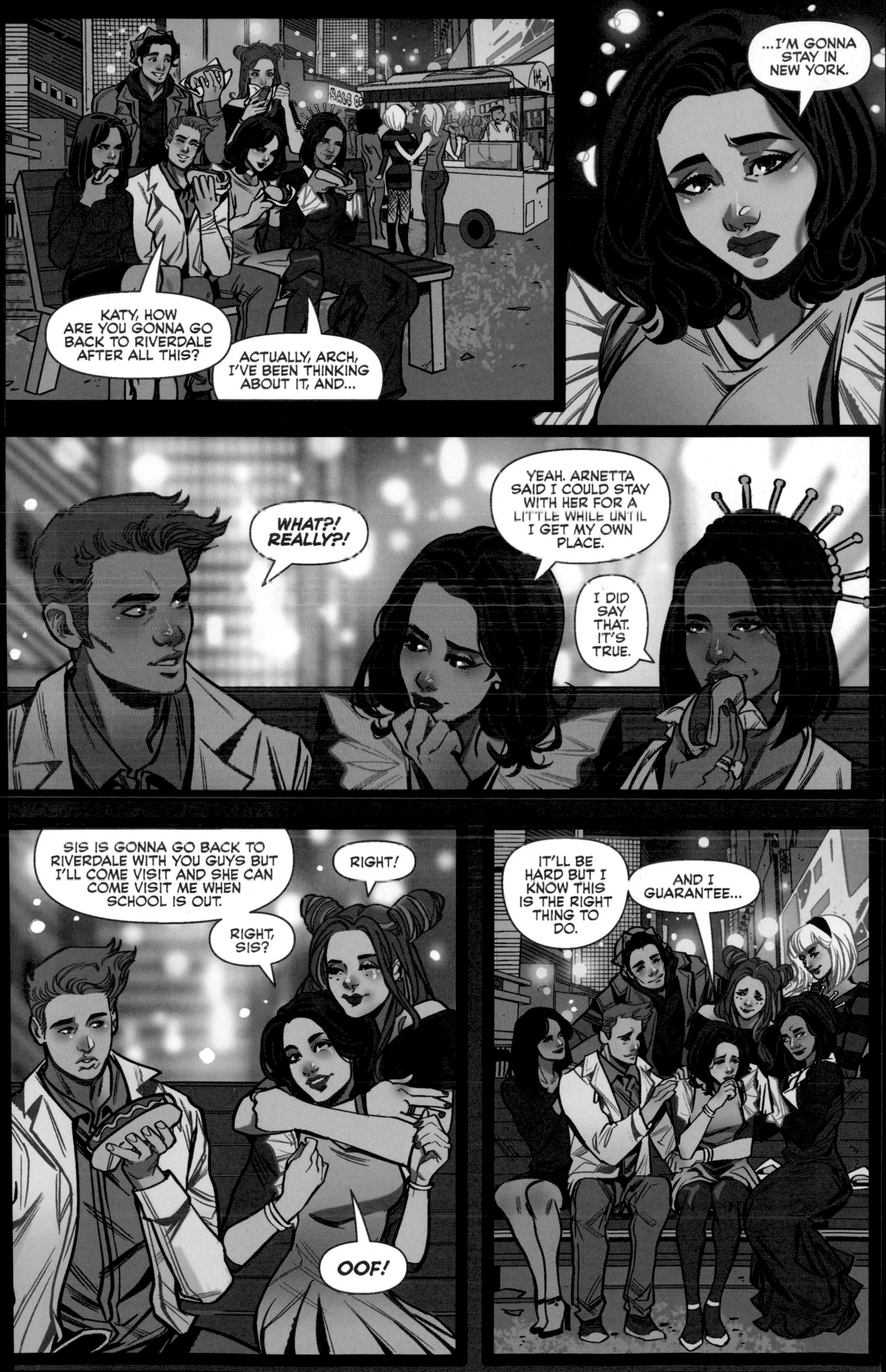
KATY, HOW ARE YOU GONNA GO BACK TO RIVERDALE AFTER ALL THIS?
ACTUALLY, ARCH, I'VE BEEN THINKING ABOUT IT, AND...
...I'M GONNA STAY IN NEW YORK.
WHAT?! REALLY?!
YEAH. ARNETTA SAID I COULD STAY WITH HER FOR A LITTLE WHILE UNTIL I GET MY OWN PLACE.
I DID SAY THAT. IT'S TRUE.
SIS IS GONNA GO BACK TO RIVERDALE WITH YOU GUYS BUT I'LL COME VISIT AND SHE CAN COME VISIT ME WHEN SCHOOL IS OUT.
RIGHT!
RIGHT, SIS?
OOF!
IT'LL BE HARD BUT I KNOW THIS IS THE RIGHT THING TO DO.
AND I GUARANTEE...

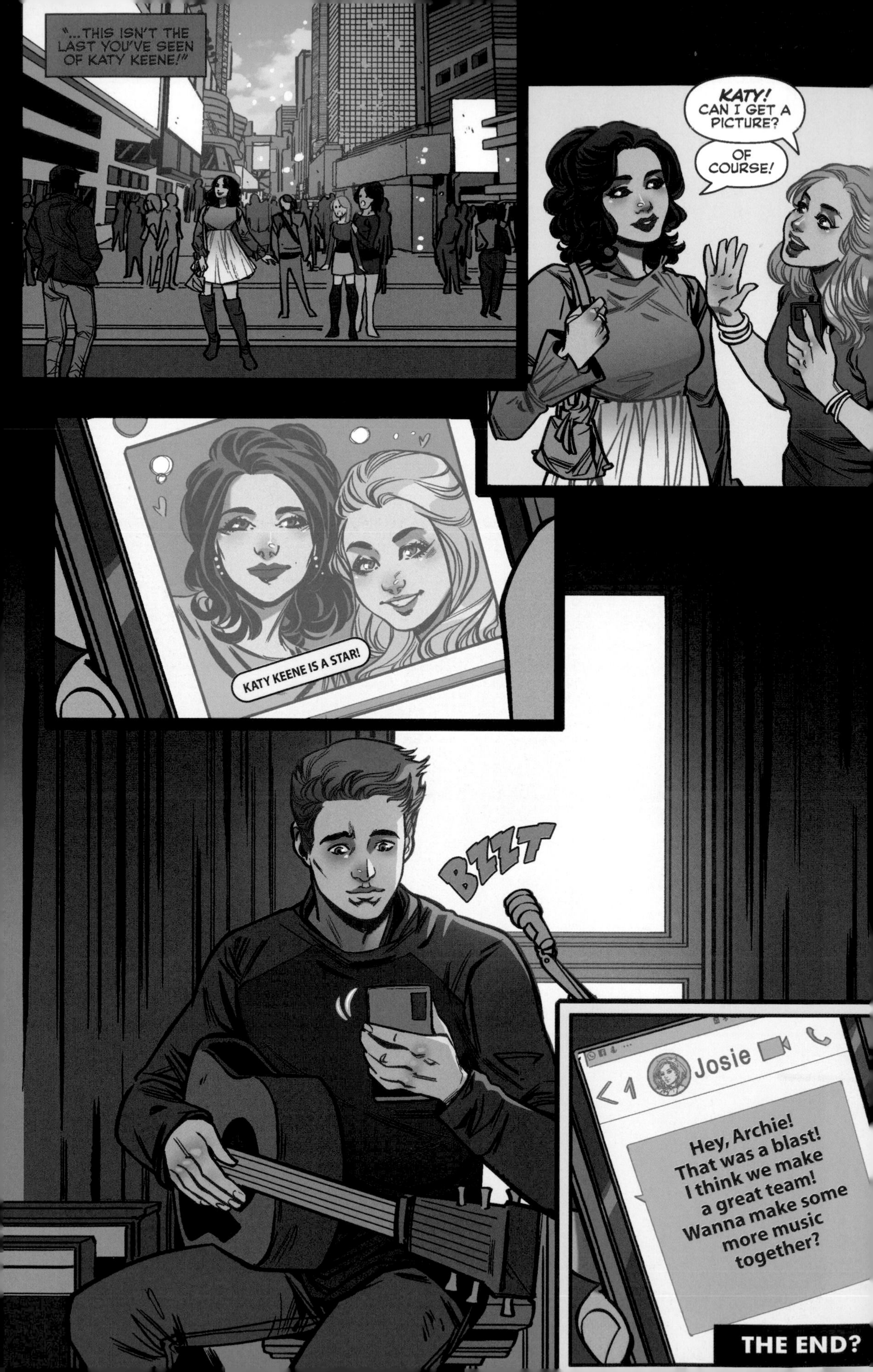

"...THIS ISN'T THE LAST YOU'VE SEEN OF KATY KEENE!"
KATY! CAN I GET A PICTURE?
OF COURSE!
KATY KEENE IS A STAR!
BZZT
Josie
Hey, Archie! That was a blast! I think we make a great team! Wanna make some more music together?
THE END?

Archie® and Katy Keene™

VARIANT COVER GALLERY

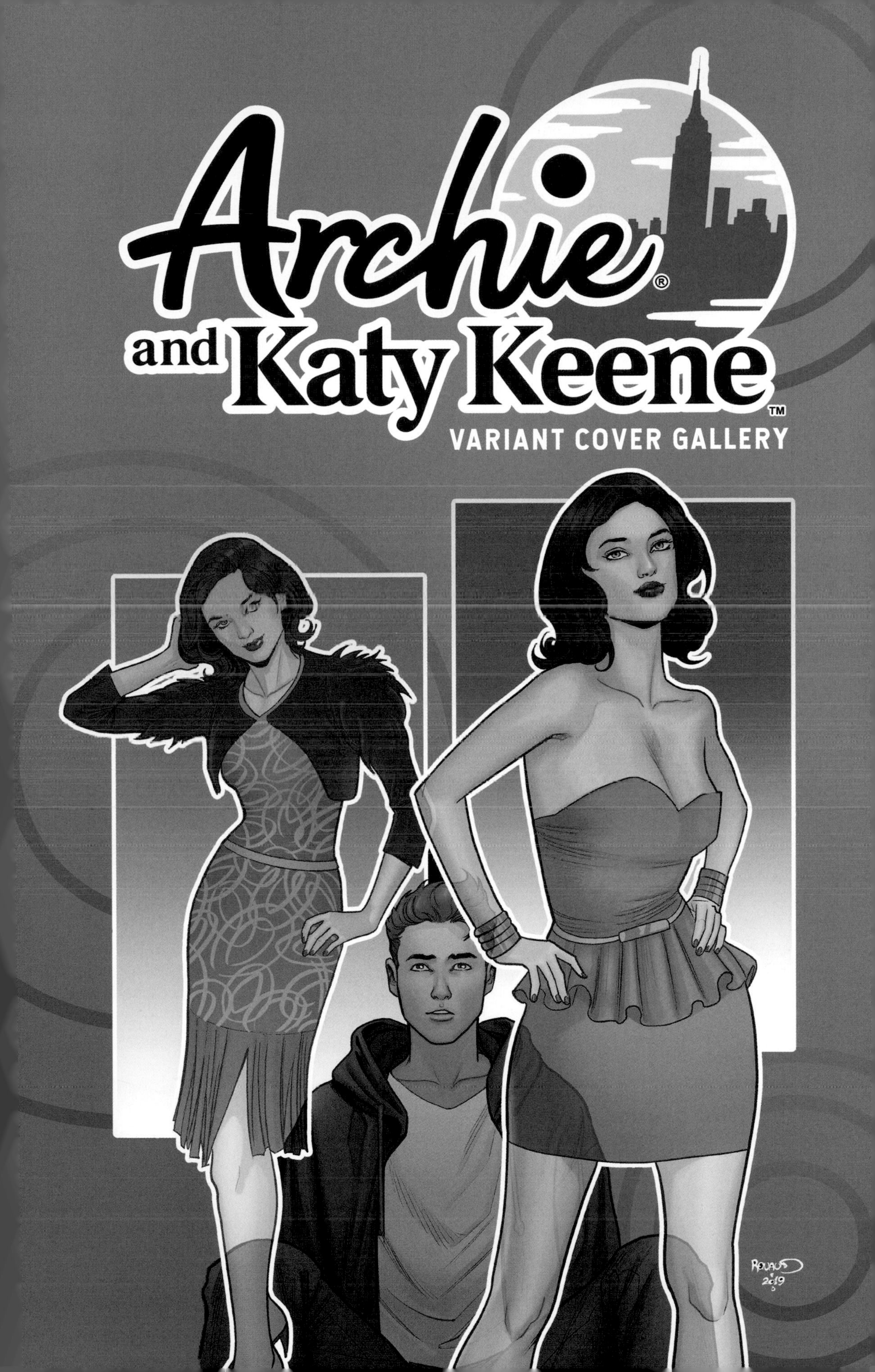

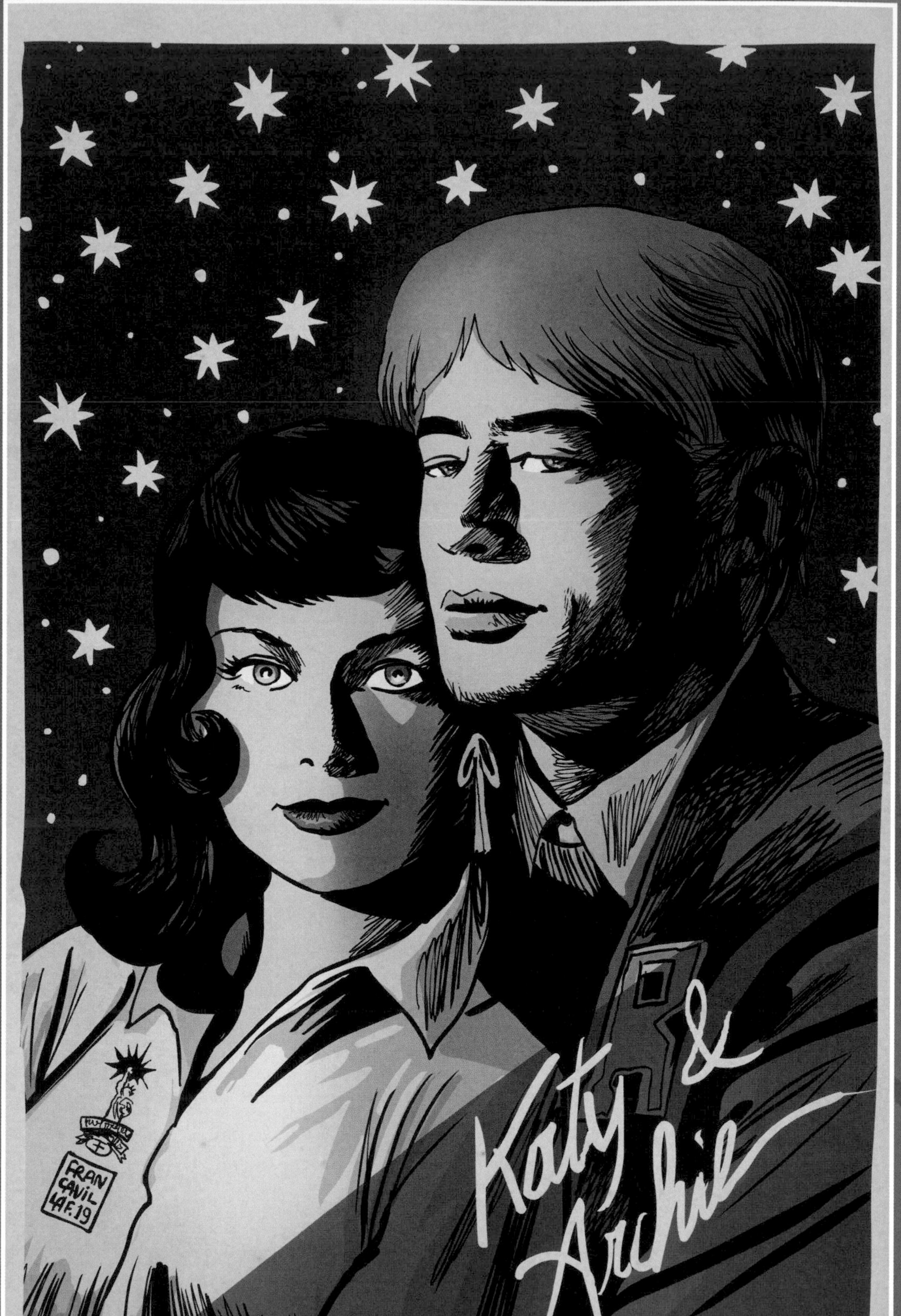
Katy & Archie
FRANCAVILLA F.19

COVER ART: **FRANCESCO FRANCAVILLA**

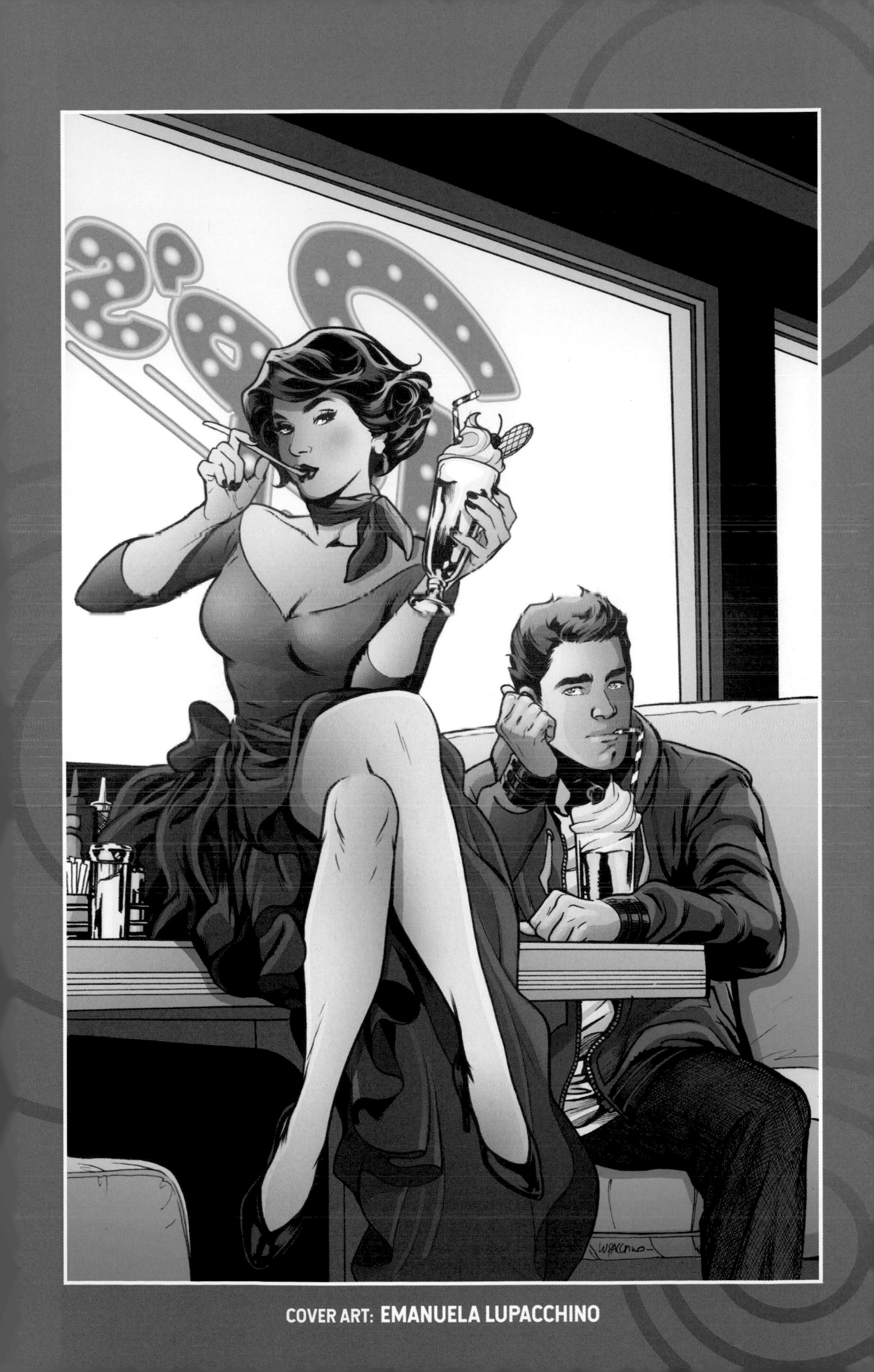

COVER ART: EMANUELA LUPACCHINO

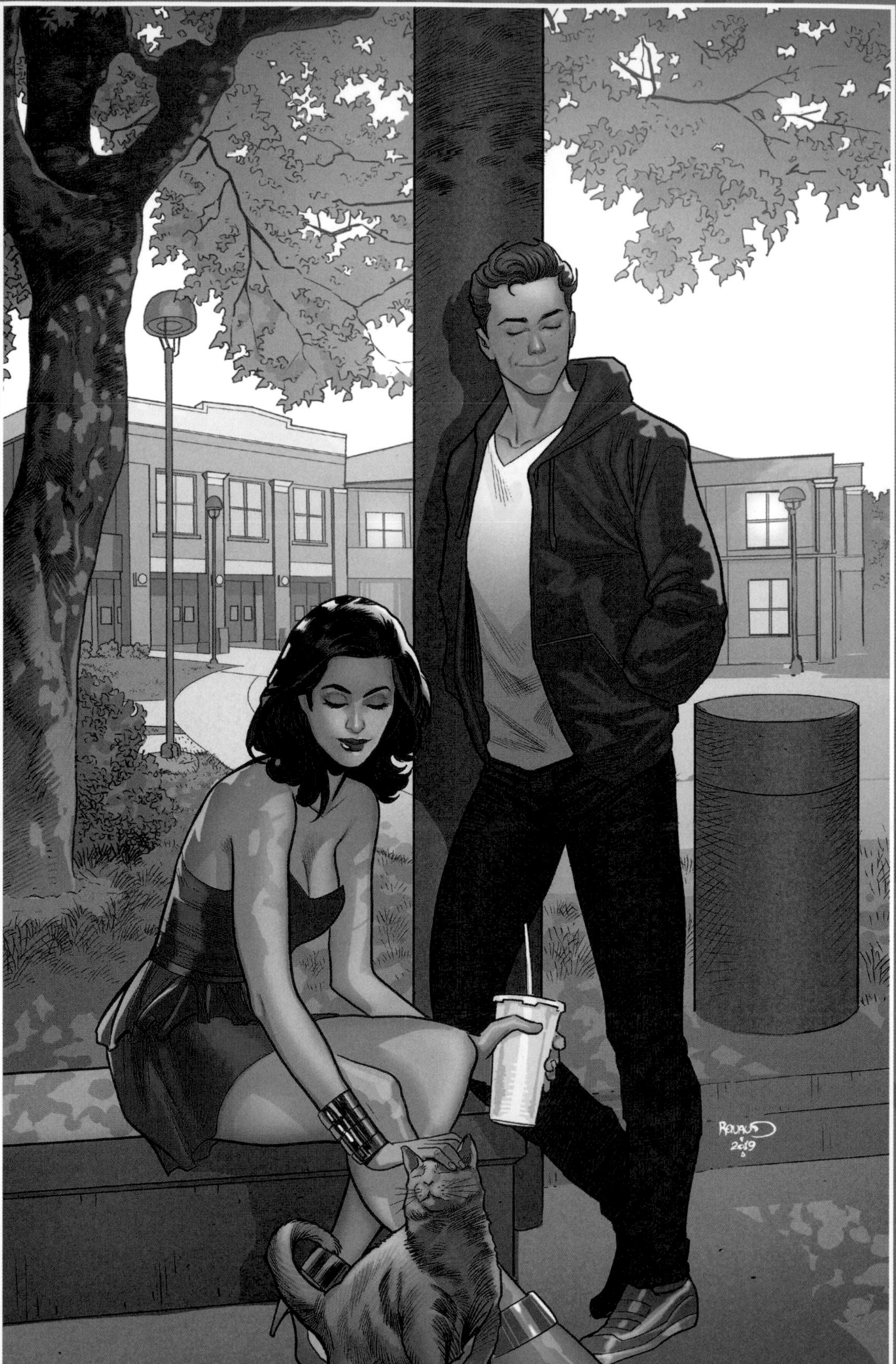

COVER ART: **PAUL RENAUD**

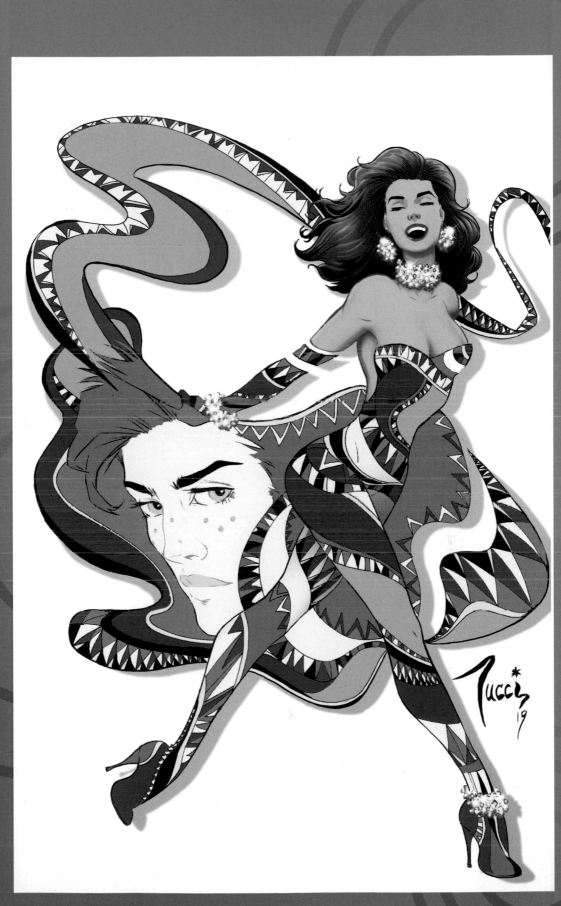

COVER ART: **BILLY TUCCI** WITH **WES HARTMAN**

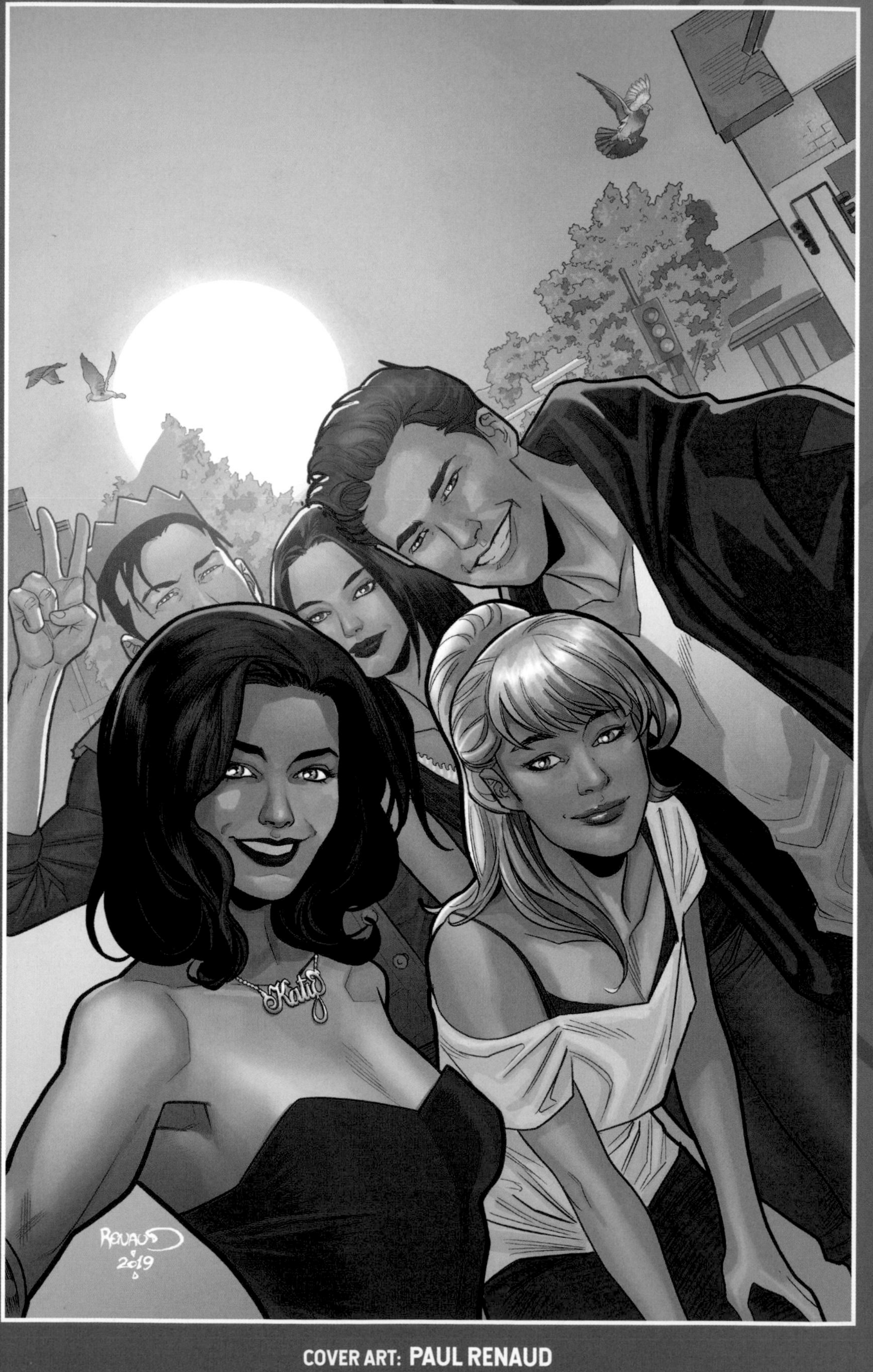
Katy
RENAUD
2019

COVER ART: **PAUL RENAUD**

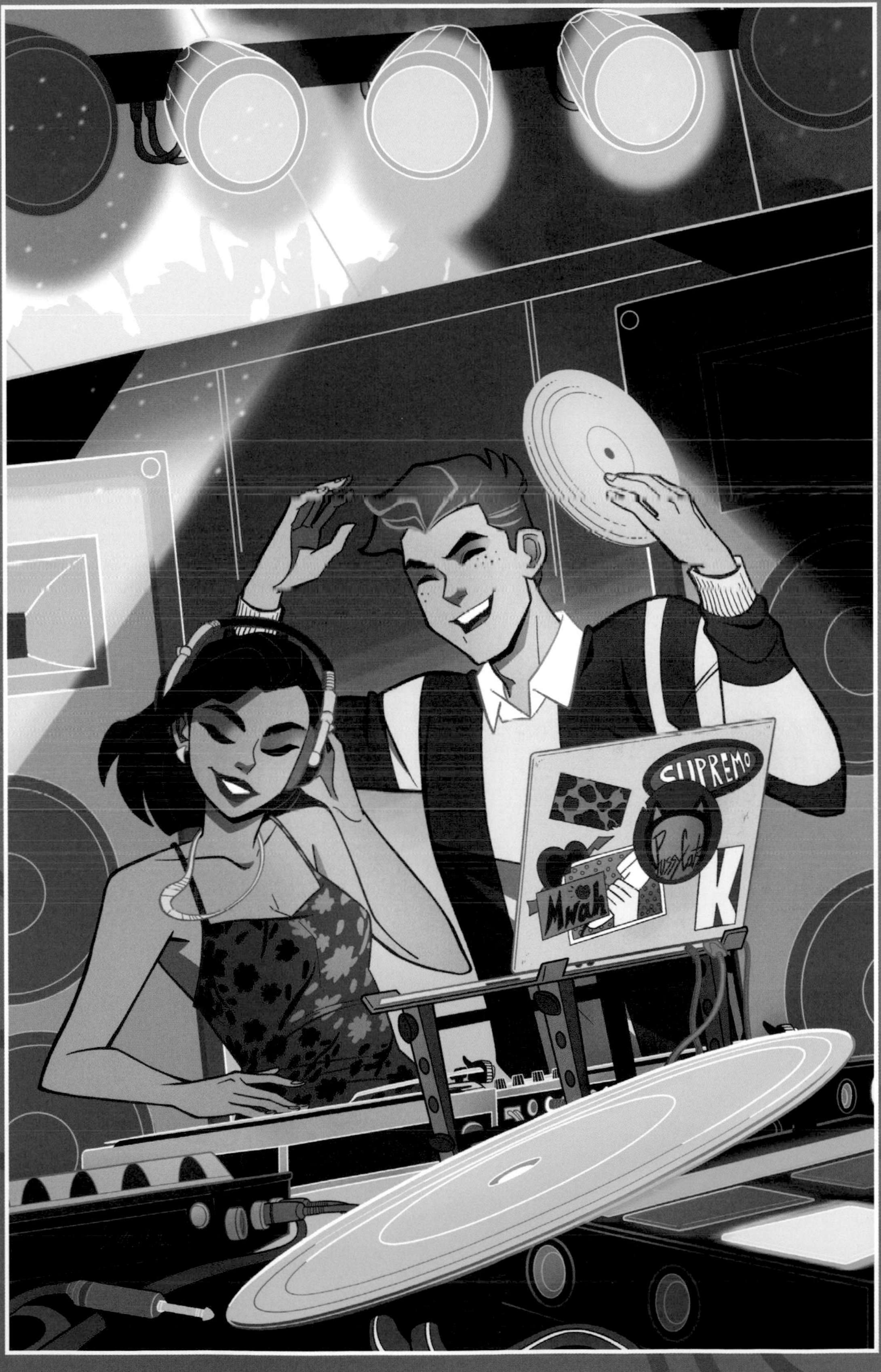
SUPREMO
PussyCats
Mwah
K

COVER ART: **BRITTNEY WILLIAMS**

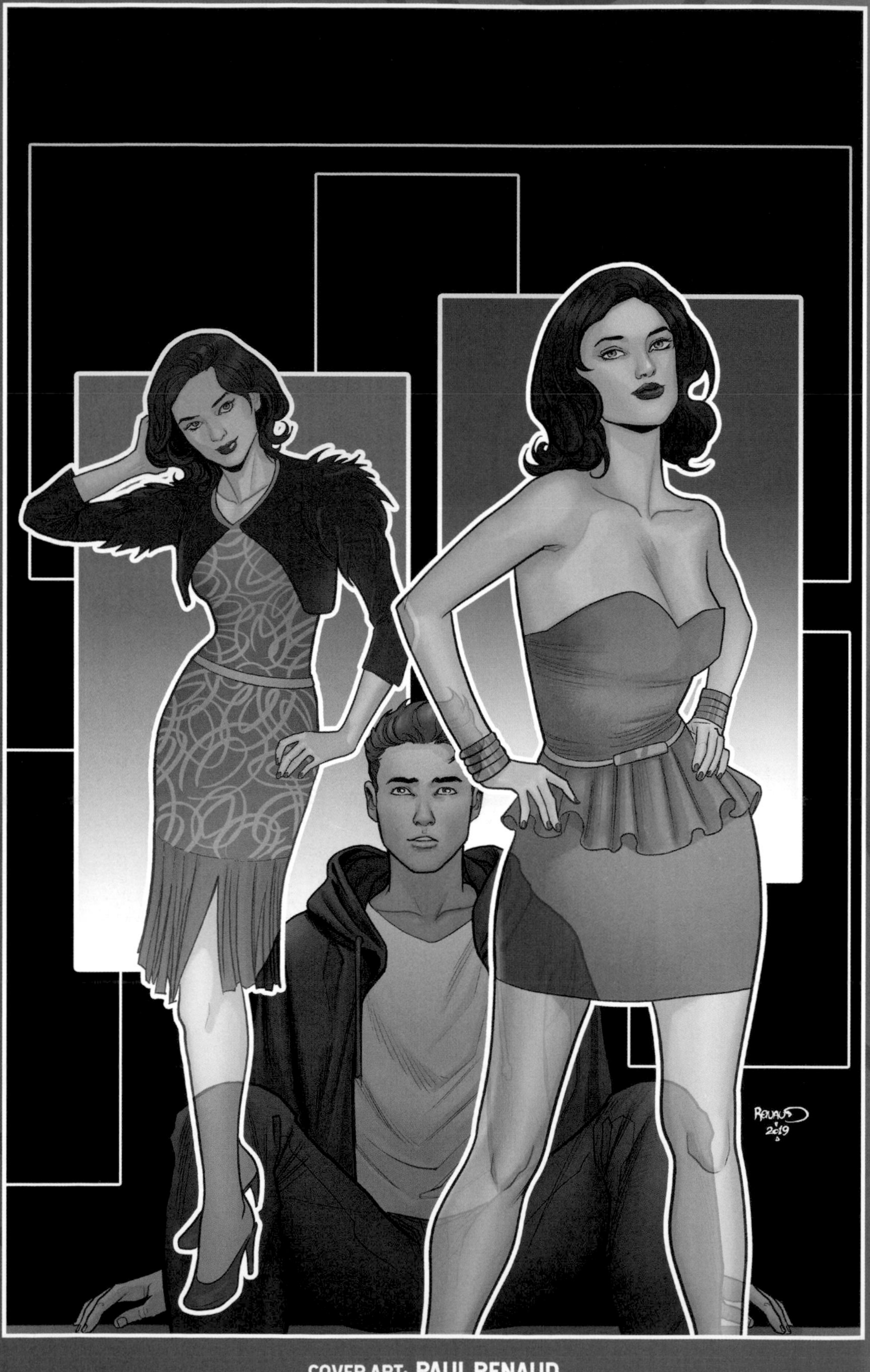
RENAUD
2019

COVER ART: **PAUL RENAUD**

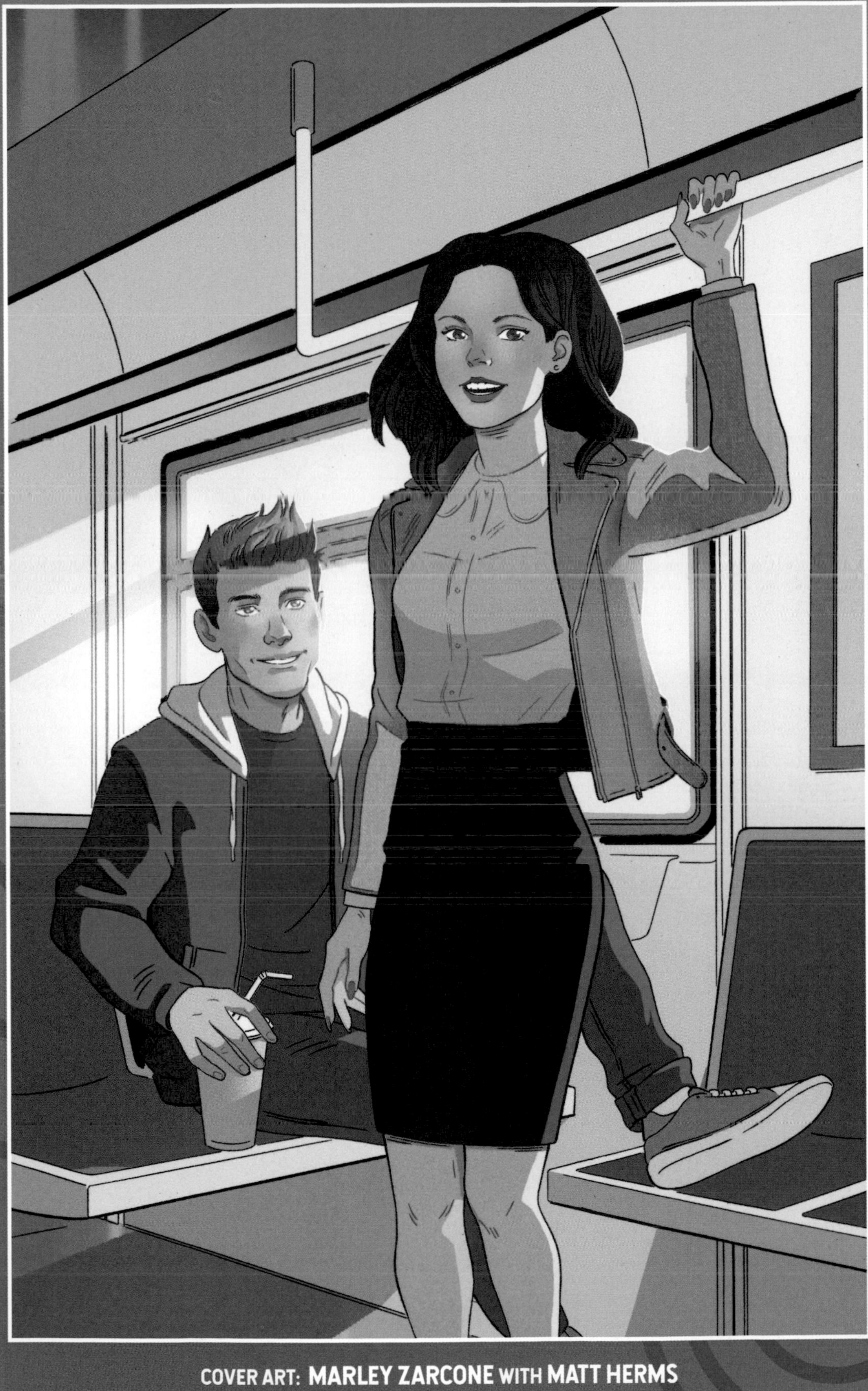

COVER ART: **MARLEY ZARCONE** WITH **MATT HERMS**

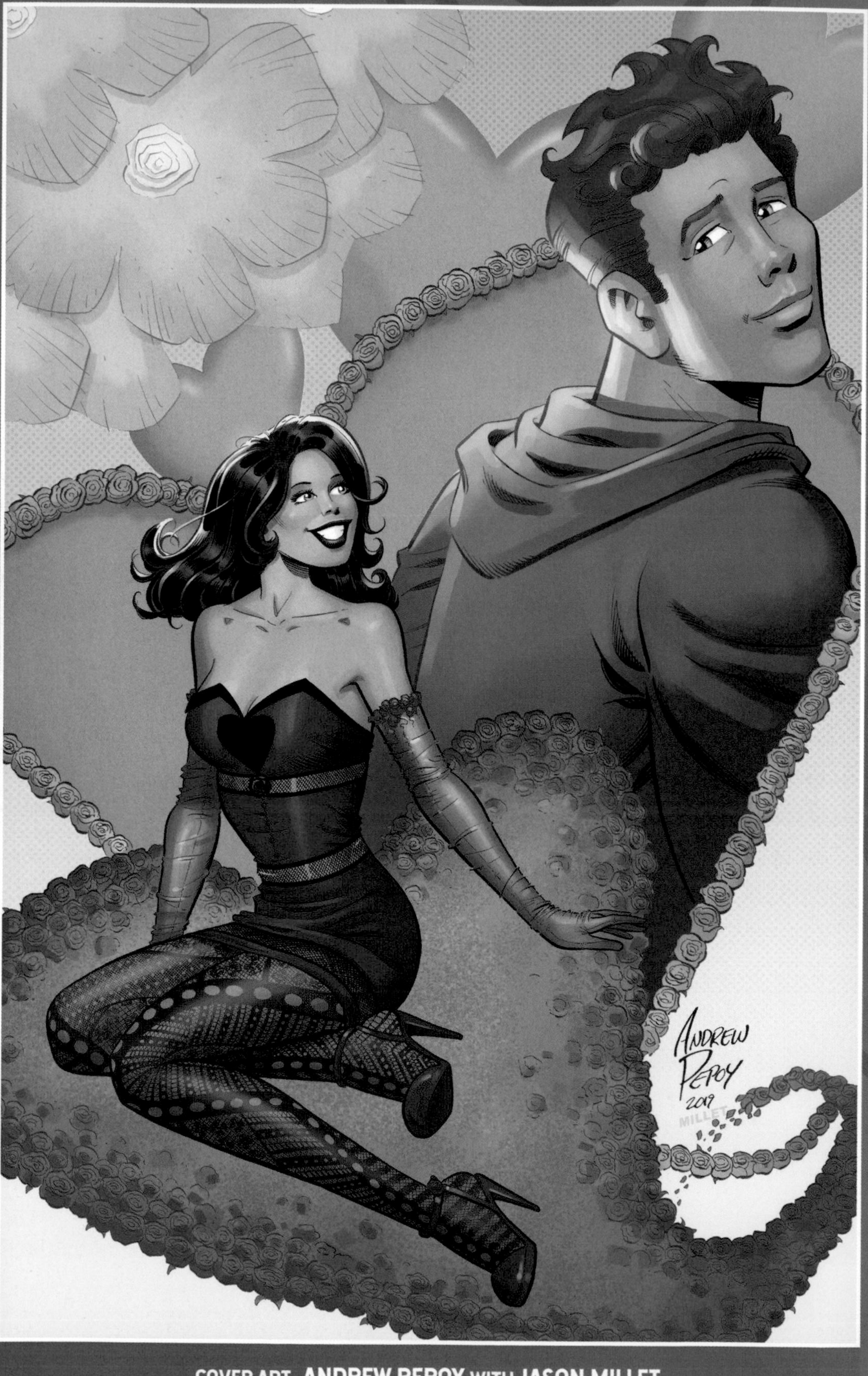
ANDREW PEPOY 2019
MILLET

COVER ART: **ANDREW PEPOY** WITH **JASON MILLET**

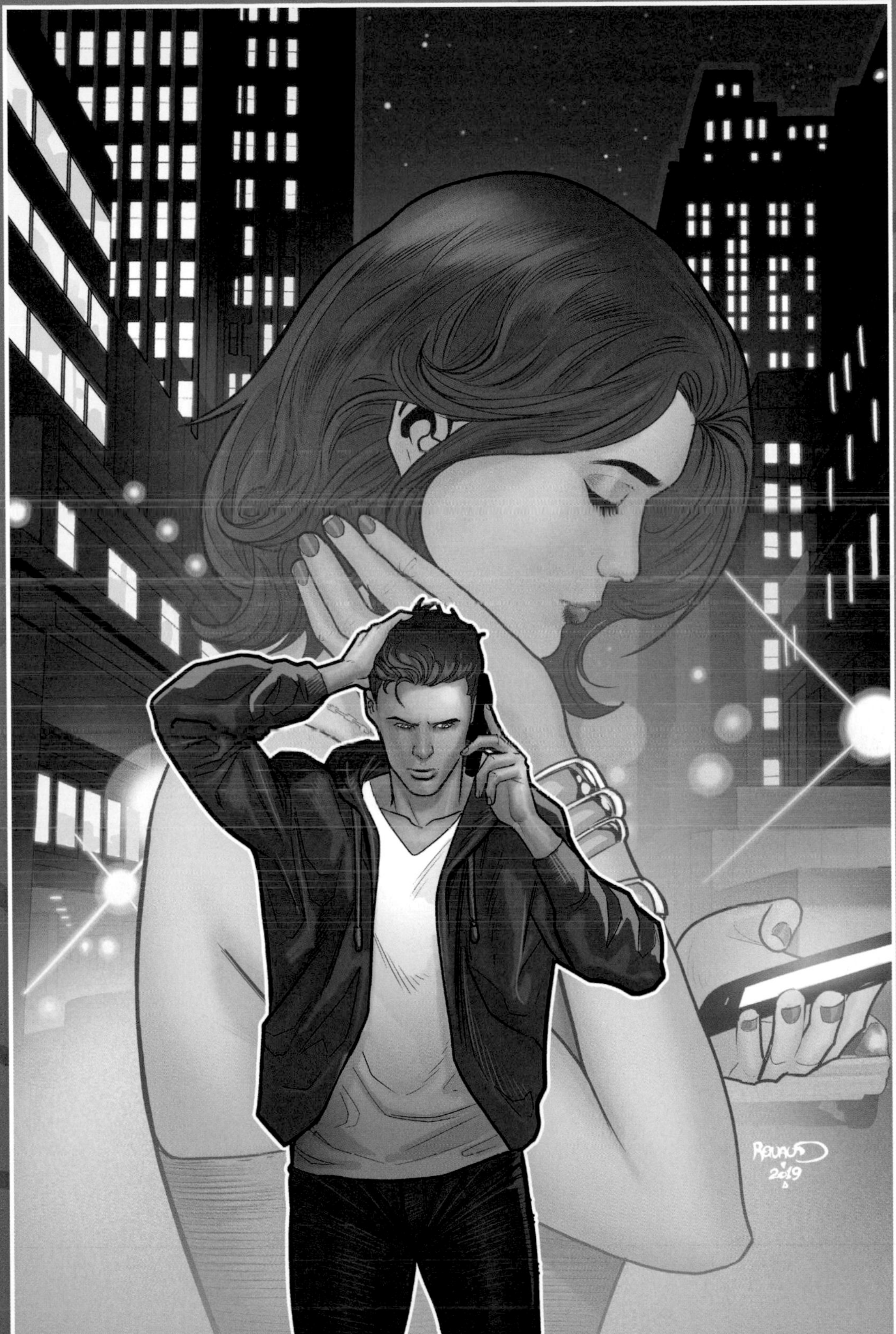
RENAUD
2019

COVER ART: PAUL RENAUD

RETRO FASHION PAGES

Katy Keene was one of the first interactive comic book series, inviting readers to send in fashion suggestions of their own that were turned into pin-ups and paper dolls that they could cut out and keep!

Here's a look at some retro fashion design pages from the 1950s!

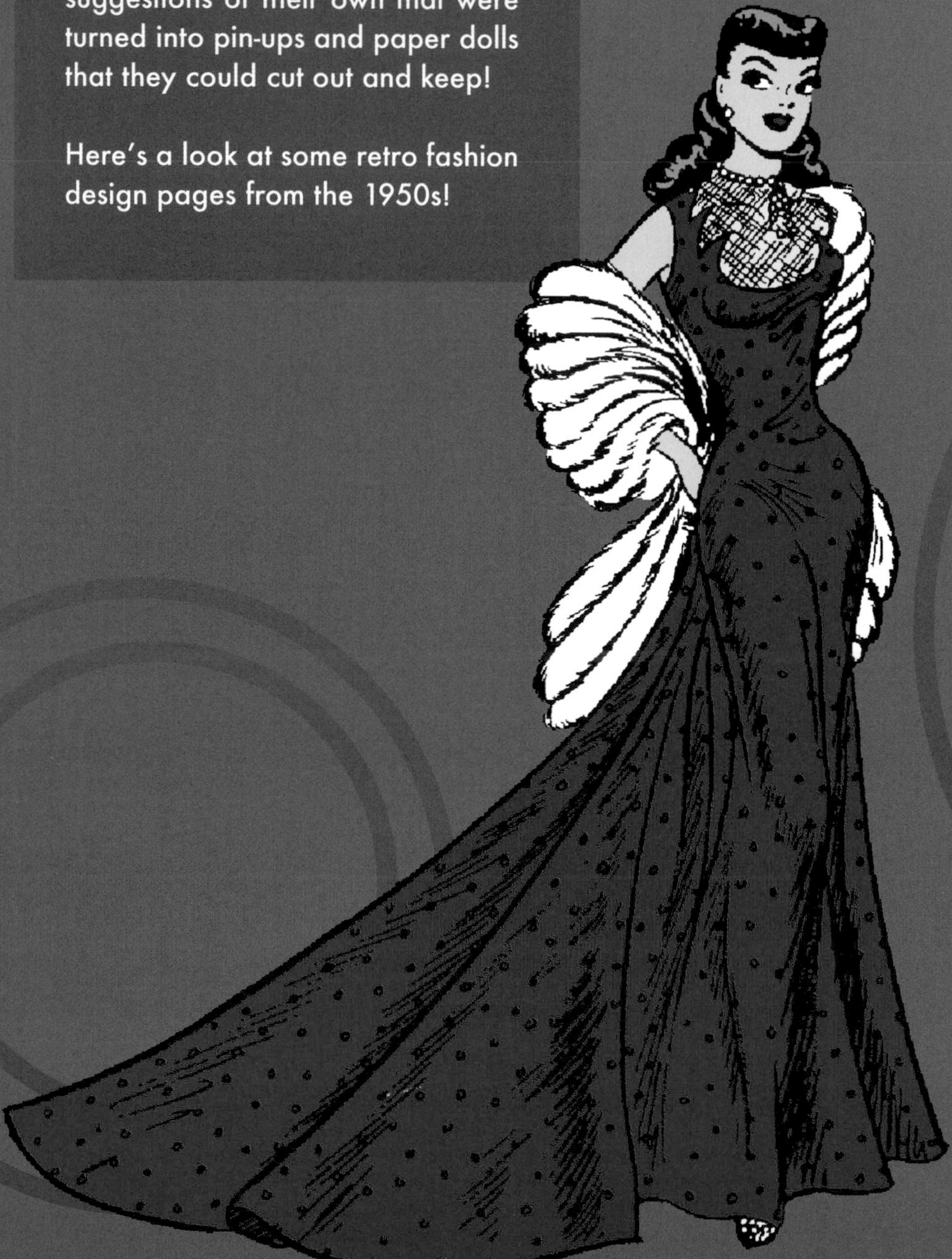

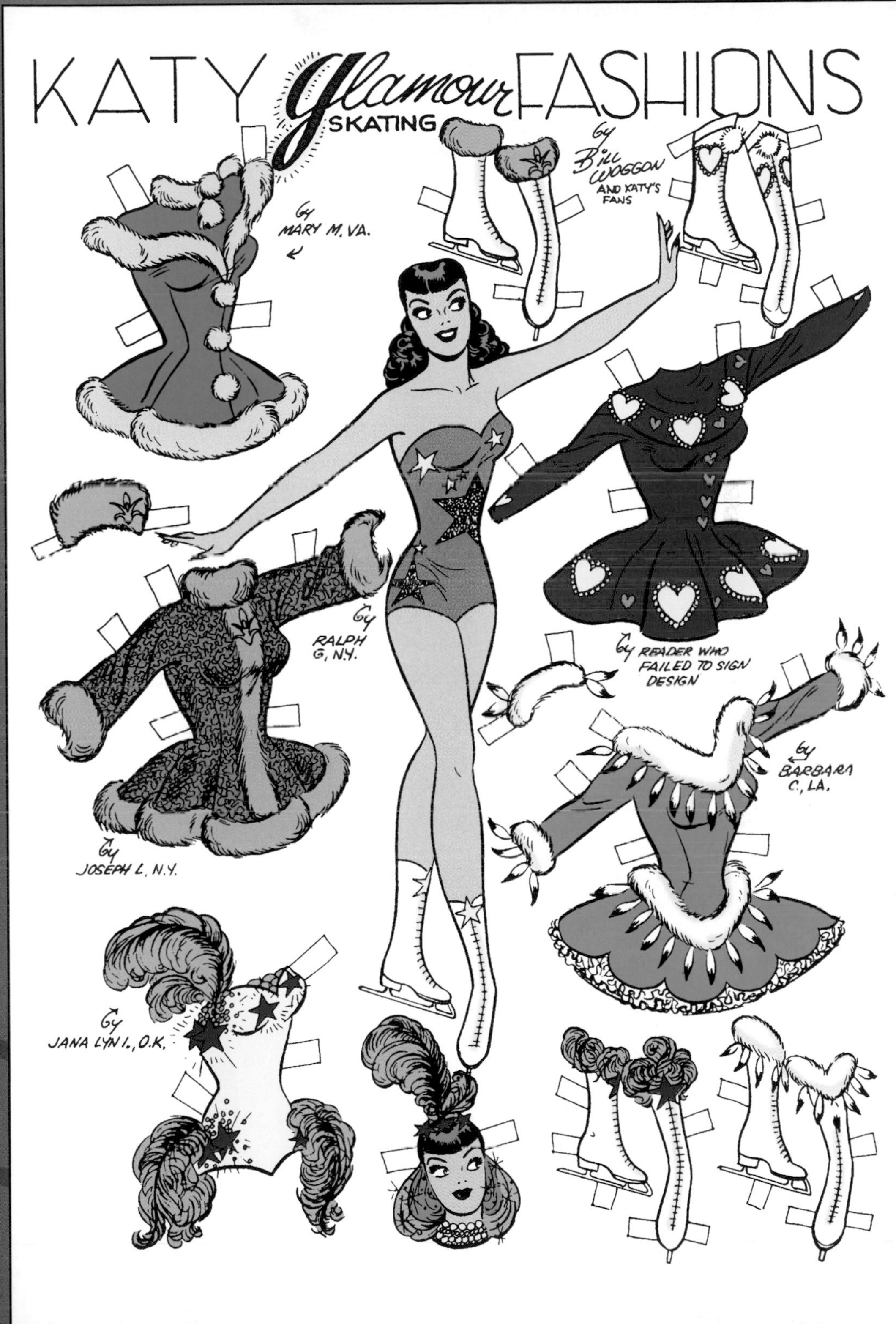
KATY Glamour FASHIONS
SKATING
by BILL WOGGON AND KATY'S FANS
by MARY M. VA.
by RALPH G. N.Y.
by READER WHO FAILED TO SIGN DESIGN
by BARBARA C. LA.
by JOSEPH L. N.Y.
by JANA LYN I., O.K.

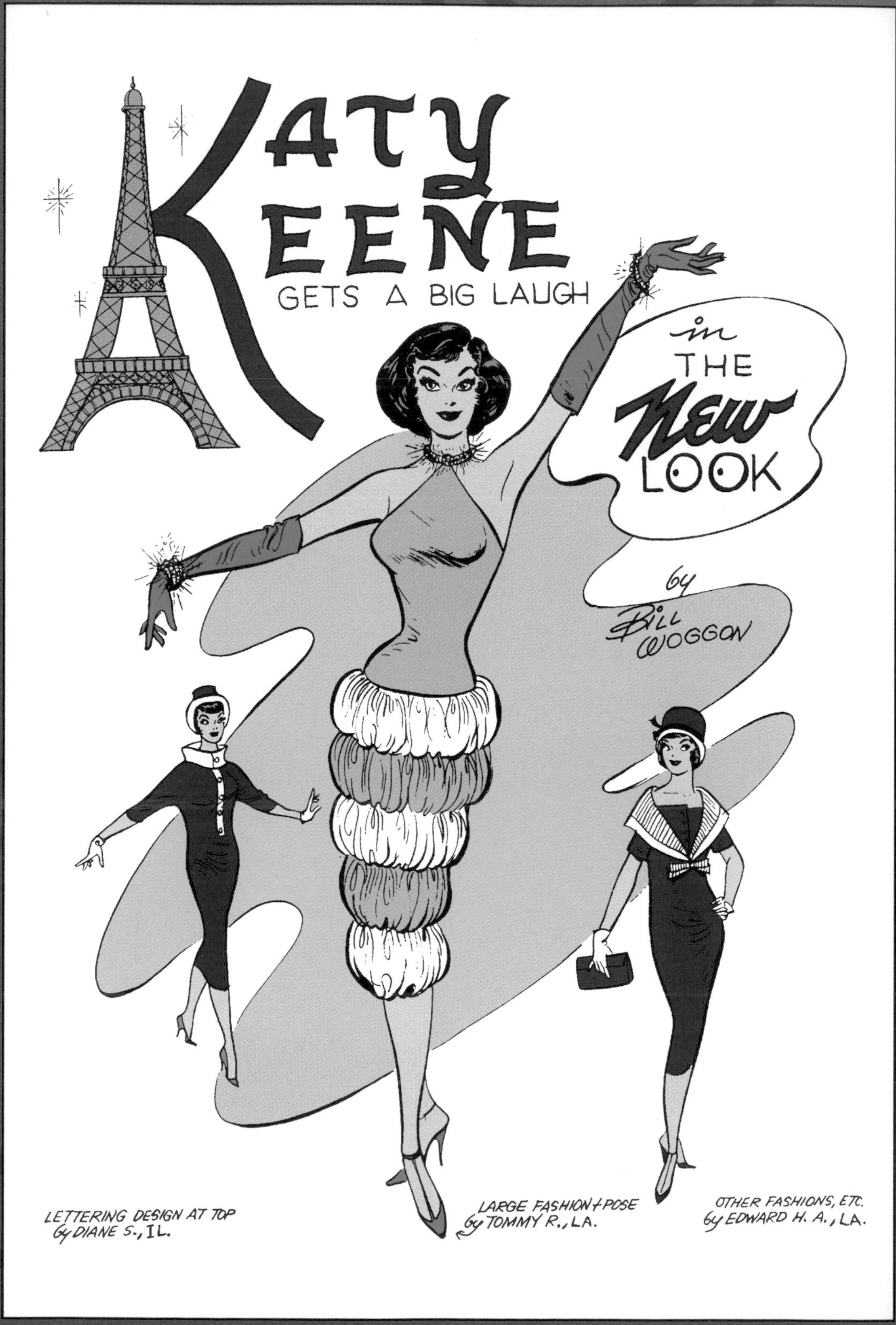
KATY KEENE
GETS A BIG LAUGH
in THE NEW LOOK
by Bill Woggon
LETTERING DESIGN AT TOP by DIANE S., IL.
LARGE FASHION + POSE by TOMMY R., LA.
OTHER FASHIONS, ETC. by EDWARD H. A., LA.

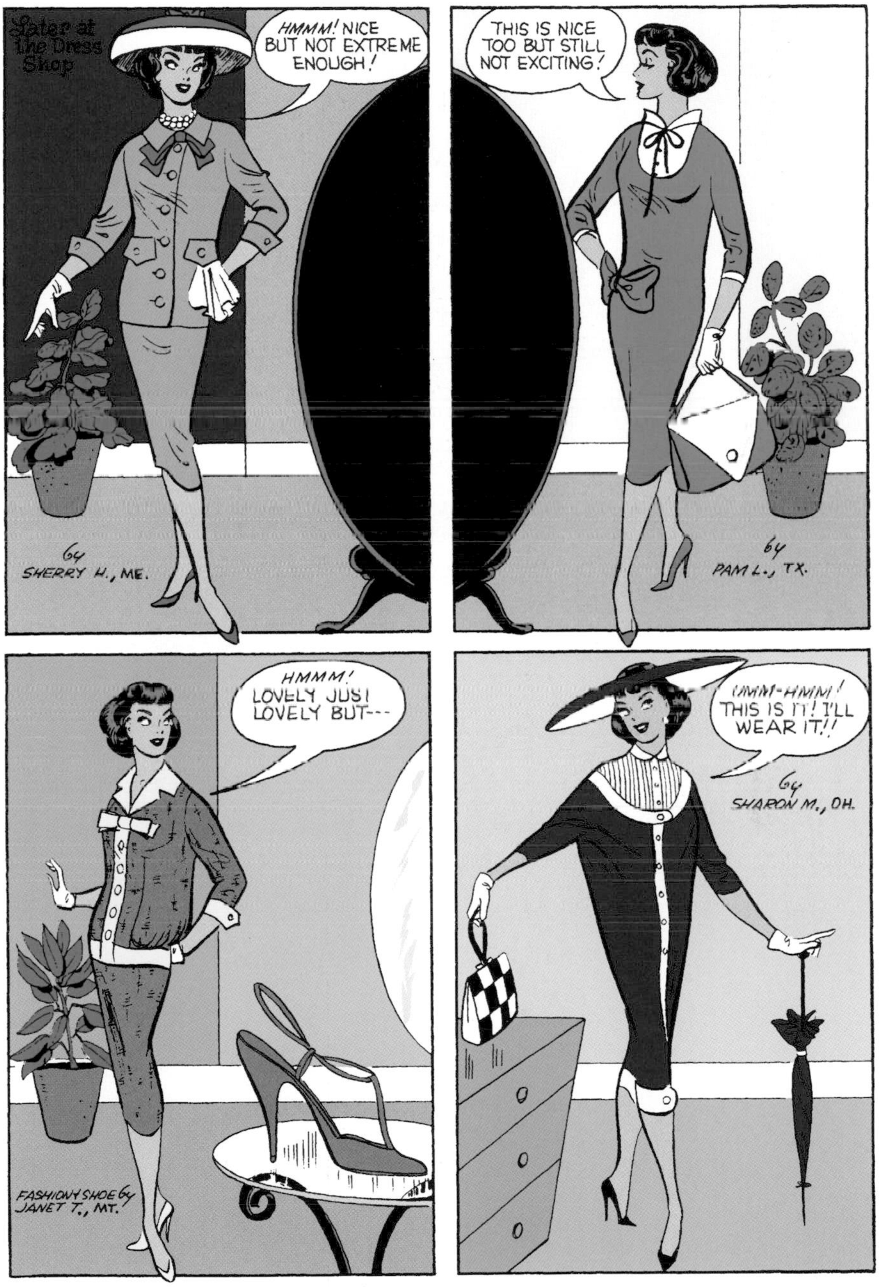
Later at the Dress Shop
HMMM! NICE BUT NOT EXTREME ENOUGH!
by SHERRY H., ME.
THIS IS NICE TOO BUT STILL NOT EXCITING!
by PAM L., TX.
HMMM! LOVELY JUST LOVELY BUT---
FASHION & SHOE by JANET T., MT.
UMM-HMM! THIS IS IT! I'LL WEAR IT!!
by SHARON M., OH.

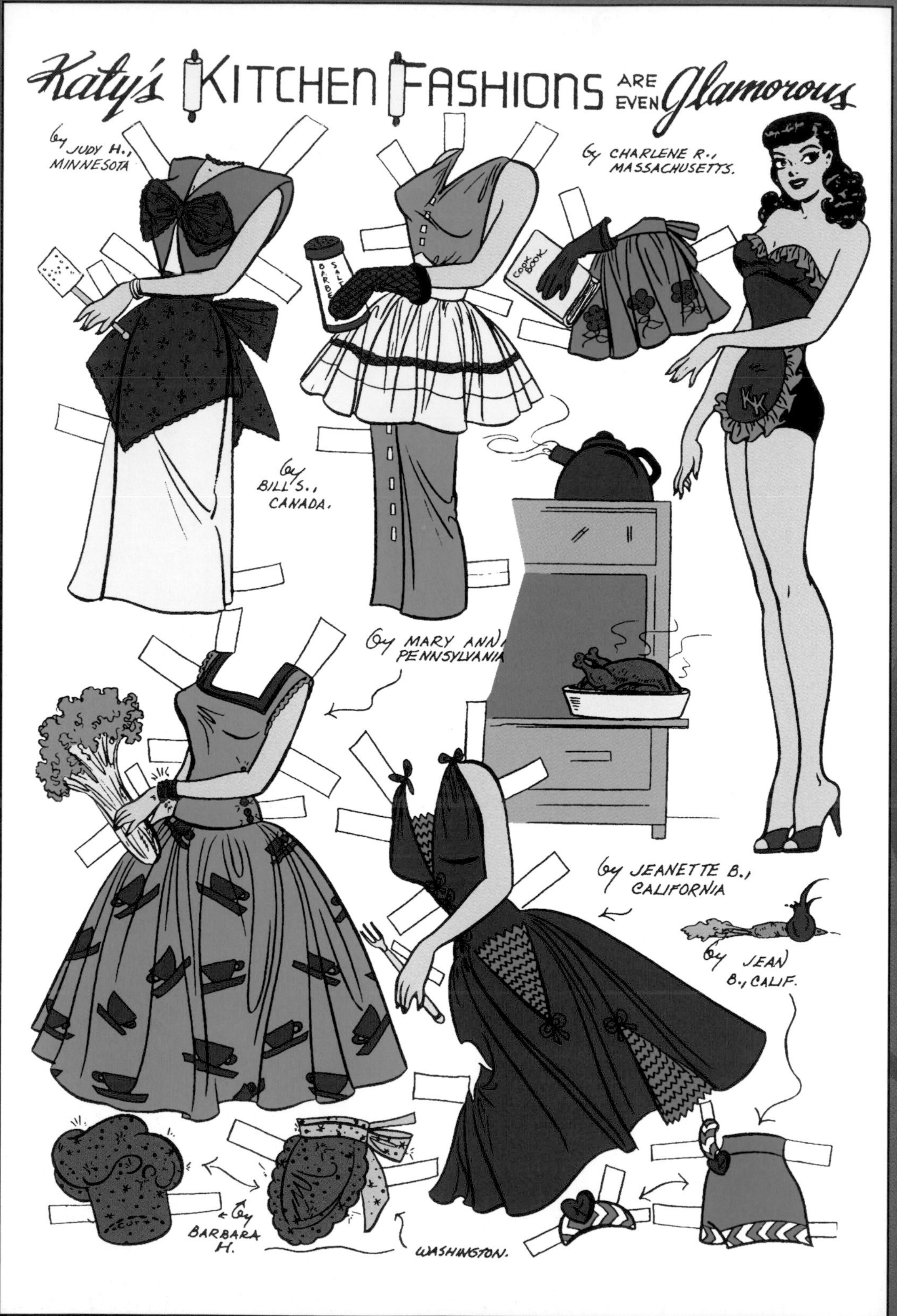
Katy's KITCHEN FASHIONS ARE EVEN Glamorous
by JUDY H., MINNESOTA
by CHARLENE R., MASSACHUSETTS.
COOK BOOK
BARBE SALT
by BILL S., CANADA.
KK
by MARY ANN, PENNSYLVANIA
by JEANETTE B., CALIFORNIA
by JEAN B., CALIF.
by BARBARA H.
WASHINGTON.

BONUS COMIC RIVERDALE: THE TIES THAT BIND

Archie's second original graphic novel, written by Micol Ostow and illustrated by Thomas Pitilli, features the world of The CW's *Riverdale*! Four interconnected stories trap each of our main characters in a unique high-stakes conflict over the course of a few pressure-cooker hours! Will Archie and company even make it to sunrise? If they do, will they ever be the same again?

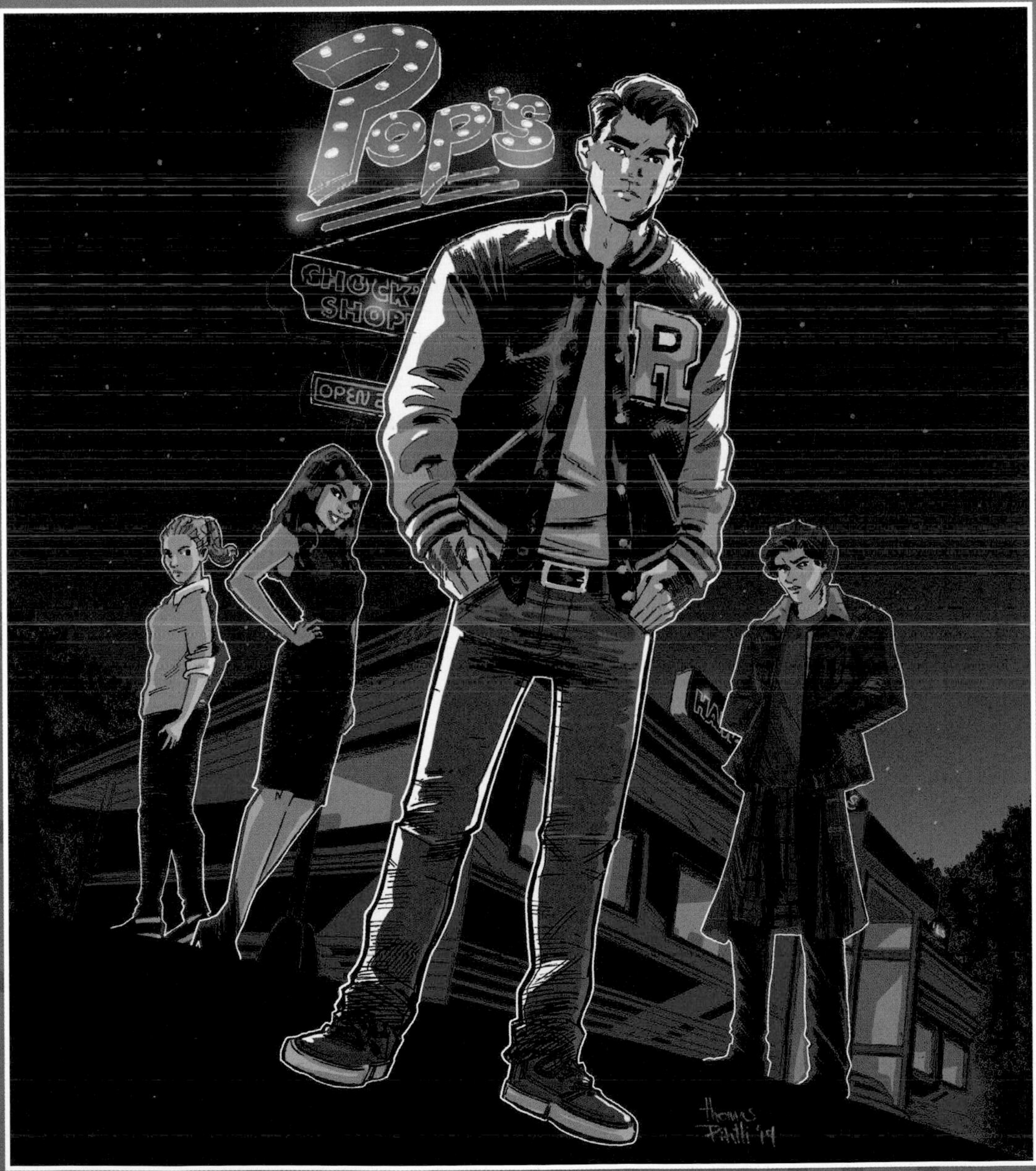

Pop's
OPEN
Thomas Pitilli '19

ART BY
MICOL OSTOW

ART BY
THOMAS PITILLI

LETTERING BY
JOHN WORKMAN

COLORS BY
ANDRE SZYMANOWICZ

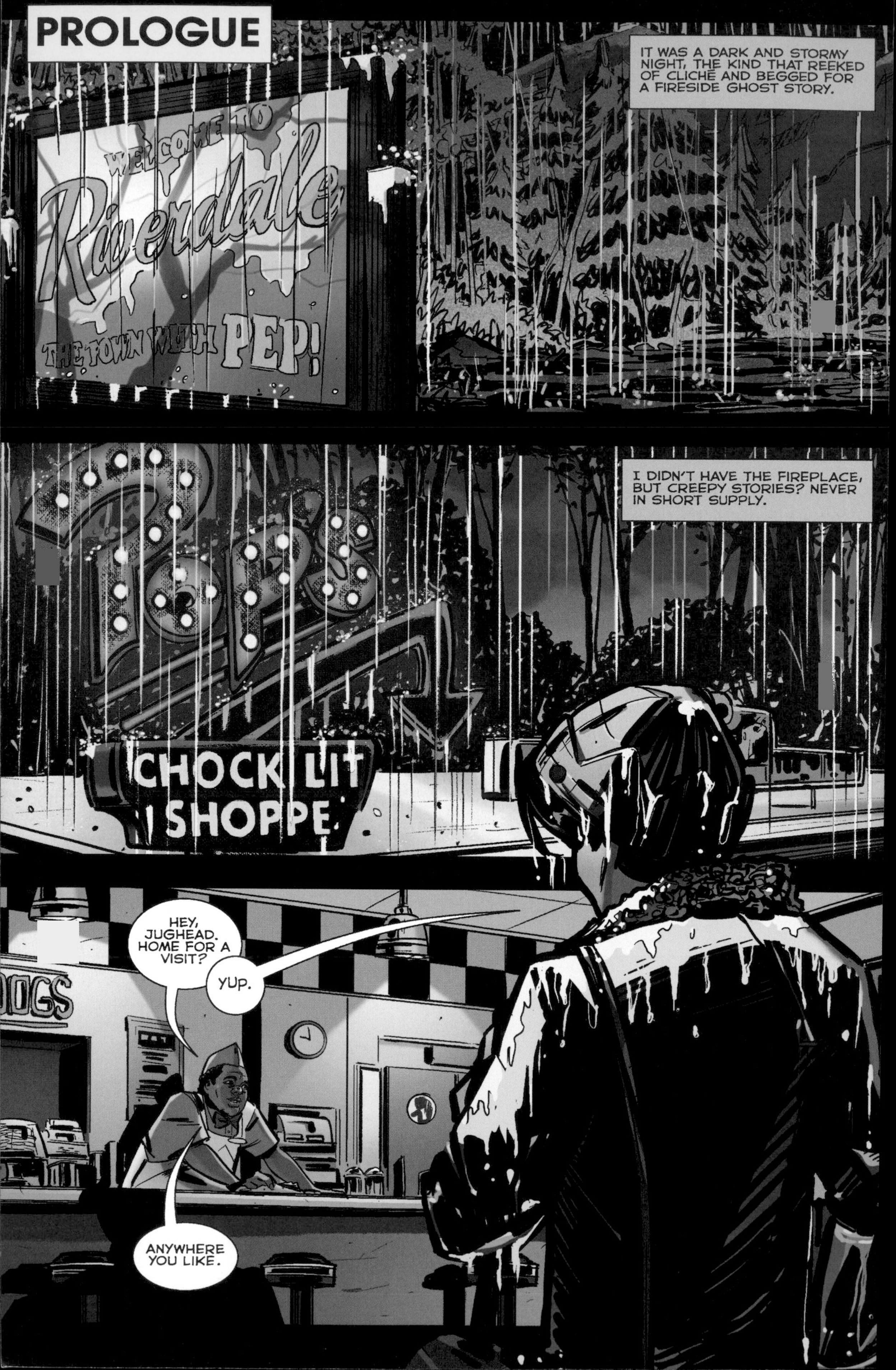
PROLOGUE
WELCOME TO
Riverdale
THE TOWN WITH PEP!
IT WAS A DARK AND STORMY NIGHT, THE KIND THAT REEKED OF CLICHÉ AND BEGGED FOR A FIRESIDE GHOST STORY.
I DIDN'T HAVE THE FIREPLACE, BUT CREEPY STORIES? NEVER IN SHORT SUPPLY.
CHOCK LIT SHOPPE
HEY, JUGHEAD. HOME FOR A VISIT?
YUP.
ANYWHERE YOU LIKE.

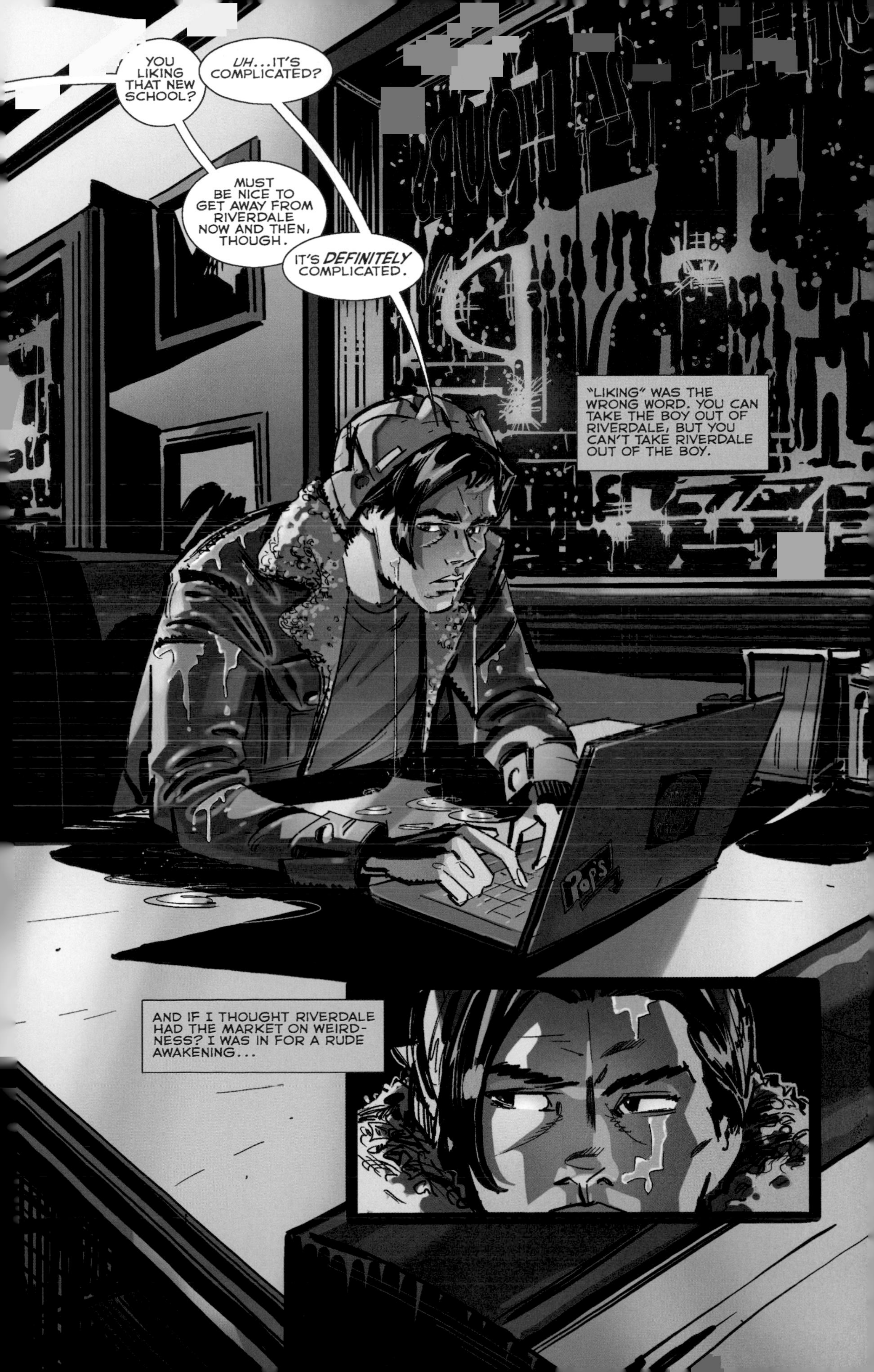
YOU LIKING THAT NEW SCHOOL?
UH...IT'S COMPLICATED?
MUST BE NICE TO GET AWAY FROM RIVERDALE NOW AND THEN, THOUGH.
IT'S DEFINITELY COMPLICATED.
"LIKING" WAS THE WRONG WORD. YOU CAN TAKE THE BOY OUT OF RIVERDALE, BUT YOU CAN'T TAKE RIVERDALE OUT OF THE BOY.
POP'S
AND IF I THOUGHT RIVERDALE HAD THE MARKET ON WEIRD-NESS? I WAS IN FOR A RUDE AWAKENING...

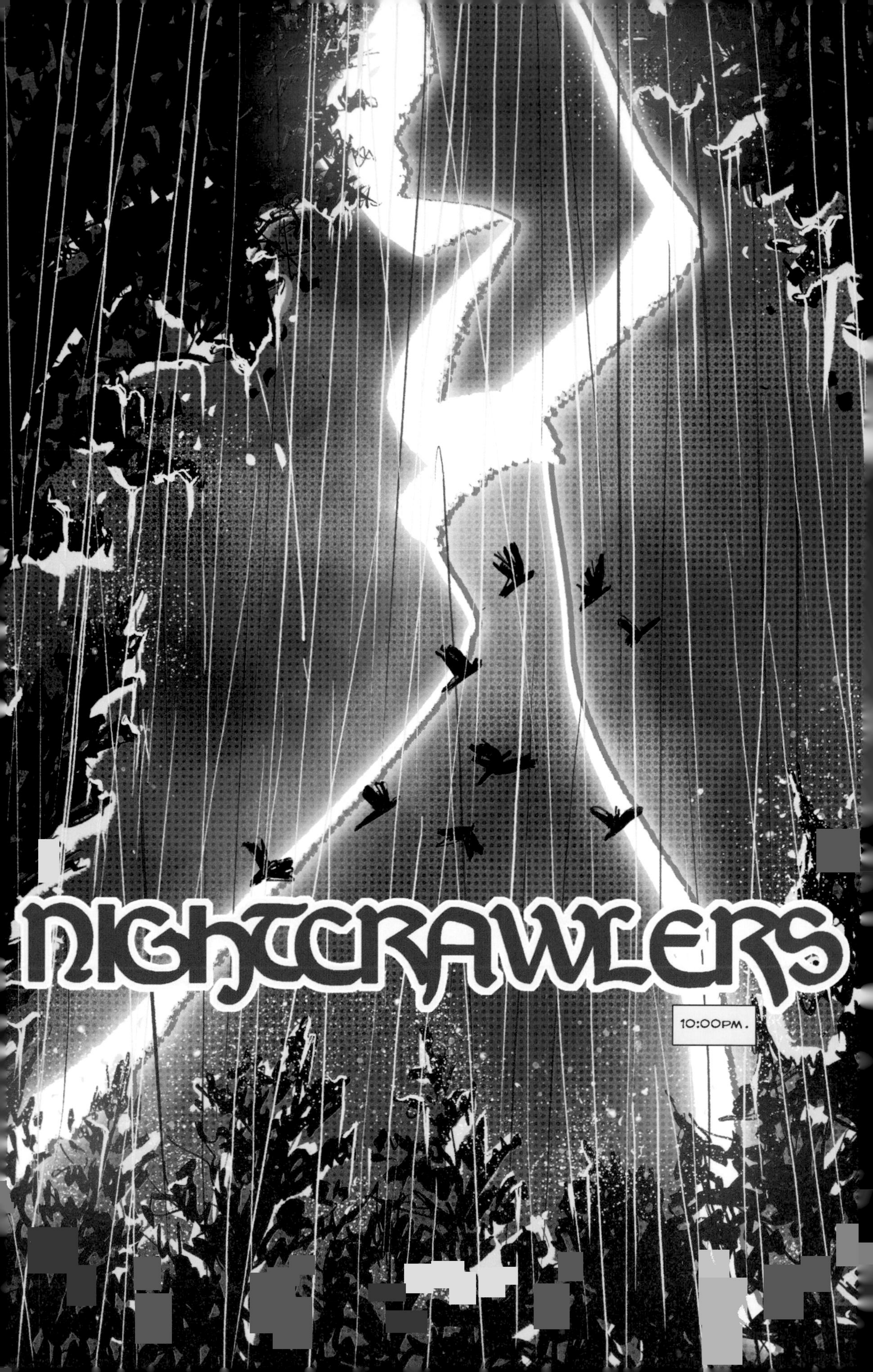
NIGHTCRAWLERS
10:00PM.

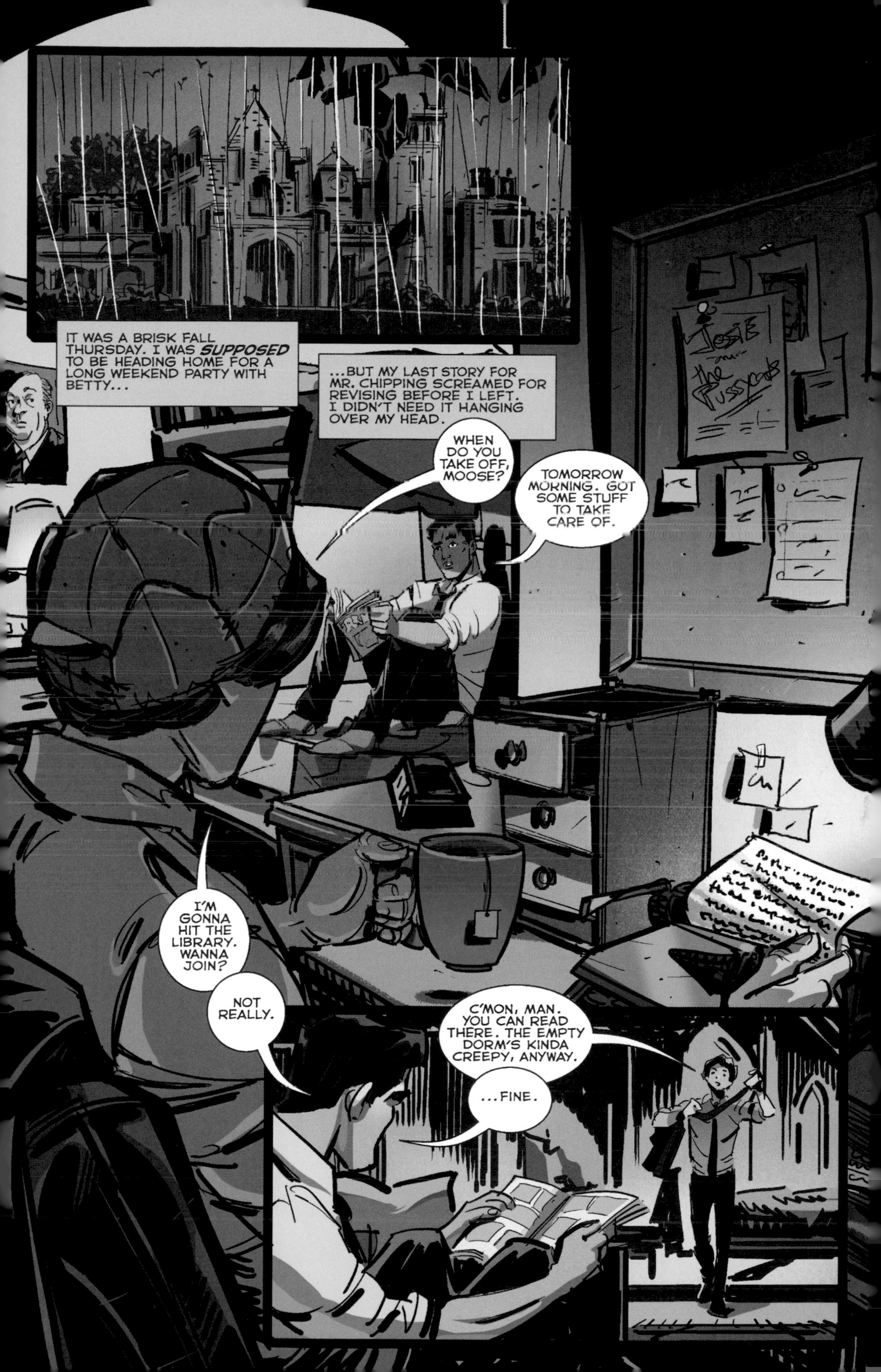

IT WAS A BRISK FALL THURSDAY. I WAS *SUPPOSED* TO BE HEADING HOME FOR A LONG WEEKEND PARTY WITH BETTY...
...BUT MY LAST STORY FOR MR. CHIPPING SCREAMED FOR REVISING BEFORE I LEFT. I DIDN'T NEED IT HANGING OVER MY HEAD.
WHEN DO YOU TAKE OFF, MOOSE?
TOMORROW MORNING. GOT SOME STUFF TO TAKE CARE OF.
Josie and the Pussycats
I'M GONNA HIT THE LIBRARY. WANNA JOIN?
NOT REALLY.
C'MON, MAN. YOU CAN READ THERE. THE EMPTY DORM'S KINDA CREEPY, ANYWAY.
...FINE.

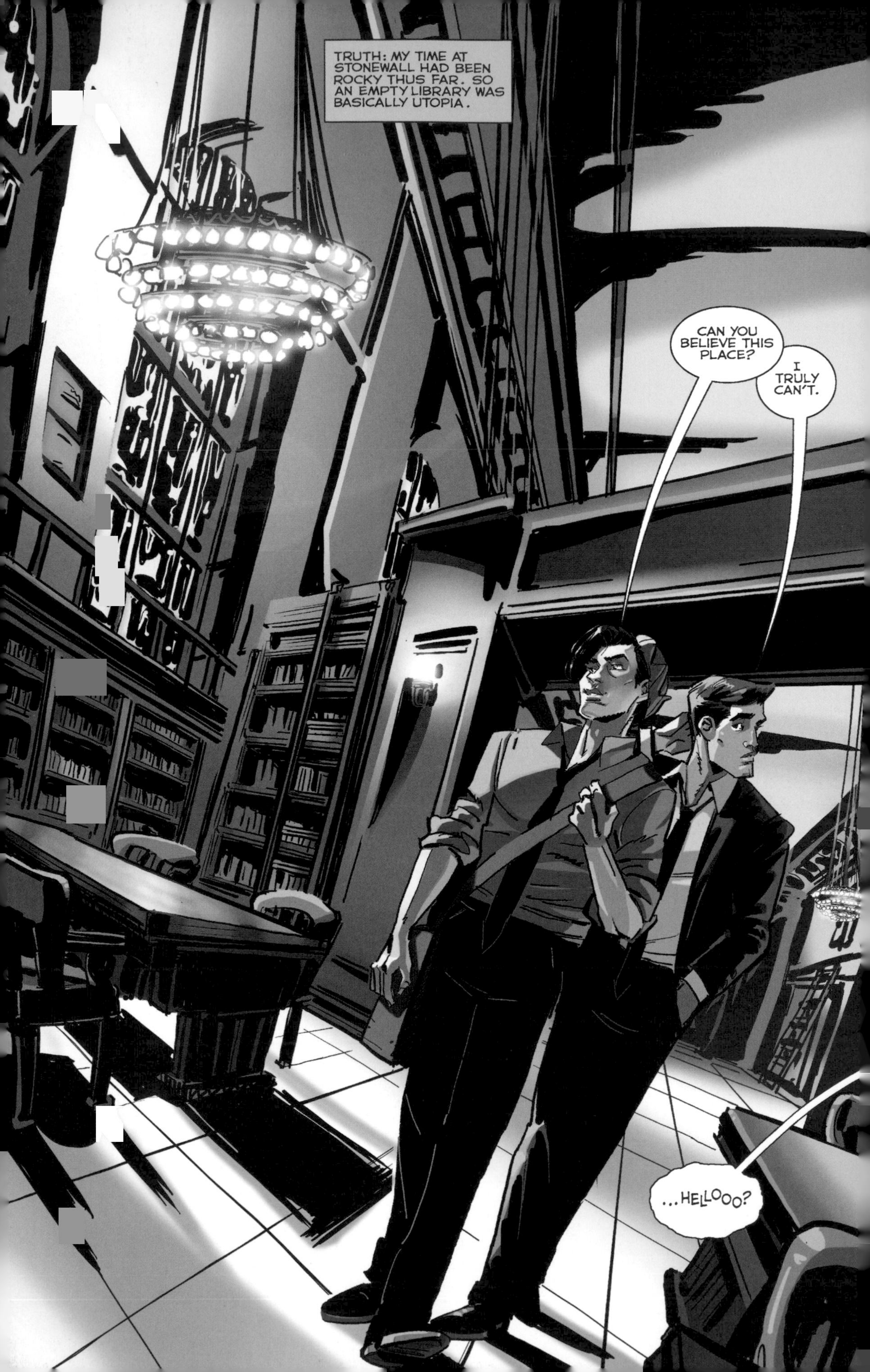
TRUTH: MY TIME AT STONEWALL HAD BEEN ROCKY THUS FAR. SO AN EMPTY LIBRARY WAS BASICALLY UTOPIA.
CAN YOU BELIEVE THIS PLACE?
I TRULY CAN'T.
...HELLOOO?

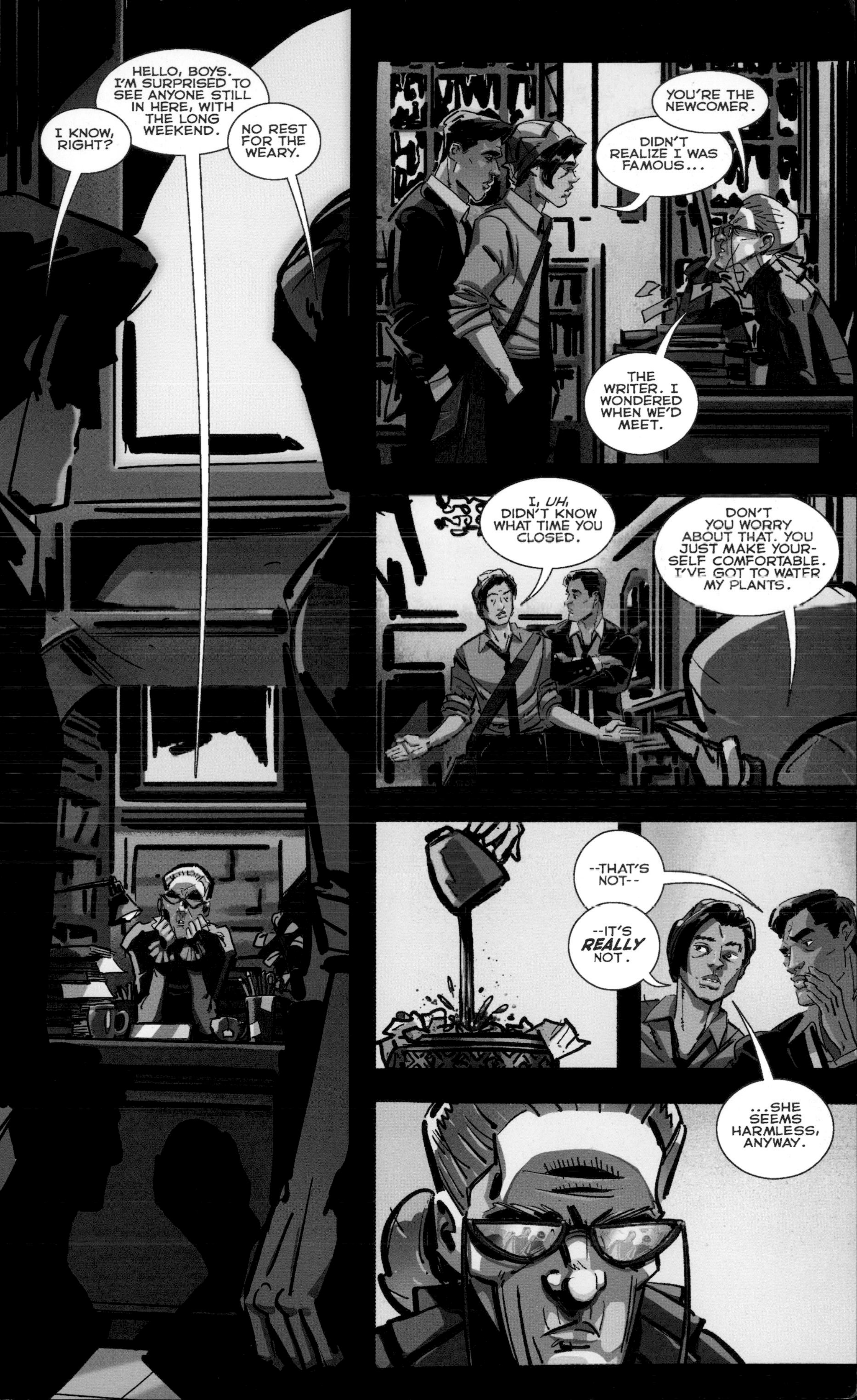
HELLO, BOYS. I'M SURPRISED TO SEE ANYONE STILL IN HERE, WITH THE LONG WEEKEND.
I KNOW, RIGHT?
NO REST FOR THE WEARY.
YOU'RE THE NEWCOMER.
DIDN'T REALIZE I WAS FAMOUS...
THE WRITER. I WONDERED WHEN WE'D MEET.
I, *UH*, DIDN'T KNOW WHAT TIME YOU CLOSED.
DON'T YOU WORRY ABOUT THAT. YOU JUST MAKE YOURSELF COMFORTABLE. I'VE GOT TO WATER MY PLANTS.
--THAT'S NOT--
--IT'S ***REALLY*** NOT.
...SHE SEEMS HARMLESS, ANYWAY.

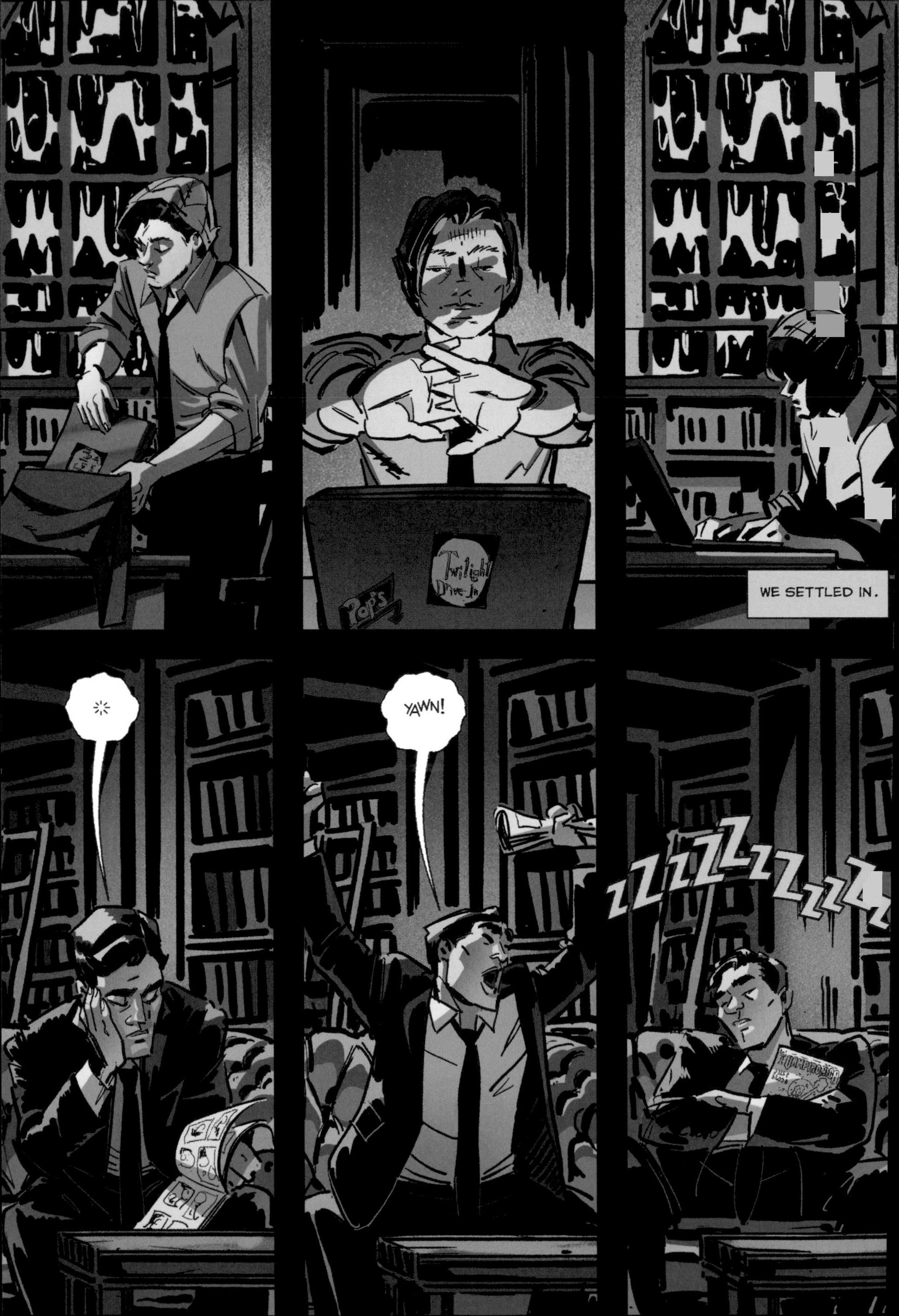
Pop's
Twilight Drive-In
WE SETTLED IN.
YAWN!

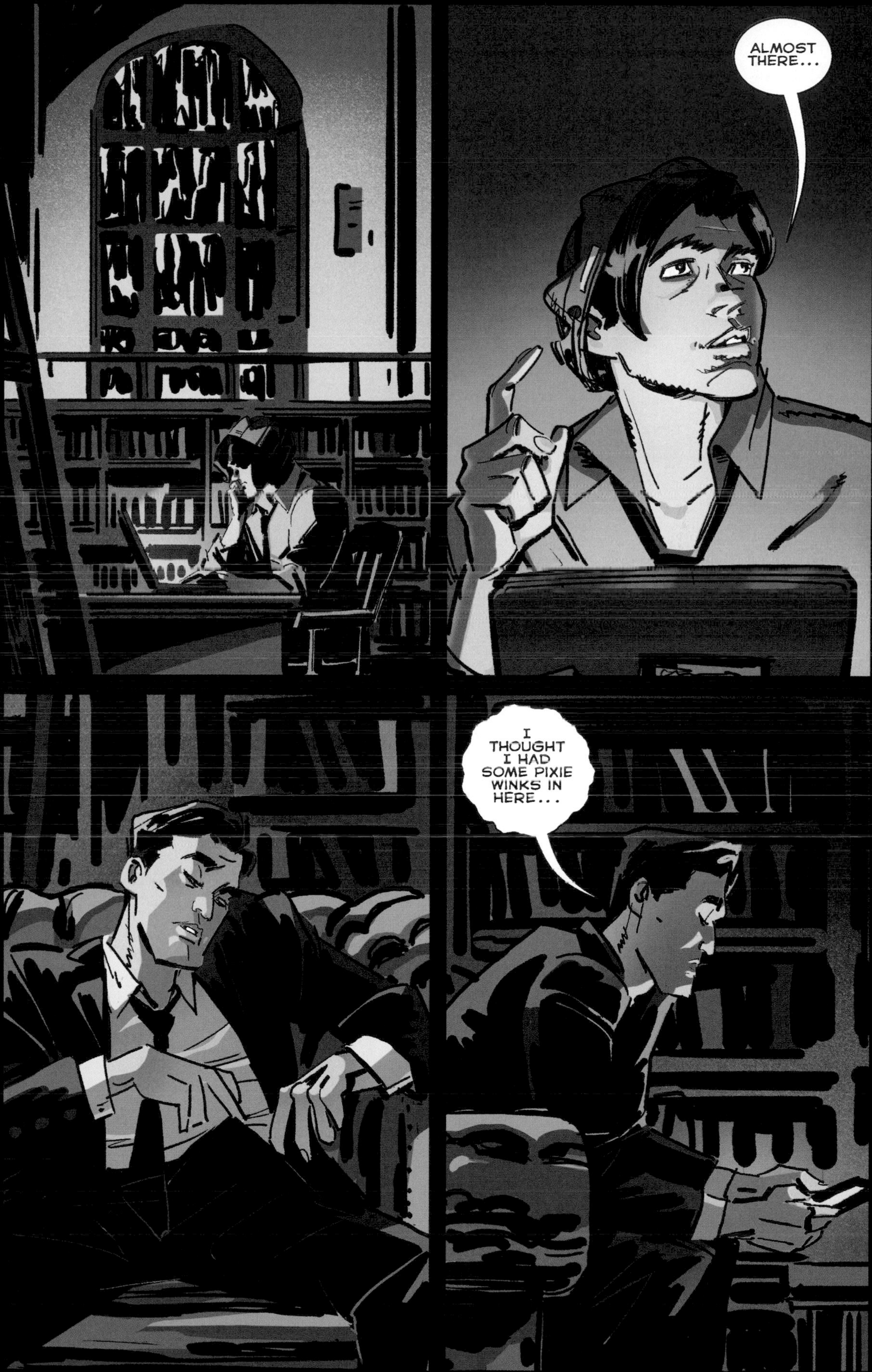
ALMOST THERE...
I THOUGHT I HAD SOME PIXIE WINKS IN HERE...

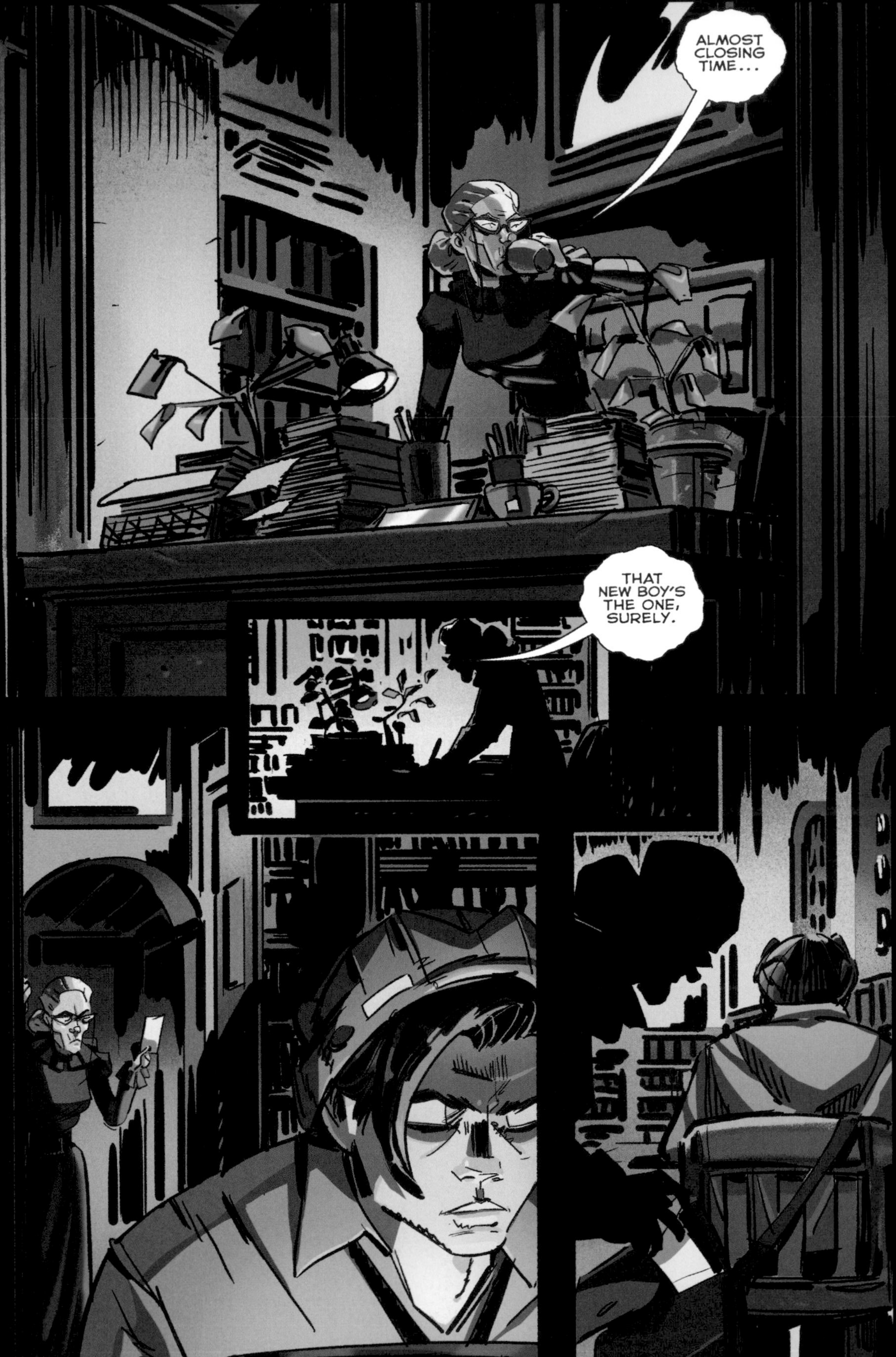
ALMOST CLOSING TIME...
THAT NEW BOY'S THE ONE, SURELY.

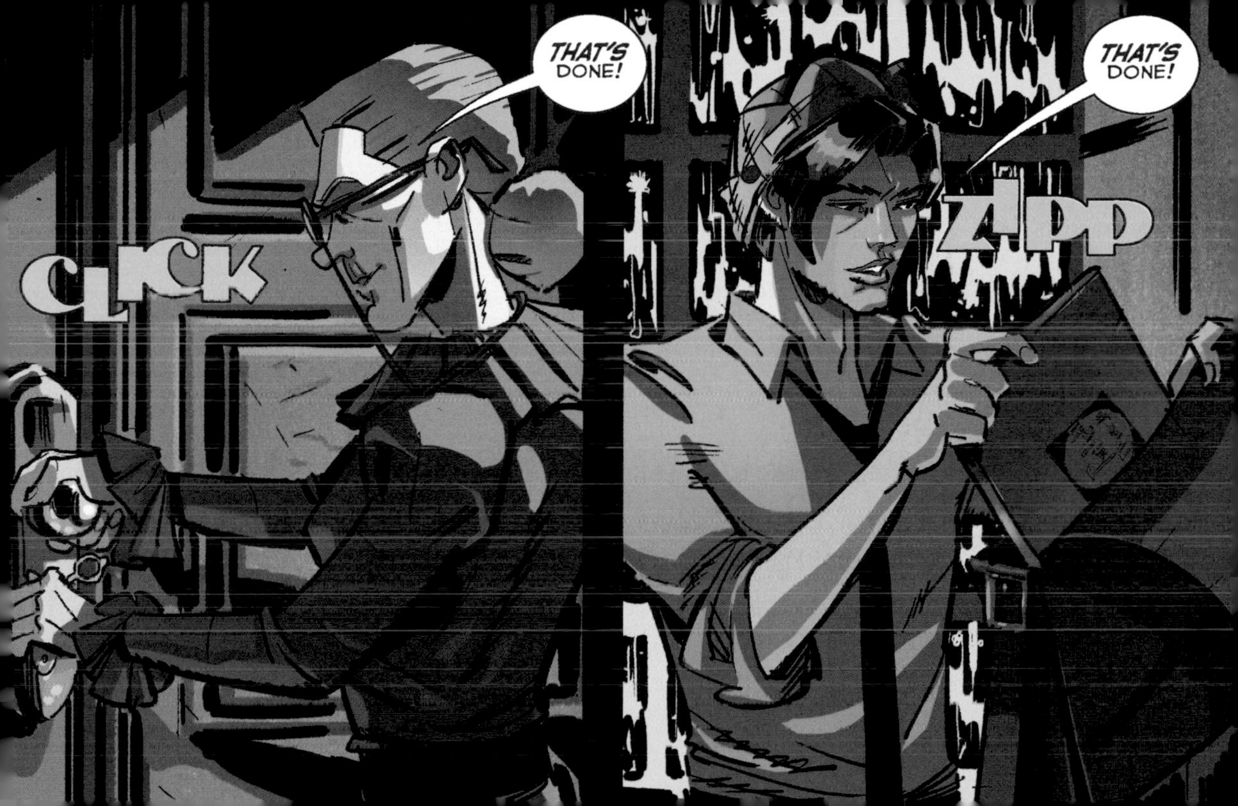
THAT'S DONE!
CLICK
THAT'S DONE!
ZIPP

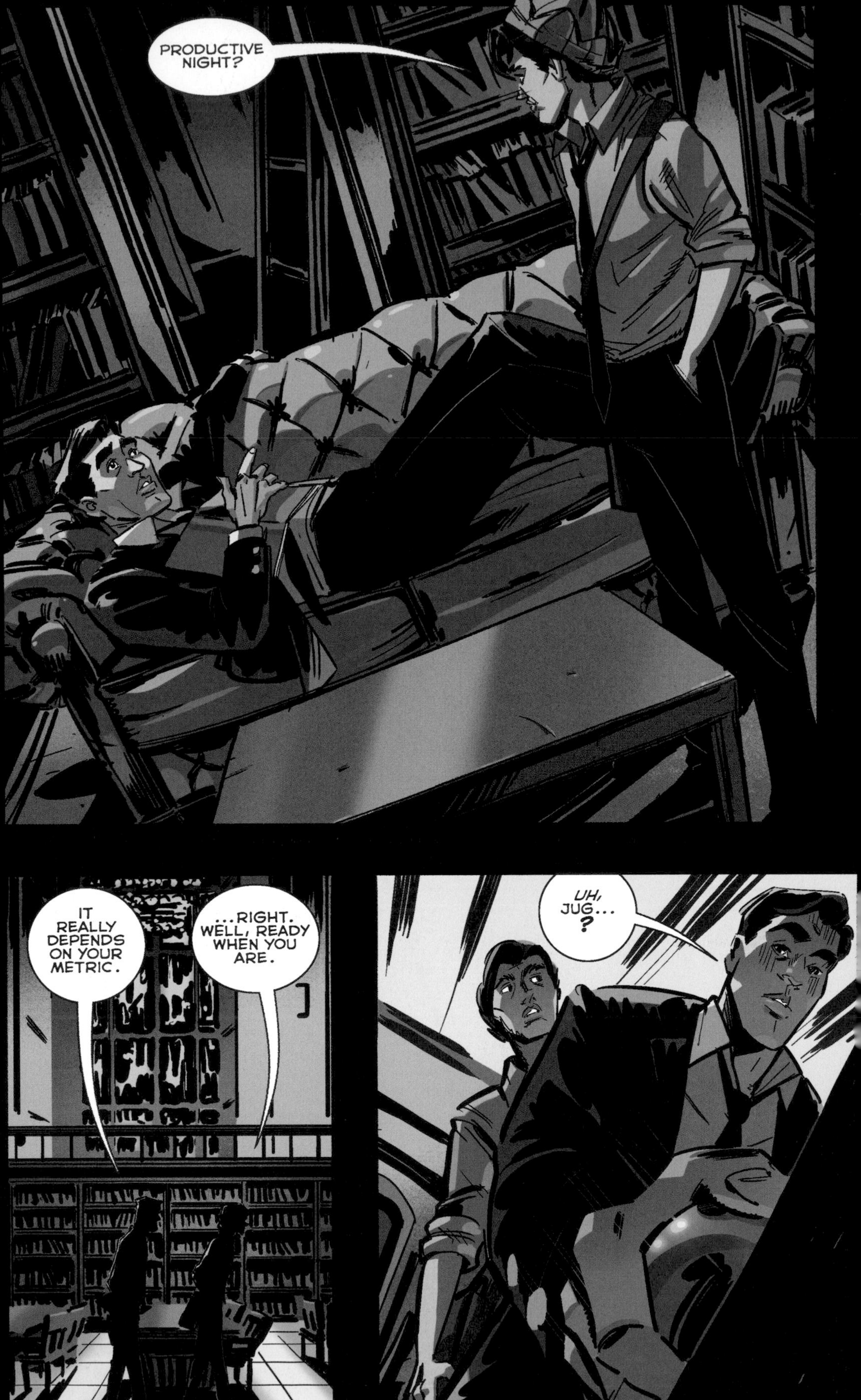
PRODUCTIVE NIGHT?
IT REALLY DEPENDS ON YOUR METRIC.
...RIGHT. WELL, READY WHEN YOU ARE.
UH, JUG...?

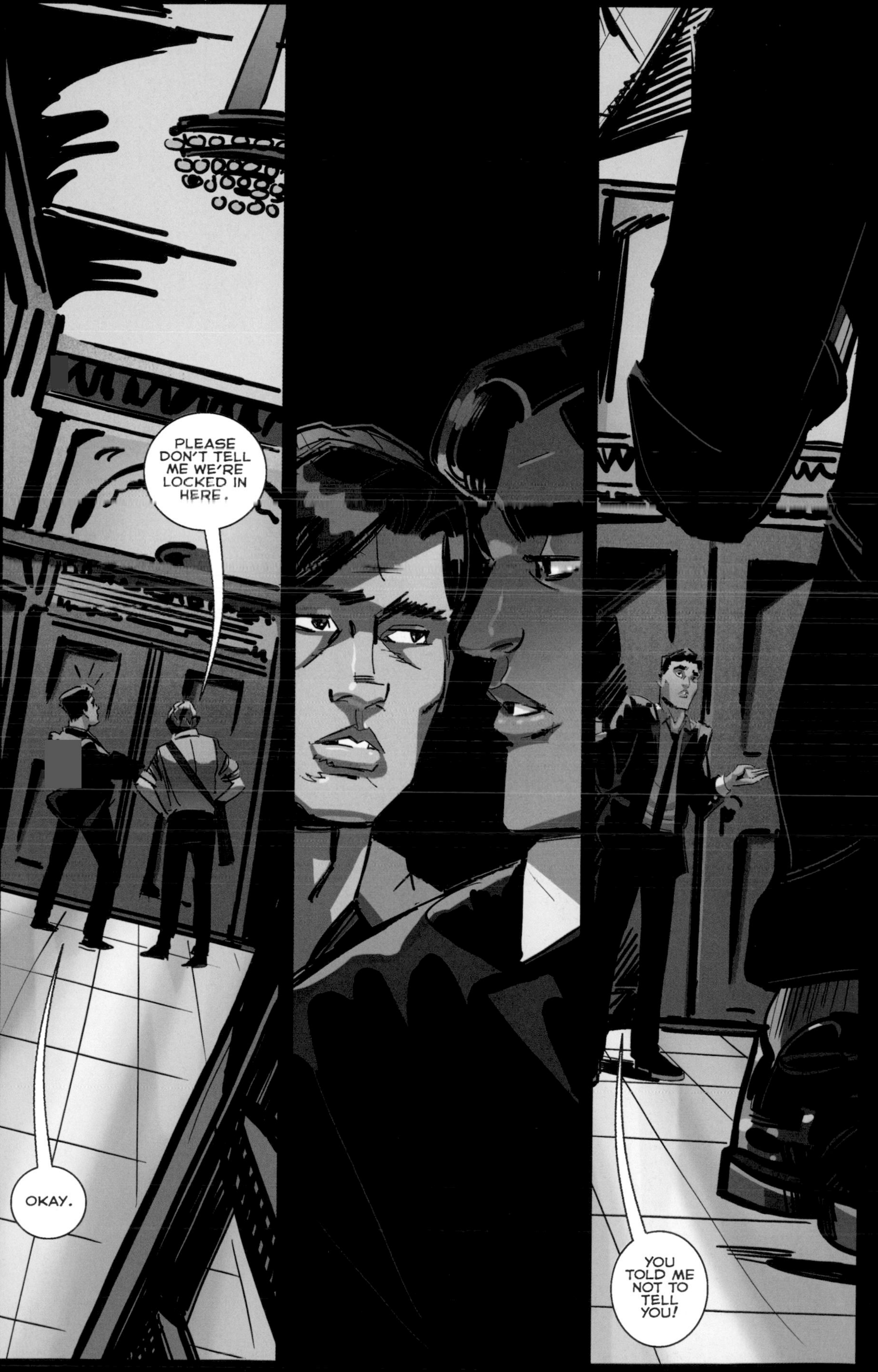
PLEASE DON'T TELL ME WE'RE LOCKED IN HERE.
OKAY.
YOU TOLD ME NOT TO TELL YOU!

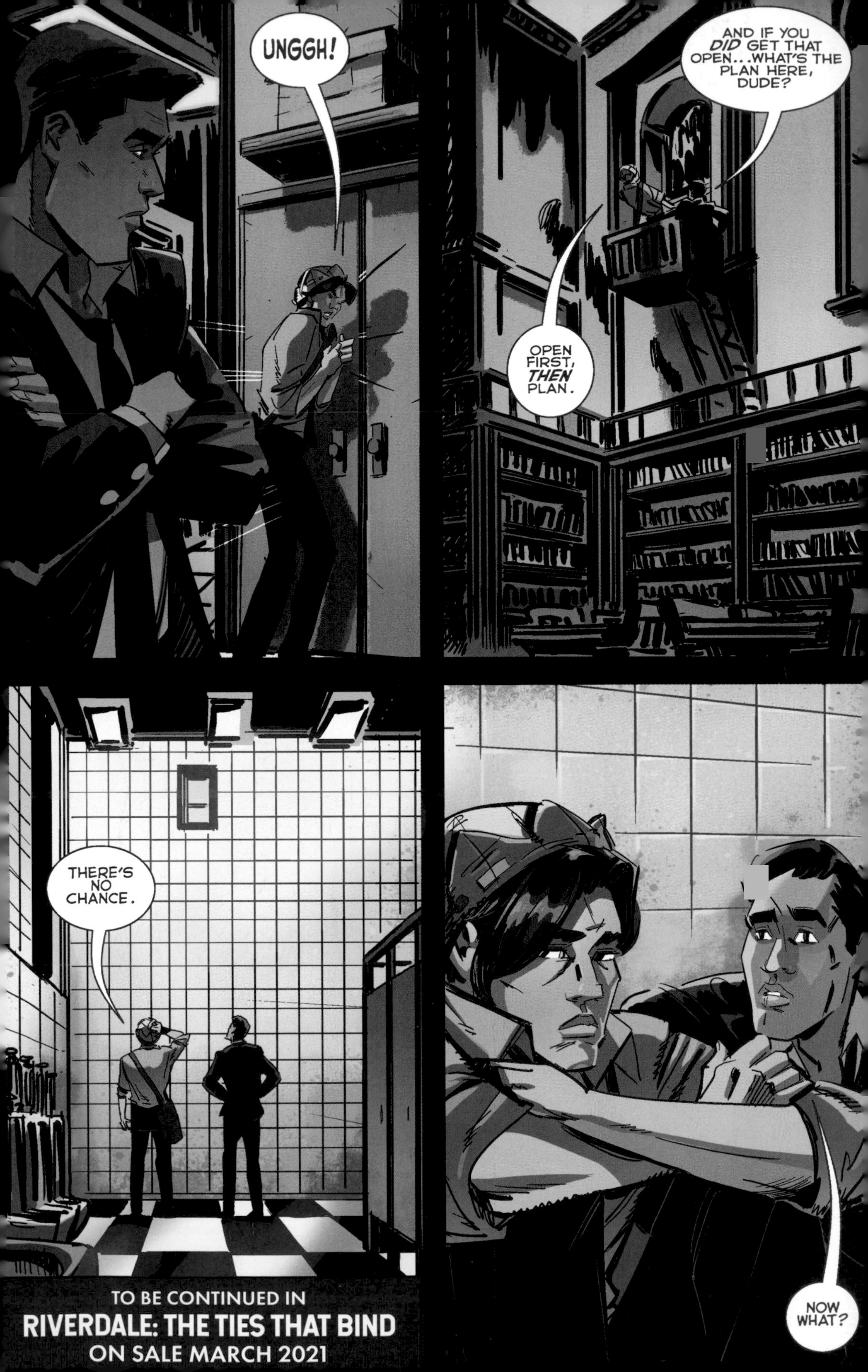
UNGGH!
AND IF YOU DID GET THAT OPEN...WHAT'S THE PLAN HERE, DUDE?
OPEN FIRST, THEN PLAN.
THERE'S NO CHANCE.
NOW WHAT?
TO BE CONTINUED IN
RIVERDALE: THE TIES THAT BIND
ON SALE MARCH 2021